Eva M. C. Kellog

The War Islands, Cuba and other islands of the sea by Eva M.C. Kellogg

Eva M. C. Kellog

The War Islands, Cuba and other islands of the sea by Eva M.C. Kellogg

ISBN/EAN: 9783743323360

Manufactured in Europe, USA, Canada, Australia, Japa

Cover: Foto ©ninafisch / pixelio.de

Manufactured and distributed by brebook publishing software (www.brebook.com)

Eva M. C. Kellog

The War Islands, Cuba and other islands of the sea by Eva M.C. Kellogg

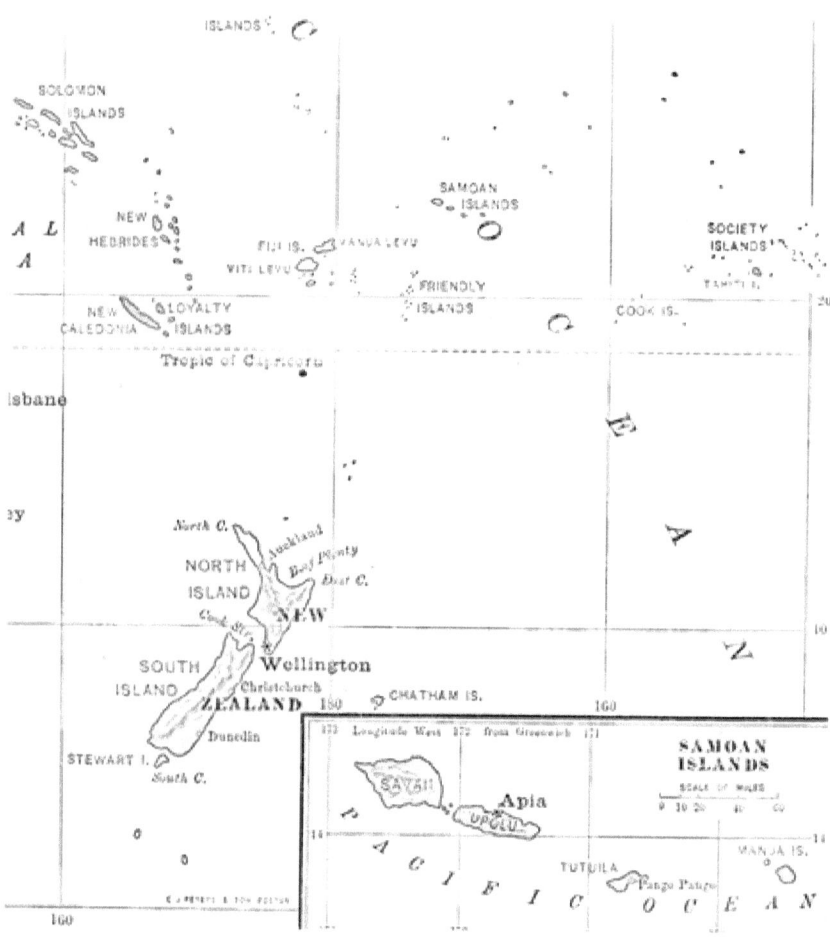

THE WAR ISLANDS

CUBA

AND OTHER

ISLANDS OF THE SEA

BY

EVA M. C. KELLOGG

EDITED BY

LARKIN DUNTON, LL.D.
HEAD MASTER OF THE BOSTON NORMAL SCHOOL

SILVER, BURDETT & COMPANY
NEW YORK   BOSTON   CHICAGO
1898

COPYRIGHT, 1898,
BY SILVER, BURDETT & COMPANY.

Norwood Press
J. S. Cushing & Co. — Berwick & Smith
Norwood Mass. U.S.A.

PREFACE.

WITHOUT a knowledge of Australia and the islands of the sea, our idea of the world and its people would be very incomplete. The continent of Australia, with only a century of growth, is one of the marvels of modern times. Its peculiar physical features, its strange flora and stranger fauna, give it a distinction not enjoyed by sister continents. Used at first only as a penal station, it now ranks in civilization and modern improvements with the most progressive countries of the world. Its resources are limitless, and its possibilities boundless. Its people are enterprising and ambitious, but they are sufficiently docile and open-minded to learn valuable lessons from the experience of older civilizations.

All of the important islands and groups of islands have found a place in this book, with the exception of the British Isles and Japan, which have been ably treated in this series in connection with the continents of which they form, politically, such important parts.

It is almost needless to say that the author has availed herself of the records of the most reliable travelers and writers of recent years. Whatever is interesting, instructive, and impressive, she has endeavored to incorporate in this work. In order to prevent a dry detail of dates and figures, pen pictures of the people as they are now, with their homes and their customs, make up a large part of the book.

The subject treated is of rare and fascinating interest; and to those who have always regarded the islands as small and unimportant places on the face of the earth, this book will be a revelation. Even their location is interesting. They are confined to no particular sea. They have the trackless waste of waters for their own, and where they will they break its limitless expanse. Their formation is often peculiar; while frozen river systems, jokuls, hot springs, pitch lakes, luxuriant forests, or other equally distinctive characteristics give to each its own individuality.

Notwithstanding their diversity, each one is, or has been, inhabited by human beings peculiarly adapted to the clime in which they were found. They dressed, and ate, and lived in accordance with their environment. They elicit sympathy, if our own method of living is our only standard of happiness. But, when seen in their native condition, their crude pastimes seem to afford them genuine satisfaction. Attempts to elevate them in the scale of living have been attended no doubt with excellent results; but in nearly all cases the promotion of civilization, as we have it, means ultimately the extinction of the native tribe.

The earnest desire of the author is that a careful perusal of this book shall result in present pleasure and permanent profit to its readers, and in questionings which shall lead some to a deeper investigation of the social, industrial, and political needs of the people who inhabit Australia and the Islands of the Sea.

CONTENTS.

CHAPTER		PAGE
I.	A Pen Picture of Australia .	13
II.	Melbourne	26
III.	Sydney, Brisbane, Perth, and Adelaide	31
IV.	The Bush . . .	45
V.	Mining and Shepherding	52
VI.	The Great Barrier Coral Reef of Australia	60
VII.	Tasmania	71
VIII.	New Zealand	82
IX.	A Pen Picture of Greenland . .	95
X.	Life in an Igloo . .	105
XI.	A Pen Picture of Iceland . .	112
XII.	The Capital, the Council, and the People .	123
XIII.	The Faroes, Shetlands, Orkneys, and Hebrides	137
XIV.	Nova Zembla and Other Islands of the North	150
XV.	Newfoundland, Cape Breton, and Prince Edward Islands . . .	160
XVI.	The Bermudas and the Bahamas .	172
XVII.	The West Indies — Cuba . . .	187
XVIII.	Haiti	207
XIX.	Jamaica	213
XX.	Porto Rico	220

CONTENTS.

CHAPTER		PAGE
XXI.	Trinidad	226
XXII.	The Lesser Antilles	233
XXIII.	Cape Verd Islands and St. Helena	242
XXIV.	The Azores	248
XXV.	The Canary and Madeira Islands	255
XXVI.	The Channel Islands	266
XXVII.	The Isles of Wight and Man, and Heligoland	273
XXVIII.	The Balearic Isles	282
XXIX.	Sardinia, Corsica, and Elba	288
XXX.	Sicily and Malta	299
XXXI.	The Ionian Islands	314
XXXII.	Crete and the Grecian Archipelago	319
XXXIII.	Islands on the East African Coast	330
XXXIV.	The Laccadive and Maldive Islands	344
XXXV.	The Malay Archipelago — Singapore and Borneo	350
XXXVI.	Sumatra and Java	360
XXXVII.	Timor and New Guinea	369
XXXVIII.	The Moluccas and Celebes	374
XXXIX.	The Philippine Islands	378
XL.	Island Groups of Oceanica	383
XLI.	Samoan, Friendly, and Society Islands	403
XLII.	The Hawaiian Islands	418
XLIII.	Tierra del Fuego and other Islands of South America	431
XLIV.	Kurile, Aleutian, and Pribilof Islands	437
INDEX		445

MAPS

Australia, East Indies, and Isles of the Pacific, *Opp. Title*

North Circumpolar Map . 97

West Indies, etc. . . 193

Islands of Mediterranean, Indian Ocean, etc. . . 289

	PAGE
New Zealand Scenery	12
An Australian Aborigine	13
Mount Kosciusko, Australian Alps	16
An Australian Waterfall	19
Miter Peak, New Zealand	21
Cliffs on Great Australian Bight	24
Government House, Melbourne	29
Pitt Street, Sydney	32
University of Sydney	35
Government House, Brisbane	37
Perth, Western Australia	39
King William Street, Adelaide	41
Birds of the Bush	43
A Fern Gully, Australia	45
Laughing Jackasses	47
Cockatoos	48
Australian Crane	49
Gold Prospectors	53
An Australian Warbler	55
A Stock Rider	58
Great Barrier Coral Reef of Australia	61
Atoll, or Ring Island	65
Coral Formations	68
Aborigines fishing by Night	71
Cape Pillar, Tasmania	73
Government House, Hobart	75
Aborigines of Tasmania	77
Tasman's Arch	79
Queenstown, New Zealand	81
Maori Warclub	82
Wellington, New Zealand	83
Maori Woman and Child	85
Rotomahama Hot Springs, New Zealand	87
Auckland, New Zealand	89
Christchurch, New Zealand	91
Hot Water Basins, White Terrace, New Zealand	93
Maori Idols, New Zealand	94
A Greenland Guide	95
In Greenland Waters	97
The Governor's Home, Greenland	100
A Greenland Glacier	102
An Old Greenland Ruin	104
A Native Greenlander	105
Umanak Church	107
Umanak Village and Fiord	110
An Ice Giant	113
A Geyser	121
Port of Reikiavik, Iceland	124
Great Chasm worn by a Glacier	127

LIST OF ILLUSTRATIONS.

	PAGE
Thor, the Norse God of Thunder	131
Odin, the Chief God in Norse Mythology	133
A Native of the Faroe Islands	138
Hoy Express, Orkney Islands	140
Stromness, Orkney Islands	142
Ponies, Shetland Islands	144
A Croft in the Hebrides	146
A Skye Octogenarian and his Grandson	147
Staffa	149
A Spitzbergen Glacier	152
Nordenskjold in the Arctic Seas	154
A Fisherman's Camp, Newfoundland	162
Queen's Square Gardens, Charlottetown	170
The Land of White Houses	173
Avenue of Palms in the Bahamas	178
Avenue of Spanish Laurels	180
Shore Road, Nassau	181
Donkey Express, Bahamas	183
A Native Hut, Grant's Town	185
A Cuban Sugar Plantation	189
A Casino near Havana	194
Port of Santiago de Cuba	198
Plaza, Cienfuegos	205
Cutting Sugar Cane, Haiti	208
Kingston, Jamaica	214
Coolies preparing Rice, Jamaica	219
A Country Road in Porto Rico	223
Trunk of a Silk-cotton Tree	228
Cabbage Palms, Trinidad	232
Breadfruit, Barbados	235
St. Helena	244
Napoleon's Tomb, St. Helena	246
St. Michael, Azores	249
Preparing Yarn for the Loom	251
Fayalese Costumes, Azores	252
Returning from Market	254
A Carrinho, Madeira	260
A Carro, Madeira	263
Tennyson's House, Isle of Wight	277
Heligoland	280
A Man of the Balearic Islands	283
A Woman of the Balearic Islands	286
Tunny Fishing, Sardinia	289
A Woman of Sardinia	291
Calvi, Corsica	293
Birthplace of Napoleon, Corsica	296
Elba	298
Catania and Mount Etna	300
Sicilian Types	303
Palermo, Sicily	305

LIST OF ILLUSTRATIONS.

	PAGE
The Cathedral, Palermo	307
Malta	310
A Street in Malta	312
The Gate of Corfu	315
Island of Scio	325
A Hova Woman and Child	332
Tattooing a Chief, Madagascar	334
A Fakir of Zanzibar	341
A Zanzibar Village	343
Palm Grove and Natives, Laccadive Islands	346
A Sultan of Borneo	352
Elephant at Work, Singapore	355
A Dyak of Borneo	359
A Young Antelope, Sumatra	361
A Girl of Sumatra	362
Drying Coffee, Java	364
A Javanese Fruit Girl	366
East Point, Java	367
A New Guinea Council House	370
Port Moresby, New Guinea	372
The Calao, Moluccas	375
Vegetation and Malay Types in Celebes	377
Mestizo Girls, Manila	380
Volcano of Mayon, Philippine Islands	382
Hogolen Islanders in Canoe	384
Native Sword and Drums	387
Native of the Solomon Islands	390
A Tambu House, Solomon Islands	391
Sugar Loaf Mountain, Fiji Islands	394
Native Canoe, Fiji Islands	396
Fan Palm, New Hebrides	398
House in New Caledonia	400
A New Caledonia Fisherman	402
House of the King, Samoa	404
Samoan Princesses	407
Harbor of Pango-Pango, Samoa	409
A Lane in Samoa	411
Native House, Friendly Islands	413
A Woman of the Friendly Islands	415
Island of Tahiti	417
Native Canoes, Hawaiian Islands	419
A Cocoanut Grove, Hawaiian Islands	421
A Grass Hut, Hawaiian Islands	423
Native Musicians, Hawaii	425
Avenue of Royal Date Palms	427
A Hawaiian Belle	430
Yahgans	432
Natives of the Falkland Islands	435
Cape Horn	436
A Kurile Mother and Child	438
Aleutian Islanders	441

NEW ZEALAND SCENERY.

AUSTRALIA AND THE ISLANDS OF THE SEA.

CHAPTER I.

A PEN PICTURE OF AUSTRALIA.

AN AUSTRALIAN ABORIGINE.

THE island-continent of Australia, with its record of but one century of colonization, is no longer the "great unknown land" which until lately it has been to the inhabitants of sister continents. The growth of its commerce, and the great advance made along the line of intercommunication, have practically bridged over the thousands of miles which separate it from the rest of the world. They have tended also to spread the knowledge of its colonial affairs, which until recently has been confined to those directly interested in the country.

The general physical characteristics of Australia are the prevalence of far-reaching plains, and the absence, with the exception of the Murray, of rivers of any importance.

We are told by geologists that the oldest parts of this country are two long narrow strips of high land. These are the Pacific Slope, which is the smaller one, and the Indian Slope, better known as the coastal range of Western Australia. By a slow upheaval of the intervening space, these two islands, separated by a distance of two thousand miles or more, were finally united.

By some geographers, Australia is treated as an island, the largest island of the globe; but its proportions are so vast that, by general consent, it is now regarded as a continent, and is so classed in all recent geographies. It is known as the Australian or Southeastern Continent.

Australia lies in the southern hemisphere, reaching nearly from the tenth to the fortieth degree of south latitude, and the Tropic of Capricorn passes through its center. It is situated southeast of Asia, and is bounded on the north by the Indian Ocean, Timor Sea, Arafura Sea, Torres Strait, and the Gulf of Carpentaria; on the east, by the Coral Sea and the Pacific Ocean; on the south, by Bass Strait and the Great Australian Bight; and on the west, by the Indian Ocean.

Its greatest length, which is from east to west, is twenty-four hundred miles, and its greatest breadth about eighteen hundred. It has an area of nearly three million square miles, and the length of its coast line is about eight thousand miles.

It is about one hundred years since the first European settlements were made in this great southern land. There was not much at first to invite settlement. The country was utterly isolated. Few rivers flowed from the interior, which made it exceedingly difficult of penetration. Gold was discovered there in 1851, and within the half century since, the enterprise and courage of the English have fringed the shores with colonies, several of which are both more powerful and more wealthy than some of the old, established states of Europe. Its chief cities are of the first order in every respect, and its population numbers upwards of three millions. Its trade is immense, and it has millions of acres of land under cultivation. Thousands of miles of railroad have been built, and the submarine telegraph unites Australia with every other part of the world.

Australia is singularly compact; and when its great extent is taken into account, it presents little variety of surface or irregularity of outline. The only remarkable indentation is that made by the Gulf of Carpentaria on the north coast, which is the most broken of any. This gulf penetrates inland five hundred miles from Cape York on the east, and four hundred from Cape Arnhem on the west. Though there are several other good harbors and capacious bays, yet all of them taken together hardly equal this one. Spencer Gulf and the Gulf of St. Vincent, both on the south coast, are next in size.

MOUNT KOSCIUSKO, AUSTRALIAN ALPS.

The mountains run north and south, at a distance of from twenty to one hundred miles from the coast, rising from two thousand five hundred to four thousand five hundred feet in rough, inaccessible elevations. The highest peak yet discovered, Mount Kosciusko, in the Australian Alps, is in the southeast, and measures seven thousand three hundred feet. The valleys along the coast are rich and well-watered, but out of the reach of the sea breezes the country is arid and waterless. The mountains of the west coast, which are inferior to those of the east, approach nearer the coast line.

Along the shore of the Great Australian Bight are sand cliffs from two hundred to four hundred feet in height. Behind these cliffs are waterless plains, which depend upon the uncertain rainfall for moisture. Throughout the whole length of the Great Australian Bight, not even the smallest rivulet empties into the sea. Certain portions of the north shore are low and flat. The land on all four sides descends gradually to the interior, which consists of immense level plains elevated but little above the sea, and unbroken except by hills in the northeast, by gum tree forests, and by other herbage, which, in Australia, is termed "bush." Some of these plains are deserts, and are likely to remain such, as there is no water with which they may be irrigated. Others are like South American llanos or Russian steppes, only not so high. In the rainless season, which occurs at uncertain intervals, they are sandy or stony wastes; but at other times they are covered with a fair amount of grass. There are, however, strips of tolerably well-watered land throughout the interior.

The rivers of the east coast of Australia are perennial, but are not navigable, even for small vessels, more than seventy miles inland. Those of the west coast often dry up during the dry season, and become a series of water holes. The Murray is the largest of the rivers, and is nearly eleven hundred miles in length. It is formed by the union of smaller streams and rivers, and may be navigated for more than eight hundred miles during the wet season. It drains the southeast part of the country, and discharges its waters into the Gulf of St. Vincent on the south coast. There are no large rivers in the interior, and most of the creeks, like the Stuart, which is three hundred miles long, flow for a considerable distance and then dwindle away or else end in salt lakes. Sometimes they become mere chains of ponds or water holes, which are valuable to the settler, as they supply him with water until the river fills again. The conformation of the interior is peculiar, perhaps owing to the fact of the land having been, at a comparatively recent period, the bed of the ocean.

The lakes of Australia scarcely deserve the name. The largest of them resemble marshes, and depend for their supply of water upon the rivers which flow into them, instead of being themselves the sources of rivers. As a result they are often dried up, and present the appearance of vast, reedy swamps. Even when filled with water, they are more like submerged flats than lakes, and have such low muddy shores as to render the water unapproachable.

AN AUSTRALIAN WATERFALL.

Australia is as peculiar in regard to climate as in other features. From the sterile central plains come burning hot winds, which fill the air with a fine dust, and raise the temperature to one hundred and ten, and even one hundred and twenty, in the shade, between latitudes twenty-five and thirty-five. But though the state of the temperature seems almost incredible, looking merely at figures, the people do not suffer nearly as much as they would if the mercury in the thermometer were lower and the amount of moisture in the air greater. In a country of such extent, the temperature necessarily varies a great deal. In New South Wales the average temperature of spring is sixty-five degrees; of summer, seventy-two; of autumn, sixty-six; and of winter, fifty-five. In general the winters are everywhere so mild that cattle seldom need housing.

Politically, the country is divided into five parts. Western Australia comprises the western third. South Australia with its Northern Territory takes in nearly a third more. The eastern third is divided into three colonies of unequal size: Queensland, the largest, is on the north; New South Wales, the next in size, is in the center; and Victoria, the smallest, is at the South.

The colonies are directed by a Governor appointed for each by the Crown, and by a Legislative Council and Assembly, one or the other body being elected by the people.

Within the past few years the subject of Australian Federation has been greatly agitated, and on several different occasions, conferences, either by delegates or by premiers of the various colonies, have been held for

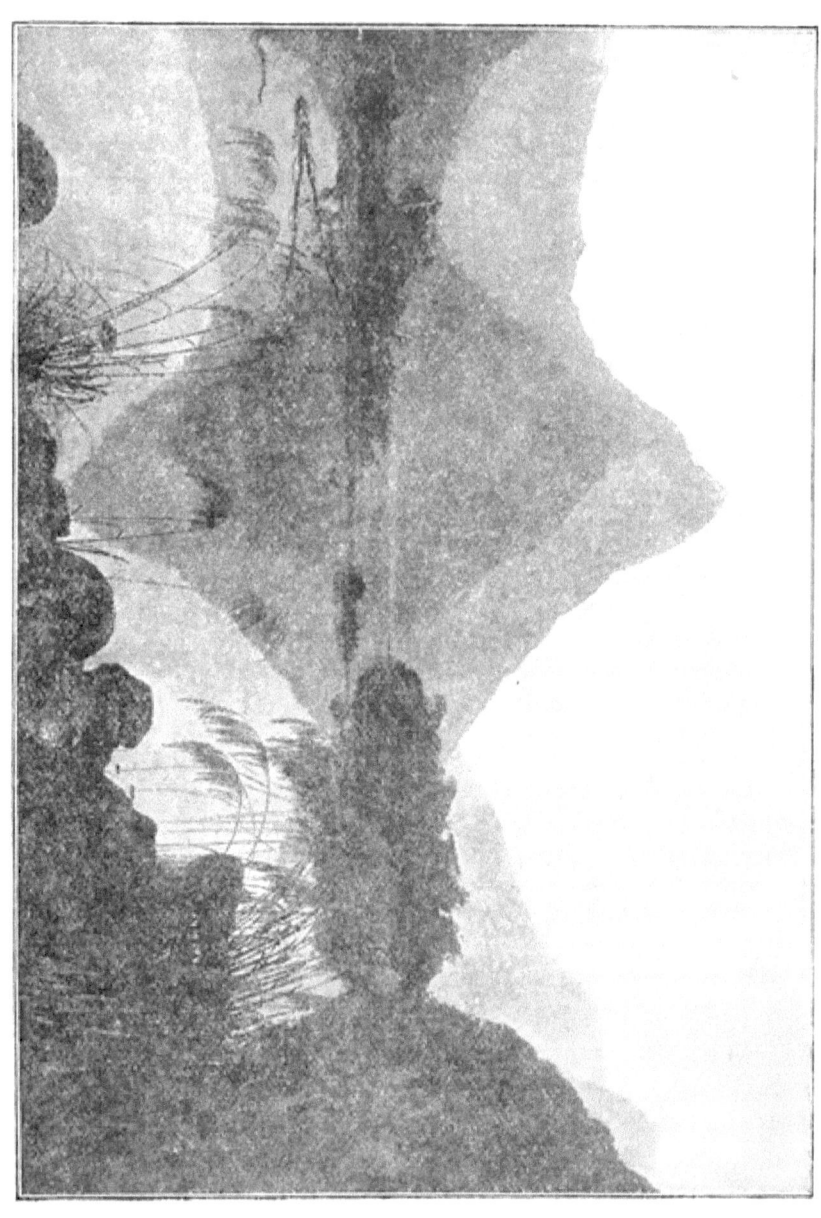

the purpose of ascertaining whether some method of union were not feasible. The last of these conferences was held at Hobart, Tasmania, in January, 1895, at which it was agreed "that an identical bill, termed the Australian Federal Enabling Act, should be introduced into the Parliaments of the various colonies, and if it should meet the approval of not less than three of them, then the proceedings toward drafting a constitution were to be forthwith agreed upon."

It was hoped that Tasmania and New Zealand would join with the five colonies of Australia in perfecting such a scheme. But the government of New Zealand insisted that such a course was inexpedient, since, although they had a number of common imperial interests, they had few if any local interests. Therefore New Zealand was omitted from the plan. But in case it should wish to join the federation at a later date, should such a form of government be established, it would be at liberty to do so. The bill proposed "that each of the remaining colonies should elect, at a popular election, ten delegates, who were to meet on the last day of March for the purpose of drafting a federal constitution. When a draft of this great charter had been prepared, the convention was to adjourn for not more than sixty days, for the purpose of having the draft submitted to popular criticism, with a view of finding out the extent of approval or disapproval it met with."

In accordance with the provision of the bill, this convention met on the last day of March, 1897. After the completion of its work and the expiration of the recess, the convention will hold another session, perfect the draft, and submit it to the people. Within a limited time they will vote upon its acceptance, "the popular approval carrying the measure without any further reference to the colonial Parliaments."

Though all the colonies did not take part in preparing the federal constitution, they will doubtless come within the bounds of the federation finally, if three or four of them lead the way at present by adopting the constitution. The insurmountable difficulty in the past, and the one which threatens to embarrass present action, is the strong feeling, prevalent in all the colonies, in favor of local independence, and the fear that union will deprive them of some privileges which they now enjoy.

Thus, Tasmania and South Australia fear that the "policy of the federation" may be dictated too largely by their more wealthy and populous neighbors, Victoria and New South Wales. Queensland is tender upon the labor question. Much sugar is raised within its limits, and the laborers are largely south sea islanders who work for low wages. Wealthy owners of large plantations, who possess considerable power at Brisbane, are afraid that a federal government, which looked at things from a national rather than a local standpoint, might impose upon them undesirable restrictions. There exist in Australia to-day conditions very similar to those which existed in our country at the time of the drafting of the constitution of the United States.

Federation in Australia will probably not be possible unless each colony is accorded equal representation in

CLIFFS ON GREAT AUSTRALIAN BIGHT.

the Senate. The intention at present is to allow each colony to choose six senators. These will probably be elected; "for, unlike the Canadian system, the Australian federation is to be popular in both branches of Parliament." It has not yet been made known under what conditions the lower branch of Parliament will be elected, but the probability is that the two branches of Parliament will bear a reasonably close resemblance to the Senate and the House of Representatives of the United States.

There are many powerful arguments in favor of a well-considered combination, and no argument can be cited against this mode of union, if federation is placed on such a footing as will harmonize with the internal self-government of each colony.

The aborigines of Australia belonged to the negro race. They were lithe and agile, and not so stoutly built as the Africans. They were of a chocolate color, and had small heads, with long, coarse, black hair, and large, full, penetrating eyes, and they were tolerably quick of apprehension. Some of the tribes were mild and gentle, while others were cruel and vindictive. They have, however, almost disappeared before the march of civilization.

CHAPTER II.

MELBOURNE.

GOLD made Victoria, and Melbourne owes its rapid growth to the same precious metal. Melbourne stands on Port Philip Bay, near the mouth of the Yarra River. It is the capital of Victoria, and the chief city of Australia, with a population of 450,000.

Having rounded Cape Otway, the southern extremity of Victoria, we soon reach the Heads at the entrance of Port Philip. These are low necks of sandy hillocks guarding the entrance to the bay. On one side is Point Lonsdale, and on the other Point Nepean, upon each of which strong fortifications have been erected. Farther on is the village of Queenscliff, built on a bit of abrupt headland. Cozy dwellings appear nestled down amid well-cultivated hills, and the village church is a pleasing object in the more distant landscape.

But we are rapidly losing sight of land, for Port Philip is a spacious inlet thirty-five miles long by twenty-five broad, and we are sailing straight for its most northern shore. As we near it, the port of Williamstown comes in sight. Its crowded masts indicate that it is full of shipping. On the right is the village of St. Kilda, and farther round is Brighton. Sandridge, lying straight ahead of us, is the landing place of Melbourne. Over the masts of its shipping, our attention is called to a mass of houses in the distance, and we are told that there is the city of Melbourne.

We are soon alongside the large wooden railway pier

of Sandridge. We buy our tickets for Melbourne two miles away, and in less than fifteen minutes are safely landed in the largest city in the southern hemisphere.

The scenery around Melbourne is not remarkable, but the internal appearance of the city is magnificent. It is built upon two hills and in the broad valley which separates them, and is laid out on the rectangular plan. The streets are all straight and of great width, and large spaces within the city limits are devoted to public gardens.

Collins and Bourke streets are usually considered to rank first. As we walk down Bourke Street, we pass an imposing structure which, though deserted in the daytime, is crowded in the evening with a richly dressed throng. It is the Royal Theater. Farther up the street we come to the market place, where crowds of people are moving about. Trade seems to be brisk, judging by the way the vegetables, fruit, and meat are changing hands. At the farther end of the street everything is much more quiet. There, in a large open space, stand the Parliament Houses, which were built at a cost of two million dollars.

Standing on the high ground at one end of Collins Street, and looking down through the valley and up the hill on the other side, we obtain a striking view. This street is not less than a mile long. Here and there on each side of it are grand edifices used as bank buildings. On the farther hill we note a white, palatial structure with a richly ornamented façade and tower. This is the Town Hall. The Bourke and Wills monument, erected in memory of two brave men who lost their lives when exploring the interior of the country, stands in the center of the roadway; while, at the very end of the perspective, rises the handsome gray front of the Treasury building.

We must remember, however, that Melbourne is a young city. Less than sixty years ago the aborigines used to hold their savage meetings on the very ground where the University now stands. And so it happens that, as yet, there is no street which is magnificent throughout; for between large imposing structures we sometimes see small, insignificant buildings, that remind us of the earliest days of the city.

There is little that bespeaks extreme poverty, and beggars are unknown. Work is plentiful, and no one can complain of being unable to find something to do. The poorest part of the city is the Chinese quarter. Here the streets are narrower and dirtier than anywhere else, and you may see the yellow-faced Mongolians standing and jabbering at their doors,— a very novel sight.

Melbourne is justly proud of its public institutions. Among these, the Library ranks first. It contains more than sixty thousand volumes, and is free to all the people from ten in the forenoon until ten at night. Here, in the evening, you may see the workingmen in their working dress. As many as five hundred workingmen visit the Library daily. The only requirements are that they shall sign their names on entering, and observe proper behavior while they remain. The Victorian Collection of pictures is in the same building, and the galleries are very attractive.

GOVERNMENT HOUSE, MELBOURNE.

The Post Office is another splendid building, and one of the most commodious institutions of its kind in the world. The University has hardly attained the success that the Library has had. The building is a modest, quadrangular one, three sides of which have been completed. These contain the lecture rooms, a library, and the residences of the professors. Behind this building stands the Museum, which is open to the public without charge.

But the most attractive part of Melbourne is its seashore, especially in its pretty, rapidly growing suburbs along the shores of Port Philip. St. Kilda is but three miles from the city, and is a favorite resort of the people. Many of them reside here, and go back and forth to their business houses. A fine promenade runs along the beach, and the bathing is unusually good. Large inclosures surrounded by piles are built for the bathers, and above them, raised high on platforms, are commodious dressing rooms. The beach has a sandy bottom, and slopes gently from the shore to any depth of water, affording a fine opportunity for swimmers. They must, however, be careful not to encounter the "cobbler." This creature is like a small octopus. It has legs, or arms, nearly equal in size and very long in proportion to its body. They are used for creeping on the land, swimming in the water, and seizing its prey. If it comes near any one, it will administer a sharp slap, at the same time squirting out a horrid, acrid juice. A thick rash quickly follows this infliction, accompanied by swelling and much pain, and for a while the delights of bathing have to be foregone.

CHAPTER III.

SYDNEY, BRISBANE, PERTH, AND ADELAIDE.

NOTWITHSTANDING the fact that Melbourne is the phenomenal city of Australia, there are others as worthy of description. These have had as marvelous, if not as rapid, a growth, and have had much to do with the general development of the continent.

One of these is Sydney. It is the capital of New South Wales, and is the oldest city in Australia. It has a population, including its suburbs, of over 408,500. It is a well-built city, with fine, broad streets and imposing public buildings, which, combined with its commanding situation on a splendid harbor, has gained for it the title of "The Queen of the South."

Sydney is situated on Port Jackson, near the thirty-fourth degree of south latitude. The choice of this precise spot for settlement was determined by the circumstance of a stream of fresh water being found there, flowing into a deep inlet, afterward known as Sydney Cove, one of the numerous bays into which Port Jackson is divided.

This last-mentioned body of water forms a magnificent harbor, extending some twenty miles inland. It is completely landlocked, and can be entered only through a narrow passageway between the "Heads," as they are termed. It accommodates vessels of the largest size. Its shores present a succession of picturesque landscapes. The cliffs which form the general outline of the harbor often rise to the height of two hundred and fifty feet. In the intervening spaces the shore consists of terraces and smooth sandy beaches.

There are, perhaps, few places more suitable for the foundation of a great metropolis. The city is situated at a distance of about eight miles from the sea, and the whole circumference of the bay around which it is built

PITT STREET, SYDNEY.

forms a series of natural wharfs, where ships of two thousand tons' burden may be moored within a distance of twenty yards of the shore.

Sydney stands near the center, north and south, of the immense coal region of Australia, which extends five hundred miles from north to south, and has a breadth of from eighty to one hundred miles. Large quantities of coal, for colonial use and for export, are mined within one hundred miles of the city. The sandstone rock, upon which the city is built, affords much valuable building material.

Sydney now consists of three distinct districts : First, the Old City, in which are George Street and other streets named after early governors. Here we find the Houses of Parliament, the Treasury buildings, and the Government House with its park and botanic gardens. The Houses of Parliament are rather disappointing in appearance. The Lower House is small, and in its arrangement resembles a music hall. The Government House is situated on a promontory commanding a view of the bay. On one side is Farm Cove, and on the other is Sydney Cove, where the large liners debark their passengers. The Government House is very different from that in Melbourne. It is like an ordinary English country house, and, though comfortable enough, is rather inadequate to meet the present requirements of this growing place. The other important buildings in Sydney are the large and imposing Town Hall, the Museum, and the railway station. There are several theaters, many handsome banks, the Exchange, and a number of elegant private residences.

The second division of Sydney is called Wooloomooloo. This is the fashionable quarter, and abounds in beautiful homes. Further away we come across numerous small watering places dotted about the harbor, the Parramatta, and Botany Bay.

The third division is called North Shore and is reached by steam ferry from Sydney Cove in ten minutes. Beside the city proper, Sydney has extensive suburbs, some of which are called by English names, such as Hyde Park, Victoria Park, and Paddington, while others have been given native names sometimes difficult of pronunciation.

The people of Sydney believe in their own city, and entertain their own opinions about the " vaunted superiority" of Melbourne; and truly there is much to justify their pride. Nature has done much for Sydney. From nearly every point may be seen the blue waters of its winding harbor; and the sunshine, as it lights up varied hues in sea and sky, seems as tender as that of Naples or Athens. The neighborhood of the city is charming. Every nook in the adjacent bay is studded with handsome villas or comfortable cottages. "The walks immediately around the city are unsurpassed for picturesqueness, while the public gardens probably excel any in the world, owing to their combination of sea and land, hill and valley, rock and wood and grassy slopes, with a climate that permits all the beautiful forms of vegetation both of tropical and temperate zones to luxuriate side by side."

The parks are many in number. Among them the most important are the Botanical Gardens, covering thirty-eight acres, exceedingly rich and beautiful; Prince Alfred Park, Belmore Park, and Hyde Park,— the last named an open, treeless plateau near the center of the city. The two largest parks are the Domain, a fine expanse of one hundred and thirty-eight acres on the northeast side of the city, and the Moor, a tract of twenty-five hundred acres southeast of the city.

UNIVERSITY OF SYDNEY.

The educational system of New South Wales consists of primary schools, the grammar school, and the University. By far the most important edifice among public buildings, not only in Sydney, but in the whole of Australia, is the University, which stands on a commanding height, and in the center of a domain of one hundred and fifty acres. The principal façade is five hundred feet long, and is flanked by a great hall at its western end. Lectures are delivered daily during each term on classics, logic, history, chemistry, natural and experimental philosophy, and jurisprudence. The University was erected out of private funds, and has a permanent endowment of five thousand pounds a year from the civil list. Instruction is limited to purely secular teaching.

Brisbane, the capital of Queensland, is situated on a river of the same name, about twenty-five miles from its mouth in Moreton Bay. It is near the twenty-seventh degree of south latitude, and more than five hundred miles north of Sydney. Including its suburbs, the city covers a very large area.

Although the population of the city proper is small, being only twenty-six thousand, yet, including South Brisbane, Rockhampton, and other suburbs within a radius of ten miles, there is a population of over one hundred thousand. The city is well supplied with public buildings. The Houses of the Legislature, still incomplete, have already cost £100,000. Beside these there are the Government House, the General Post Office, the Museum, Town Hall, and Custom House, beside two theaters, an opera house, several concert halls, and half a dozen fine bank edifices.

There is a noble iron bridge across the Brisbane River, more than one thousand feet long, with two swing openings of sixty and one half feet each, to allow the passage of ships. The actual city, surrounded on three sides by this river, is a well-built town laid out in streets which cross at right angles. Those which run

GOVERNMENT HOUSE, BRISBANE.

north and south are called by men's names, as William Street and George Street. Those running east and west assume the names of the fairer sex, as Alice Street and Margaret Street, the center and principal one being called Queen Street.

There are several clubs, that known as the Queensland Club being one of the finest in Australia. In the suburbs many forms of sport are indulged in, among which are pony races and dingo hunts.

The people of Brisbane delight in social gatherings and dances, both public and private, and entertainments are in vogue throughout the season. The Queen's birthday is always a great event in Australia, and its celebration in Brisbane is thus described by Mr. Baden-Powell, an English scientific writer : —

"It generally starts off with a great school feast. Some thousands of school children assemble in the Domain, and have a great day of it. At a given time the Governor arrives upon the scene to deliver an address, and on mounting a platform is received with solemn cheers ; but when on one occasion. I humbly followed him, arrayed in regimental uniform and wearing a bearskin, roars of laughter from thousands of young throats rose to the skies, and 'the man in the big hat' was voted quite the most comical part of the show.

"A review of the troops is the next event of the programme, and a really very fine display they make. Then follows a levée at the Government House, all the gentlemen unable to raise uniforms having to appear in evening dress.

"After this the Governor has to attend in a sort of semi-state the great race meeting of the year. Escorted by mounted orderlies, and a detachment of mounted police, he drives up the center of the course *à la* Prince at Ascot, and is received by the president and stewards of the Turf Club. But before the racing is over a return has to be made to Government House, in order to prepare for a big dinner given to all the principal Government officials. It is a great relief to get this day over."

AUSTRALIA AND THE ISLANDS OF THE SEA. 39

PERTH, WESTERN AUSTRALIA.

Perth is the capital of Western Australia, which, of all the Australian colonies, has the most extensive area, being nearly one third of the entire continent. At the same time, it has the smallest population. About forty per cent of the entire population of Western Australia resides in Perth and in villages within twenty miles of the capital city. Perth alone has about 20,000 inhabitants. Freemantle, the port of Perth, twelve miles distant at the mouth of the Swan River, has a population of 9500, and is the second city in size in the colony.

The city of Perth is picturesquely situated on the Swan River, about twelve miles from the sea. It presents a striking appearance, being built on sloping ground above a fine lake-like reach of the river. It is well laid out and beautifully planted. There are a few imposing public buildings, including two cathedrals. The City Hall, containing the Legislative Chambers, was erected recently by convict labor. The principal street is nearly two miles long, and is planted with Cape lilac, a beautiful flowering tree. An excellent macadamized road connects the city with the port of Freemantle; and it is united with all the settled districts of the colony by railway and telegraph.

The country surrounding Perth is rocky and hilly, covered with heather and rough grass, and it has, on the whole, quite a Scotch look. The chief diversion of the ladies is gathering wild flowers, which grow in profusion over the slopes.

Adelaide is the capital of South Australia, and has with its immediate environs a population of 144,000.

KING WILLIAM STREET, ADELAIDE.

It was founded in 1837 by Colonel Light, who named it after the wife of King William IV.

Adelaide is situated some seven miles inland on both sides of the Torrens River, and is connected with Port Adelaide by railway. Much intelligent foresight was manifested in laying out the original plan of the survey. Adelaide is built in a regular pattern, the streets running at right angles with one another. One half of the city is the business quarter, and the other is covered by residences. A strip of park land, half a mile wide, separates these two portions. Through the center of this the Torrens flows. Originally this stream was looked upon as a nuisance, as, according to the season of the year, it was either a muddy creek or a flooded flat. Much money and labor were expended upon earthworks to bring it under control, and now a sheet of water, spanned by several bridges, extends for two miles through the city. The sanitary system of the city is of a superior order.

The Mount Lofty range lies a few miles eastward, and in these hills reservoirs have been constructed, which are capable of storing more than a billion gallons of water for the accommodation of the city. Beside being well supplied with local railways, Adelaide is connected with the whole railway system of Australia.

Exactly in the center of the city is Victoria Square. Beside this there are four other squares similar to it, lying toward the four corners of the town. The principal thoroughfare, King William Street, runs through the center, passing through Victoria Square. The chief buildings of the city, some of which are noted for fine architectural design, are situated on this street. Adelaide is a busy place, and boasts an unusual number of churches, a university, three colleges, and a botanical garden which covers one hundred and twenty acres of land.

CHAPTER IV.

THE BUSH.

WITHIN the interior of Australia is a great, uncleared, natural forest known as "The Bush." On most sides it begins at the coast and extends for many, many miles inland. If we should sail around Australia, the view from the sea would be dull and monotonous. There are trees, trees, and nothing but trees, as far as the eye can see in any direction. All the land seems to be covered with trees. No green hills or pieces of open country break the sameness. Everywhere is seen the gloomy, somber shade of the Australian forest.

In the interior, the bush does not prevail. Here the country is more like a wild, natural park. Great sand ridges, lying parallel with one another, reach across the plains, and these are covered, at certain seasons of the year, with a great variety of grasses and flowers, interspersed here and there with shrubs and clusters of trees.

The bush is for the most part a carpeted forest. There is no damp, miry soil and decaying vegetation here. Instead, natural grasses cover the ground, and their hardy roots strike deep into the stony earth; while overhead stretches a canopy of never-fading green, — for, with few exceptions, the trees do not lose their leaves in the winter time.

Here is a gigantic tree rising to the height of one hundred and fifty or two hundred feet. Its leaves have a leathery appearance, and contain a large quantity of aromatic oil. Instead of growing horizontal, with one of the surfaces toward the sky, and the other toward the earth, these leaves are vertical, so that each side is equally exposed to the light. This is the red gum tree, or iron bark tree. If a hole is cut in the bark, a red juice flows freely and hardens in the air into an inodorous, transparent mass, almost black when large, but of a beautiful ruby red in small or thin fragments.

The stringy-bark tree is also striking in appearance.

A FERN GULLY, AUSTRALIA.

It attains a lofty height and yields a beautiful red gum, which is found filling the cavities in the stem, between the concentric circles of wood. The timber of the gum trees cannot be used for cabinet-making purposes. But farther inland there are many trees which are very good for this purpose, such as the cedar, satinwood, pine, and rosewood.

The myall is a small tree with close-grained wood, strongly scented, and is highly prized for making spears and handles for whipstocks. Cattle are fond of eating the leaves, and, as a result "myall country" is very much prized. The apple tree has no apples upon it. It is so named because its leaves bear a strong resemblance to those of the ordinary apple tree. The cherry tree, so called, is only a large shrub of the pine species with small red berries upon it. There are other trees whose names are misleading. The oak resembles a pine tree, and is never found except beside a creek or river. The honeysuckle tree doubtless received its name on account of its bright and shining leaves.

Here is a very peculiar-looking tree with a curious name; it is the "black boy." The stem runs up tall and straight, and is topped with a shaggy green head. The trunk is the peculiar part. A slender pith stick runs through it, and around this stick is set a sort of ring, five or six inches wide, of resinous flakes. These are black outside, while inside they look like varnished splinters, and are full of a resinous, aromatic tar or pitch. The tree is much valued by travelers, as it will burn slowly all night, and thus provide them with both light and heat.

"Scrub" is found in many places in Australia. It differs from "bush" in that it is almost impenetrable on account of the low bushes and shrubs which grow among the larger trees. The scrub on the east coast is especially dense and dark. It contains countless

AUSTRALIA AND THE ISLANDS OF THE SEA.

LAUGHING JACKASSES.

In these forests parasitical and creeping plants are to be found everywhere. Wild vines hang down in festoons, so closely interwoven with the branches of the trees, as to make entrance in most places simply impossible without the use of a hatchet. The scrub, even more than the bush, abounds in vast numbers and kinds of snakes. They vary in length from the eighteen-inch deaf adder, whose bite is fatal, to a rare kind which attains a length of fourteen feet. Some species are considered a great table luxury by the aborigines.

But what is that loud, uproarious noise coming from the very top of that high gum tree? That is the peculiar cry of the "laughing jackass," so called from the resemblance of its cry to the braying of that animal. This bird belongs to the kingfisher family; but, instead of preying upon fish, it eats beetles, reptiles, and small animals.

COCKATOO.

Here may be found the robin, the wren, the crow, the plover, and the snipe, and also those harbingers of spring, the swallow and the cuckoo. There are plenty of bats, owls, and hawks. The mountain pheasant is rare. The eagle hawk is large and is very destructive to lambs. But by far the most common birds are the parrots. There are all kinds and sizes, from the macaw, which sometimes attains a length of three feet, to the little love birds, no larger than a sparrow. Their voices are harsh, and many of them have the power of imitating human speech. They are characterized by a monkeylike restlessness and love of tricks, and,

COCKATOO.

though docile and affectionate, have naturally a very bad temper. The tongue is thick, fleshy, and round; the hooked bill is strong, and is used to help them in climbing. They use their feet as hands, holding their food and carrying it up to the mouth. One of the most beautiful, a cockatoo of a rare species, is of a creamy white color, with orange and red crest, a delicate red lining to the wings, and brilliant crimson among the tail feathers.

There are emus, native turkeys, and many kinds of water fowls, such as pelicans, cranes, black swans, wild ducks, and geese. The native has a curious way of catching ducks. Covering his head with a green sod, he swims quietly out and drops in among a flock. Then seizing a bird by the feet he pulls it down under the water and kills it. Thus he carries on the work, until nothing remains but a lot of dead bodies floating on the surface of the water.

AUSTRALIAN CRANE.

There are wood ducks, which roost in the trees at night; and musk ducks, which smell of musk; also the widely celebrated water moles, which form the connecting link between birds and beasts.

Among animals, the kangaroo and opossum have the precedence, since they supply the natives with food. The former are found in unfrequented parts of the country feeding together like a herd of deer. When frightened, the females put their young ones into their pouch by means of their small front feet, or, if the young are large enough, allow them to jump in themselves; and then away they hasten, leaping long distances over rocks and fallen trees. They are harmless, but if closely pressed, some of the males, called "old men," prove themselves dangerous antagonists. It is said that a gentleman, the owner of sixty thousand sheep, barely escaped being drowned by an "old man" once. He enjoyed calling "hilloo" to his kangaroo dogs, but "all the amusement ceased when an 'old man' came leaping toward him, clutched him round the waist with his fore feet, and commenced hopping away with him to a large water hole to drown him, — a well-known and dangerous practice which the kangaroos have of fighting their enemies. He cried out lustily, as he might under the circumstances be very well excused for doing, and the faithful dogs came to his rescue."

The wallaby is a smaller sort of kangaroo. It lives among the rocks, and is much prized as food by the natives. The opossum is also a marsupial much valued both for its flesh and its fur. "Possum shooting" is a favorite sport in Australia. The proper time for it is at night, when the moon is at the full. The dog will track him, and where he stands and barks one may be sure there is a "possum up the gum tree."

There is a large number of creatures of which little is known. They are all of small size except the harmless wombat, or native hare. The native cat is a beautiful speckled creature that does a great deal of mischief. The native dog, or dingo, is a handsome beast with a bushy tail. He howls, but does not bark, and is the sheep's worst enemy.

Australia is full of insects, but the only one deserving especial mention is the native bee. It has no sting, is slender in body, dark in color, and not much larger than a common house fly. The natives prize the honey, and have a very ingenious way of discovering the hive, which is always in a standing tree. They catch one of the bees, and then, with a piece of gum from a tree, fix a bit of white down on its back. Then they release it. Away goes the bee, and away go the natives. They keep their eyes fixed upon it until it alights at its hive. Then one native takes his tomahawk, cuts notches for his toes to rest in, and climbs to the place where the bee was seen to enter. He speedily cuts out the honeycomb, which he and his companions devour at a meal.

CHAPTER V.

MINING AND SHEPHERDING.

AUSTRALIA is rich in precious and useful minerals. Victoria has gold ; South Australia, copper ; Queensland, copper, tin, gold, iron, and coal ; Western Australia, lead, silver, and copper ; and New South Wales, gold, copper, iron, coal, silver, lead, and tin. The first discovery of gold was in 1851.

When it is reported that gold has been found, there is always a great rush to the place, which at once becomes the scene of much bustle and confusion. In the line of the march, there are immense drays drawn by bullocks, whose drivers do not hesitate to attempt any kind of road, so long as their bullocks can stand on their feet. These drays are loaded with provisions, which are to be sold at an enormous price ; and, if four yokes of bullocks cannot ascend the mountain over which they must pass, a dozen can and must. There are many people who carry their own loads by means of horses and carts. Some travel on horseback with blankets strapped to their saddles ; but by far the largest number go on foot, and carry their loads on their backs. Some take shovels and picks, but others trust to being able to buy them after they reach the fields.

Very soon long lines of white tents overtop the heaps of pipe clay, that grow higher from day to day. If the men are accompanied by their families, they generally fence in a small inclosure, which in the spring is used as a garden. Many of them keep cows, and sell milk and butter. As timber is abundant, houses of every sort soon take the places of many of the tents.

There are several processes of mining. In that of surfacing,

GOLD PROSPECTORS.

the earth is dug two or three feet deep, thrown into a trough, and the water kept running continuously through it. Two men with shovels and forks stir the gravel constantly. The gold, usually in very small pieces, falls to the bottom of the trough, and escapes with the small stones through a sheet of perforated iron at the further extremity.

Another process is called "shallow sinking," and here the pits are simply sunk deeper, the process of washing being the same. But the most common process is called "deep sinking," and the preliminary labor is the same as that performed in sinking a well. This digging is continued until "bed rock" is reached, when the shaft is said to be bottomed. The sand and gravel on the bed rock are then scraped off, and the collection thus made is put into a bucket and drawn to the surface by means of a windlass. Sometimes large quantities of gold have been found in one bucketful. The process of tunneling is carried on upon the surface of the bed rock underneath, equaling in extent the area of the claim above.

These shafts are of various depths, some sinking six hundred feet. Many lives have been lost from want of proper attention to the use of props to prevent the falling of the earth above, from accidents caused by blasting at great depths, and from the filling of the mine with water.

When mined, the pieces of gold differ very much as to size and shape. The three most common forms are the "fine" or "gold dust," the "scaly," and the "rough." The first is found in places abounding in granite; the second, where quartz and slate are intermixed; the last, where quartz predominates. When mixed with

AN AUSTRALIAN WARBLER.

quartz, steam power has to be resorted to for crushing the quartz.

The diggers all have a correct knowledge of the value

of the precious metal, and keep scales for weighing it. After a digger has amassed a quantity, or a "pile," he does not usually keep it by him. In common with all others, he intrusts it, for conveyance to the capital city, to the Government gold escort. This is a four-wheeled wagon drawn by four horses and protected by armed policemen. The gold commissioner at the gold fields receives the packages, which are incased in chamois-skin bags, and gives the miner an acknowledgment of the same. These bags, duly sealed and registered, are then forwarded to their destination.

The life of the digger is a very undesirable one. It is attended with great temptation, and a man may easily degenerate. It is impossible to take proper care of the body. The food is likely to be coarse and poorly prepared. The life is one of uncertainty, irregularity, and excitement, and utterly devoid of all opportunity of self-improvement. It is almost necessarily one of wandering; and, notwithstanding the most solid qualities of head and heart, those who follow it soon become unfit for any steady occupation.

The other great industry of Australia is stock raising. Cattle probably impose less labor than sheep, but the men who own three or four thousand cattle apiece usually have their hands full. These men are called "squatters" or "graziers." Their "runs" usually amount to twenty thousand acres or more; and, though some of them are owned, the most of them are leased for a number of years from the Government.

Their houses are usually furnished comfortably, and if the run be near a town, even luxuriantly. They live well, the food on the table being abundant; but the meals are monotonous. The breakfast, luncheon, and dinner are equally substantial, and tea is the universal beverage, both of masters and men. There is always a carriage; and as horses are cheap, they are found in profusion, both for riding and driving. The squatter is a busy man. He is often on horseback before breakfast, and never seems to slacken his labors till after the evening dews have fallen. If he keeps sheep, the shearing, selling, buying, breeding, and feeding, together with the management of a large force of hired workmen, tax his energies to the utmost. But many squatters really manage their properties by deputy. Serviceable men have grown up in their employment, and, after a while, the real work of the run falls into their hands, and they are called overseers.

As to the underworkers, any man who has sufficient eyesight to see the sheep before him, and strength enough to walk a few miles a day, may be a shepherd in Australia. Many persons who in other lands are totally unable to support themselves can manage to live here by shepherding, and even to lay up a little money. The business is an extremely indolent one; and it is a pitiable sight to see a large strong man sitting on a fallen tree, and dragging himself along over the ground, doing the work which might easily be done by a boy.

"Hut keeping" is still lazier work. The man has nothing to do but sit in his hut, cook his victuals, and, when necessary, shift the hurdles in which the sheep are folded. At night he reports to the overseer in

A STOCK RIDER.

regard to missing sheep. To guard against attacks on his sheep, he sleeps in a covered box near them, and, if native dogs come around, the howling and barking of his own wake him. When he has a wife, she receives extra wages and takes care of the hut. If she is thrifty, the place soon loses its woe-begone look and assumes the appearance of a comfortable home. Cows are kept, a garden is made, and articles of furniture, before unthought of, find their way into the humble abode.

The system of employing families is a great improvement upon the old one of hut keeping. If there are boys in the family, they tend the sheep while the father spends his time in cultivating a plot of ground, or in making shoes if he knows the trade, while, at the same time, he may see that the sheep are properly tended.

In the early history of the country, convicts, exiles, Chinese coolies, and even savages from the Fiji Islands, were employed, cheap labor being what was wanted. But the discovery of gold brought about a radical change. Nearly every one rushed off to the mines. Wages rose at once from twelve pounds to forty and sixty pounds a year, besides rations; the allowance for a man being ten pounds of meat, ten of flour, two of sugar, and one fourth pound of tea a week. At present the wages vary in different parts of the country, being governed largely by the law of demand and supply.

Great interest attaches to this industry, since it has proved a stepping-stone to comfort and even affluence for a great many people. Those who take to the occupation are saved all risk of loss. They are taken from the ship in which they arrive, and are at once housed, fed, and provided for. Their work is easy to learn, and in a little while they acquire the manners and customs of the country. This life is a lonesome one, however, and it is not surprising that, when a few hundred pounds have been saved, the family generally seek some other occupation.

CHAPTER VI.

THE GREAT BARRIER CORAL REEF OF AUSTRALIA.

The Great Barrier Coral Reef of Australia is one of the wonders of the world, and its curious structure and vast extent were first made known by that intrepid explorer, Captain Cook. Its total length is twelve hundred miles. Its northern origin is in Torres Strait, in close proximity to New Guinea, and from this point it extends in a southeasterly direction along the coast of Queensland as far as Lady Eliot Island in latitude 24° south, almost directly opposite the mainland promontory known as Bustard Head.

The width of the reef or series of reefs varies in different districts. In some places the distance from the mainland to the outer edge measures two hundred and forty geographical miles. In other places it narrows down to thirty miles, and at one or two isolated points it measures but ten or twelve miles.

The area inclosed between the mainland and the

outer edge of the reef is about eighty thousand square geographical miles. This extensive surface consists of an archipelago of detached reefs and coral islands. The majority of the former are completely submerged,

GREAT BARRIER CORAL REEF OF AUSTRALIA.

and at low water are but partially exposed to view. The outer wall is generally represented as being one continuous reef, but it is more correct to describe it as a chain of detached reefs broken by many openings, only a few of which are navigable for large-sized vessels. The Admiralty Charts specify twenty-two such channels, but of these only nine are in common use.

The reefs which form the outside barrier, together with the secondary reefs crowded closely to them, constitute a natural breakwater against which the ocean waves dash in vain. The "Inner Route" thus formed is consequently converted into a comparatively shallow and tranquil inland sea. It is, however, so thickly studded with shoals, reefs, and islets as to render its navigation extremely intricate. For vessels of heavy tonnage, the services of a pilot are absolutely necessary, and this employment is followed by a large number of experienced and efficient men.

The danger is in reality reduced to a minimum by the very excellent system of beaconing established by the Queensland government, which is cited by navigators, the world over, as among the most efficient of its kind.

But, notwithstanding the utmost precautions, many vessels are wrecked yearly upon the coral reefs. One of the most noteworthy instances was the loss of the *Quetta* at the entrance of Torres Strait in February, 1890. The *Quetta* was one of the finest and largest of the British India and Australian Steam Navigation Company's fleet. Her express mission was to carry the mails between Queensland ports and London.

Having safely passed through the Barrier Inner Channel, while sailing at full speed along the charted course between Albany and Adolphus islands, she struck an unknown rock, and in three minutes had sunk to the bottom of the sea in a depth of fifteen fathoms of water. Of 282 people, only 162 escaped, and in some cases the escape seemed almost miraculous.

One young woman, sixteen years old, swam and floated on the surface of the water for thirty-five hours before being picked up by a rescue boat. In about the same length of time, another, swimming and drifting with the help of a plank, reached Adolphus Island. Of the cargo, only a small percentage was ever recovered.

There is another story of shipwreck, similar to this one, but of much earlier date. "In this instance, all painful associations of loss of life are, happily, absent, the narrative resolving itself into an almost romantic record of discovered treasure-trove. The good discovery on this occasion fell to the lot of Mr. Frank Jardine, the genial owner of the cattle ranch and fishing station at Somerset, in the Albany Pass, to whose ready and unlimited hospitality, extended to them in the day of their sore distress, the survivors from the *Quetta* accident owe their lifelong gratitude. In the minds of many, doubtless, there will seem to be an almost providentially directed connection betwixt these good deeds and this fortunate episode.

"It so happened that one of Mr. Jardine's boats, prospecting in pastures new for a remunerative fishing ground, was driven, through stress of weather, to take shelter in one of those naturally protected coves that abound among the Barrier Reefs. Lying to in the secluded haven, the flukes of a time-worn anchor were discerned at a short distance from the boat at low ebb-tide. Acting on the idea that the instrument might in some way prove useful, steps were taken to remove it. The surprise and gratification experienced on a mass of coin being laid bare on the immediate resting ground of the eroded anchor, can well be imagined. Further investigation led to the discovery of a larger mass of coin than could be transported by the fishing lugger in a single voyage, several trips from Somerset being eventually undertaken before the little mine was exhausted."

The specie exhumed consisted of Spanish silver dollars, with a fair sprinkling of gold coins. The money was in a remarkable state of preservation, and the aggregate value of the treasure amounted to several thousand pounds.

The Great Barrier Reef doubtless has many secrets, and hides within its coral caves many treasures which will never come to light. Among these are Captain Cook's six guns, thrown overboard from the *Endeavor* when she was temporarily aground on a reef. These are of classic interest to all Australians, and the supposed vicinity of the disaster has been searched with the aid of divers many times without success. In all probability the guns have long since been buried beneath a mass of growing coral.

Before we go farther, it may be well to inquire what formed this great coral reef. The coral insect? Not so. There is no such thing as a coral *insect*. A great many people labor under the delusion that held Punch's railway porter, who, puzzled as to the classification of the old lady's tortoise, affirmed that being "neither a dawg nor a bird, it must needs be a hinsec."

An insect in the normal adult condition has several legs, associated with a distinctly articulated body and a complex nervous and circulatory system. The coral animal has none of these. "It is individually a single polyp, comparable in every essential detail with the ordinary simply organized sea anemone, with the exception that it possesses the property of secreting a dense, calcareous skeleton out of the lime held abundantly in suspension in probably every sea."

The coral reef-building polyps are found only in water whose temperature never falls below 68° F. Therefore, as a rule, they live only in tropical seas, be-

ATOLL, OR RING ISLAND.

tween the parallels of latitude $23\frac{1}{2}°$ north and south of the equator.

In the Barrier district, the highest elevation at which growing corals are found is low-water mark, and the lowest is thirty fathoms deep. Their most luxuriant development is limited by a depth of fifteen fathoms.

As originally classified by Mr. Darwin, there are three distinct varieties of coral reefs: Lagoon Islands, or Atolls; Barrier, or Encircling, Reefs; and Fringing, or Shore, Reefs.

The atolls are singular rings of coral land which rise abruptly out of the unfathomable sea.

Between the atoll and barrier reef there is no essential point of difference. The former incloses a simple sheet of water; the latter encircles an expanse with one or more islands rising from it.

"With respect to fringing, or shore, reefs, there is little in their structure that needs explanation; and their name expresses their comparatively small extension. They differ from barrier reefs in not lying far from the shore and in not having within them a broad channel of deep water."

The Capricorn group forms the southern extremity of the Great Barrier Reef, and of this group Lady Eliot Island lies farthest south. This island was visited by Professor Jukes in 1843. Then many sea birds inhabited it. Now it is the site of a first-class lighthouse, which, with another on Sandy Cape, illumes the entrance to the Inner Route along the coast of Queensland to Torres Strait.

Coarse fragments of bleached coral and broken shells form the beach of Lady Eliot. Back of this is a ridge of the same material, four or five feet in height and measuring several yards across. This ridge, which is occupied by a growth of small trees, encircles the island, which is about a quarter of a mile in diameter. In the center is a sandy plain covered with scrubby vegetation a foot or two high. On the northwest side of the island, is a sloping bank of coral, which, at the distance of a fourth of a mile, is about two fathoms under water. Here it ends suddenly, and the water measures fifteen fathoms deep.

In Moreton Bay, opposite Brisbane, are found at the

present day masses of dead coral of two species. Beside these are found several species of living corals, one of which resembles the Red Sea variety.

Proceeding north from Lady Eliot Island, we fall in with a chain of islands about fifty-five miles long, belonging to the Bunker and Capricorn groups. They all lie within thirty or forty miles of the mainland. None of these islands are more than a mile in length, and all closely resemble the Lady Eliot.

The Torres Strait group practically forms the western boundary of the Great Barrier area. It comprises twelve islands, and, with the surrounding reefs and shoals, they stretch northward to the center of the strait. The largest, Prince of Wales Island, is irregularly circular, and has a diameter of nearly twelve miles. It reaches its greatest height in a hill which rises 761 feet above the level of the sea.

Banks Island lies twenty miles north of this and has about the same area. All the rest are much smaller. Thursday Island, although one of the smallest, takes the precedence commercially. It is the headquarters of the Torres Strait pearl shell fisheries, and it is also the port of call and coasting station for ocean steamers passing to and from the ports of India and China. The population of the island is small, being less than three thousand. But the number of nationalities represented, twenty-four, is in excess, comparatively, of what is to be found in any other quarter of the globe.

Some idea of the monetary importance to Queensland of the Great Barrier Coral Reef may be gained from the fact that raw material to the value of over £100,000

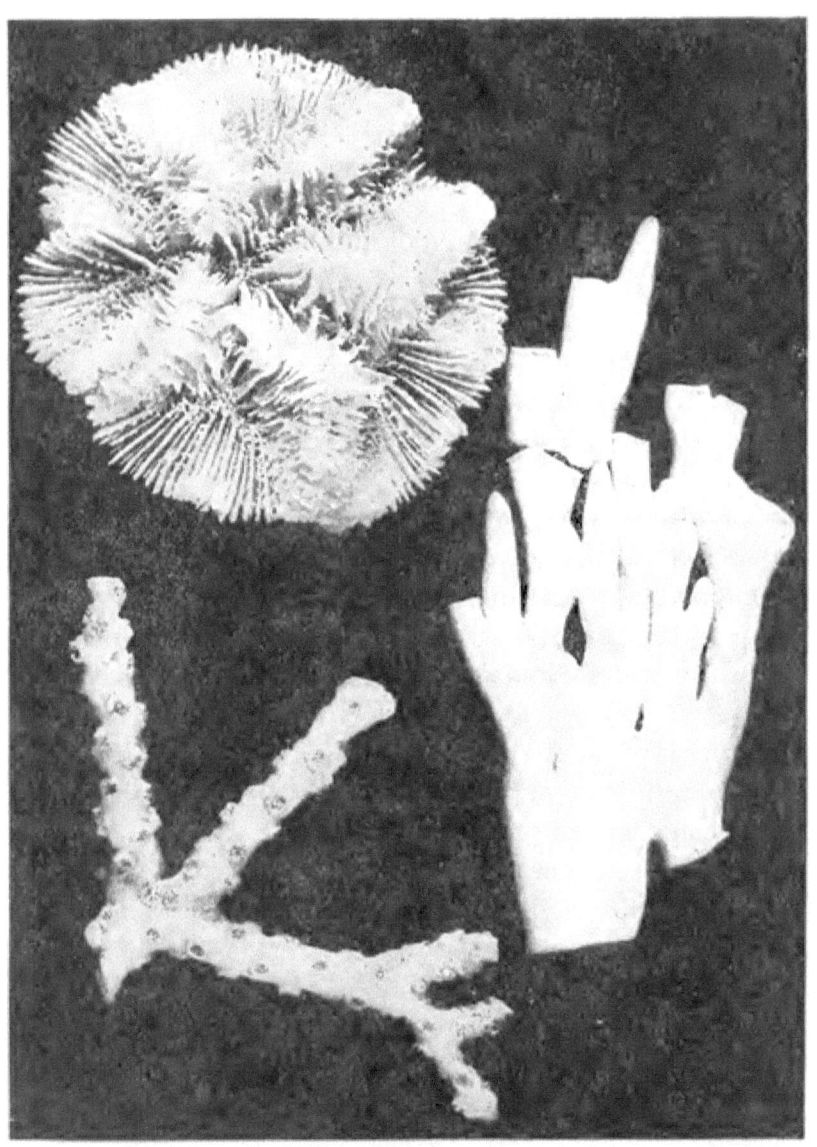

CORAL FORMATIONS.

is obtained annually from the reefs and the intervening waters, and exported from the colony.

When the prolific resources of the region have been fully developed, this sum will be considerably increased. The pearl, pearl shell, and trepang fisheries have contributed most largely to bring about this result. These industries are capable of almost unlimited development, and in addition to them are other allied industries, which will in time yield a rich increase to the colony's wealth.

In former years mother-of-pearl was obtained in large quantities at little expense, and even now it is found in some places in shallow water, where, at low spring tide, it may be gathered with the hand. But the average depth of water from which it is now collected is seven fathoms. The greatest depth at which it may be gathered with profit is twenty fathoms. Even at this depth there are few divers who can work very long at a time, on account of the great pressure of the water.

The vessels employed in this industry are chiefly strong lugger-rigged crafts, which average ten tons' burden. The crew of the lugger is made up of a diver, who acts as sailing master and takes command, a tender, who holds the life lines and attends to the signals given by the diver when at work, and four other men, who, in pairs, alternately attend to the pumping apparatus which supplies air to the diver.

As a rule, the entire crew is composed of colored men of various nationalities, — aborigines from the mainland, south sea islanders, and natives from islands in Torres Strait. Some of the best divers, however, are

Chinese, Japanese, Manila men, and Malays. There are but few European divers, and these are generally the owners of their own vessels.

Of the typical mother-of-pearl taken from Queensland waters there are two varieties. One has a golden edge, and the other is of a uniform silvery appearance throughout. The latter is of the greater value, since it cuts up to better advantage. As may be seen in a recent report of one of the principal mother-of-pearl mercantile houses of London, the Queensland shell occupies a leading position in the market. The "fine white, selected bold" brings no less than $1125 per ton, which is seventy-five dollars in advance of the best shell procured from any other waters.

In this connection, an interesting study might also be made of the pearls obtained from these shells. It is only one shell out of many thousands which produces a pearl weighing as much as thirty or forty grains. Such a pearl, if perfect, sells for about twelve hundred dollars. Occasionally larger ones are found, which, if they are unblemished, bring a correspondingly higher price. Thus a perfectly spherical one weighing eighty-eight grains was sold by the owner for two thousand dollars. Pearls vary much in shape. A pear-shaped one, weighing twenty-eight grains, is valued at about five hundred dollars.

Next to the pearl and pearl shell fisheries, those of the trepang, or bêche-de-mer, are of most importance. The term "bêche-de-mer" is a French word signifying a sea slug or sea worm. The term was applied by the older Portuguese navigators to that product of the sea,

AUSTRALIA AND THE ISLANDS OF THE SEA. 71

ABORIGINES FISHING BY NIGHT.

which, from remote times, has constituted such an important article of commerce with China. The terms "sea slug" and "sea worm" have reference to the general shape of the animals. They are distinguished from their allies, the starfishes and sea urchins, by their elongate, somewhat cucumber-shaped bodies, which are capable of great contraction or expansion. The mouth, which is situated at one end of the body, is surrounded by a series of tufted tentacles.

The bêche-de-mer fisheries are carried on by luggers of five or six tons' burden. Still larger schooners are fitted up with all the appliances necessary for curing the fish, and these simply change their anchorage from time to time, sending out their boats in every direction to collect the fish.

The fish are taken during the low tides in the new and full phases of the moon, and eight or ten days in each lunar month are thus utilized. The greater part of the fish are simply picked off the reefs and thrown into sacks. But the finest red and black fish, and the prickly fish, are obtained at the depth of two or three fathoms by diving.

Arrived at the curing station, the fish are thrown into boiling water and boiled for twenty minutes. They are then split lengthwise with a sharp knife, and cleaned. Then they are laid on the ground to dry, and after this they are smoked for twenty-four hours, the favorite wood in use being the red mangrove.

By this time they are so shrunken as to measure only about six inches. They are then ready for bagging and shipping to market. The greatest care now is to

CAPE PILLAR, TASMANIA.

keep them dry, and this is a difficult matter, since they absorb moisture readily. "Properly cured and maintained in first-class condition, the dried animals should rattle like walnuts in their bags." In transporting them to Hong Kong, they are sometimes placed in cases lined with tin.

Third upon the list of Queensland fisheries stands that of the oyster. The annual export value is much lower than that of pearl shell or bêche-de-mer, but the revenue accruing to the government is far in excess of that derived from either of these industries. Beside this, about half as many as are exported are kept for home uses.

The rock oyster is the only variety as yet to receive serious consideration from a purely commercial standpoint. The coxcomb oyster is the largest edible oyster found in Queensland waters. It received its name on account of the regular zigzag undulations of the outer edges of the valves. A pair of shells of this oyster often weigh as much as five or seven pounds.

CHAPTER VII.

TASMANIA.

TASMANIA lies a hundred and thirty miles south of Australia, from which it is separated by Bass Strait. It was known formerly as Van Diemen's Land, and contains an area of more than twenty-six thousand square miles. The coast line is considerably broken, especially on the south. The surface of the country is mountainous, varied by deep, narrow valleys, extensive undulating tracts of country, and open plains of limited extent. Ben Lomond and Cradle Mount are each more than five thousand feet high, and there are several other peaks exceeding four thousand feet. Nestled among the central mountains, at an average height of three thousand

GOVERNMENT HOUSE, HOBART.

feet, are numerous small lakes; these feed the greater part of the rivers draining the southeast slope.

On approaching the island from the north, the first object that attracts the attention is a lighthouse one hundred and forty feet high. It marks the mouth of the Tamar River. The tide in this river is characterized by a remarkable rise and fall, the difference between high and low tide being fourteen feet. Here and there along its shores isolated houses dot the country. These are not cabins, but neat, permanent structures, near which are large barns and other appropriate buildings. These barns signify that the domestic animals have need of protection during the winter, which is not the case in Australia.

Forty miles from the mouth of the river is Launceston. Its tall smoking chimneys proclaim the fact that the people are busy smelting ores dug from the neighboring hills and valleys. This town is at the head of navigation on the Tamar River, in a beautiful valley surrounded by hills. It has a population of seventeen thousand. Like Melbourne, its streets are broad and regularly laid out. A good supply of water is brought from St. Patrick's River, fifteen miles away. Its many substantial buildings of brick and stone impart an air of unusual prosperity to the place.

A mountain range, from two to five thousand feet in height, occupies the central part of the island, while its plains and valleys give pasturage to nearly two million sheep, besides large numbers of cattle. The wool produced is of an excellent quality, and always commands the best price. In the mountain ranges and near them, gold, silver, tin, copper, and coal abound; so that the land teems with mineral wealth, as yet undeveloped.

One hundred and fifty miles from Launceston is the famous Mount Bischoff tin mine. It may be reached from the city either by land or water. The quartz, or tin-bearing rock, may be said to form the entire hill to the height of three hundred feet. Several shafts have been sunk to the depth of a hundred feet, showing that the metallic deposit reaches that depth, and is practically inexhaustible. The tin is shipped direct to England in the form of "pigs," the demand from that country absorbing the entire product of the mine.

One hundred and fifty miles south of Launceston is Hobart, the capital of Tasmania. The two places

ABORIGINES OF TASMANIA.

are connected by a narrow gauge railroad owned and operated by a private company. The city occupies a fine position, twenty miles from the sea, at the head of a sheltered estuary called Sullivan's Cove. On the other three sides it is surrounded by hills and mountains, the loftiest being Mount Wellington. The city is square, and is built upon a succession of low hills.

Its broad streets intersect one another at right angles. They are lined with well-stocked stores, and among them are several elegant bookstores which would do credit to any American or European city, their shelves containing a full assortment of both modern and classical literature.

Its public buildings and many of its private residences are constructed of light freestone, which not only gives an imposing aspect to its thoroughfares, but produces a pleasing effect whether seen in sunshine or shadow. The population numbers thirty thousand. Though the prospect is so pleasing, Hobart has not yet outlived the curse of the penal institutions which characterized its early history. Fifty years ago the British government was spending five thousand dollars a day in support of jails and military barracks. The last convict ship from England discharged her cargo in 1851. Since then the system, with all its incidental barbarities, has gradually disappeared.

The Botanical Garden covers an area of over twenty acres. It is filled with ornamental trees, flowers, and fruit trees, from every part of the world. Even in the winter, which, for the climate, is mild and wonderfully equable, sweet-scented shrubs and flowers render the dewy morning air delightfully fragrant.

In some respects the street scenes are novel. The typical miner, with his canvas bag, his pick, and shovel on his shoulder, seems omnipresent. The chimney sweep, whom we know only as belonging to olden times, is seen here, with blackened face and soiled hands, pursuing his vocation. Market men, galloping

TASMAN'S ARCH.

on wiry little horses, deliver their goods to customers, in baskets which they bear on their arms. Women, with scores of slaughtered rabbits, cry them for sale at sixpence for two, and realize a bounty, besides, for killing them, as they are counted as pests.

The fish market is also an interesting place. The inhabitants of the sea differ very much from those with which we are most familiar. The lobsters have a corrugated shell exceedingly hard, and lack the claws which are so conspicuous a part of ours. The best of their oysters are of a very inferior grade.

There are about thirty species of mammals in Tasmania, of which one half are marsupials. Among the latter are the kangaroo, wallaby, opossum, and wombat. The Tasmanian devil is also a marsupial, and is peculiar to Tasmania. It is sometimes very destructive to sheep. The skin of the kangaroo is much prized for leather, and opossum fur sells well. The majority of the birds of the island are identical with those of Australia. The black swan is now seldom seen in the settled districts. There are thirteen species of snakes, most of which are venomous, but accidents from their bite seldom occur.

About twenty miles from Hobart is a fine forest of gum trees similar to those abounding in Australia. The people say that they can show trees larger than any in Victoria. One which had fallen was of extraordinary size, being three hundred and thirty feet in length, and its trunk having a circumference of seventy-one feet. In these forests, local steam sawmills are constantly at work preparing lumber of various dimensions for market.

The aborigines of Tasmania resembled those of Australia only in color. They were well formed and

AUSTRALIA AND THE ISLANDS OF THE SEA.   81

QUEENSTOWN, NEW ZEALAND.

athletic and had flat noses, curly hair, bright eyes, and elaborately tattooed bodies. They were low in the scale of barbarism and were addicted to cannibalism. They are now utterly extinct.

MAORI WARCLUB.

CHAPTER VIII.

NEW ZEALAND.

NEW ZEALAND is a British colony in the South Pacific Ocean, about twelve hundred miles southeast of Australia. It consists of North Island, South Island, and Stewart Island, the last being much smaller than the other two. There are also numerous islets. The group is irregular in form, and, like Italy, resembles a boot in shape. North Island and South Island are each about five hundred miles long from north to south, and have an average breadth of one hundred and forty miles. The combined area of the three is one hundred and five thousand square miles. North Island is separated from South Island by Cook Strait, which is eighteen miles wide at the eastern point, and ninety at the western. The coast line measures nearly four thousand miles, and North Island has many excellent

AUSTRALIA AND THE ISLANDS OF THE SEA.

WELLINGTON, NEW ZEALAND.

harbors. New Zealand is a little larger than Colorado, and a little smaller than Italy including Sicily and Sardinia.

Wellington, at the southern extremity of North Island, is the capital; but, aside from this fact, little of importance attaches to the place. It has its asylums, a hospital, a college, botanical gardens, a Roman Catholic cathedral, and a museum. Here is also a Maori house, built by the natives, and filled with carvings, weapons, and domestic utensils used by the aborigines.

In this city may be seen a number of natives, who are called Maoris, dressed as a rule in European costume. The women have great masses of hair falling over their foreheads and shading their great, black eyes. Their cheek bones are high, and their chins are tattooed with a sort of blue dye. The men tattoo the whole face. They greet each other by rubbing noses when they meet on the street. As is the rule among savages, the women do all the work, and the men play the part of idlers. The aborigines were cannibals. Captain Cook, in order to discourage the inhuman practice of eating human flesh, introduced swine and other domestic animals into the country. But although the natives hunted the animals, which were allowed to run wild, and which increased in numbers, cannibalism received no appreciable check. While the Maoris were utter barbarians, they seemed to thrive; but now that they are semi-civilized, they yearly decrease in numbers, and, like the aborigines of Tasmania, they will probably become extinct.

The islands forming New Zealand are of volcanic

MAORI WOMAN AND CHILD.

origin. The surface is very mountainous. There are a few active volcanoes, and many more inactive ones. The loftiest mountain in North Island is over nine thousand feet in height. Mount Cook in South Island is about thirteen thousand feet high. The greatest elevation in Stewart Island is not over three thousand feet above the sea level.

There are countless running streams of the purest water, but the rivers are short and not navigable for more than fifty miles, as a rule. The principal one is Waikato River in North Island. It rises in the center of the country, and, after flowing north for a distance of two hundred miles, reaches the sea on the west coast.

The climate of New Zealand is one of the finest in the world. There are but few physical sources of disease. The average temperature is remarkably even at all seasons of the year, and the atmosphere is continually freshened by winds which blow over a great expanse of ocean. In North Island the mean annual temperature is fifty-eight degrees; in South Island, fifty-two. All the native trees and plants are evergreen. There are over a thousand species of flowering plants. Cattle as a rule feed on grass and shrubs all the year round, and the cultivation of the land may be carried on at all seasons. Of the crops, the principal ones are wheat, oats, barley, potatoes, and sown grass.

A few species of lizards and a small rat are the only native four-footed animals. Hawks are numerous. There are no snakes, and but few insects. The domestic animals introduced by colonists thrive well, and at present there are thousands of horses, cattle, and pigs,

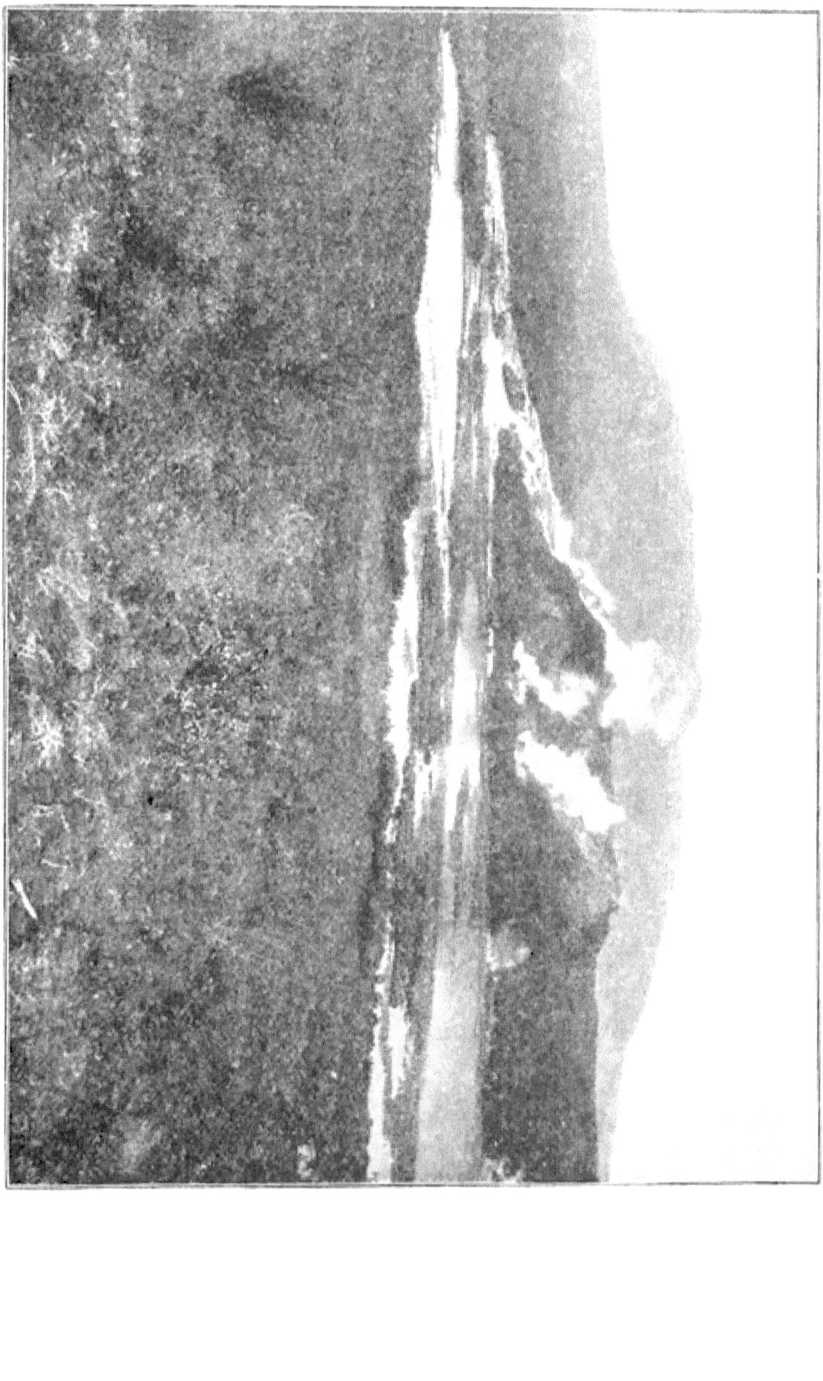

ROTOMAHAMA HOT SPRINGS, NEW ZEALAND.

and millions of sheep and poultry in the country. Coal, iron, gold, silver, copper, and tin are found in various places, and there is a great abundance of valuable timber.

Auckland, the Naples of New Zealand, is its northern metropolis and a typical city. It is built upon an isthmus in one of the most remarkable volcanic districts in the world. One mountain six thousand feet high is, even now, in constant activity. The severest earthquake occurred in 1851, raising the coast line four feet higher for many miles. It is said that within a radius of ten miles from the center of the city there are sixty-three volcanic cones where eruptions have taken place. The height of these hills varies from two hundred to seven hundred feet. A century ago, each of them was held by a native tribe who fortified its summit. The highest hill is Mount Eden, close to Auckland.

The harbor is unusually fine. It has two dry docks, one of which, five hundred feet long by eighty wide, is the largest in the South Pacific. Vessels of any size may anchor in this harbor.

The city is spread out over a large area, extending from the foot of Mount Eden to the bay, and each of the dwelling houses has a beautiful garden attached. Queen Street, reaching from the wharves to the suburbs, is the main thoroughfare. Some of the buildings with which it is lined are handsome structures. They are built of freestone, and are occupied as banks, offices, and stores. There are some very imposing brick structures, four stories in height, with handsome façades. Churches are to be seen in all parts of the city. There

AUCKLAND, NEW ZEALAND.

are also a university for boys and a high school for girls, besides primary schools. The post office, supreme court house, government house, public library, and hospital are the chief public buildings.

Near the center of the city is a popular resort called Albert Park. It is really a small mountain, with winding paths leading to the summit, on which are a flagstaff and several cannon. This park commands a fine view of the city, the harbor, and the surrounding country.

The commercial prosperity of Auckland and the adjacent territory is due to the large forests. The pine of this country, called the kauri tree, is very different from our pines. It has leaves of a somber green in place of needles. This tree makes an excellent timber, fine-grained and easily worked. It grows to an average height of one hundred feet, and its diameter is fifteen feet or more. It does not seem to relish the proximity of other varieties of trees, and sometimes occupies whole forests unmixed with any other kind. There is no undergrowth except tree ferns.

Kauri gum, which resembles amber, exudes from the bark of the kauri pine, and is gathered and exported in large quantities from Auckland. It is also found in large masses at the depth of five or six feet in the ground, and is supposed to be the product of ancient kauri forests, which, centuries ago, were destroyed by fire or decay. The deposit seems to be inexhaustible. This gum is used as a base, instead of gum mastic, in the manufacture of fine varnishes, and for other purposes.

The lakes of New Zealand are a prominent feature.

CHRISTCHURCH, NEW ZEALAND.

In South Island are two, covering areas of one hundred and thirty-two and one hundred and twelve square miles, respectively. These, and many others among the Southern Alps, are possessed of great beauty, and are objects of interest to tourists and explorers. Near the center of North Island is one covering an area of two hundred and fifty square miles. Lying between it and the White Island, in the Bay of Plenty, is the famous Hot Lake District of New Zealand. It is in the center of territory reserved for some of the Maori tribes. Geysers, boiling springs, and palatial terraces abound everywhere. Many of the geysers and springs are so hot as to blister the flesh immediately on its coming in contact with their waters. Others are of a temperature suitable for boiling vegetables, while others still are lovely natural baths, formed, as it were, of tinted marble and full of warm transparent water of a bluish color.

The Maori people of both sexes spend much of their time in these pools. Their covering, as a rule, is nothing but a blanket; and if they feel cold, day or night, they resort at once to the water. They seem to do little else than bathe and smoke, and in the use of tobacco the women indulge even more freely than the men. They live almost wholly upon pork and potatoes, the latter growing without cultivation. They boil their potatoes by suspending them in a wire net in a hot spring, or bake them by placing them upon the hot rocks that are found everywhere. They have no way of building a fire in their cabins, which consist of but one room. Their beds are composed of dried fern leaves.

AUSTRALIA AND THE ISLANDS OF THE SEA. 93

HOT WATER BASINS, WHITE TERRACE, NEW ZEALAND.

MAORI IDOLS, NEW ZEALAND.

The Maoris differ in many respects from other savage tribes. They are not revengeful like the American Indians, neither are they treacherous or deceitful. Before going to war they always give their enemy due warning. Originally their greatest ambition was to make prisoners, "and when made, to cook and eat them." At the present time they have settled down to a life of quiet and peace, and are as lazy and listless as it is possible for humanity to be.

CHAPTER IX.

A PEN PICTURE OF GREENLAND.

"For if the land have a good name, it will cause many to come hither." So said Eric the Red, a thousand years ago, when he gave the name Greenland to this desolate island. And he was right. Emigrants poured in. New towns were built, new farms were cleared, and Greenland became a land of the Northmen.

A GREENLAND GUIDE.

At what time this race became extinct, we do not

know. But the Esquimaux, a heathen people, who laid waste their homes and sanctuaries, now occupy the country.

A large part of Greenland lies within the Arctic Circle, and all of it is arctic in its character. It is separated from Europe by the Atlantic Ocean, from Iceland by Denmark Strait, and from North America by Davis Strait and Baffin Bay. According to a map made by Lieutenant Peary, its northern shore is bounded by Kane Basin, Kennedy Channel, Robeson Channel, Lincoln Sea, and Independence Bay.

The length of Greenland from north to south is thirteen hundred and eighty miles. Its greatest width from east to west is six hundred and ninety miles. Its area is estimated at five hundred and twelve thousand square miles; this allows one hundred and ninety-two thousand for the "outskirts" with their fiords, and three hundred and twenty thousand for the "inland ice." By the first term is meant the land lying on the coast; by the latter, the interior.

The country cannot be called mountainous, though heights of from three to four thousand feet are common. There are a few points, still more elevated, such as Petermann's Peak on the east coast, eleven thousand feet high, Payer's Peak, Sukkertoppen, and Saunderson's Hope.

Very little is known of the eastern coast, on account of the Spitzbergen ice stream continually pouring down that shore. Its general features are high cliffs, great glaciers, and deep inlets. The western coast is more accessible. The coast line is indented by numerous

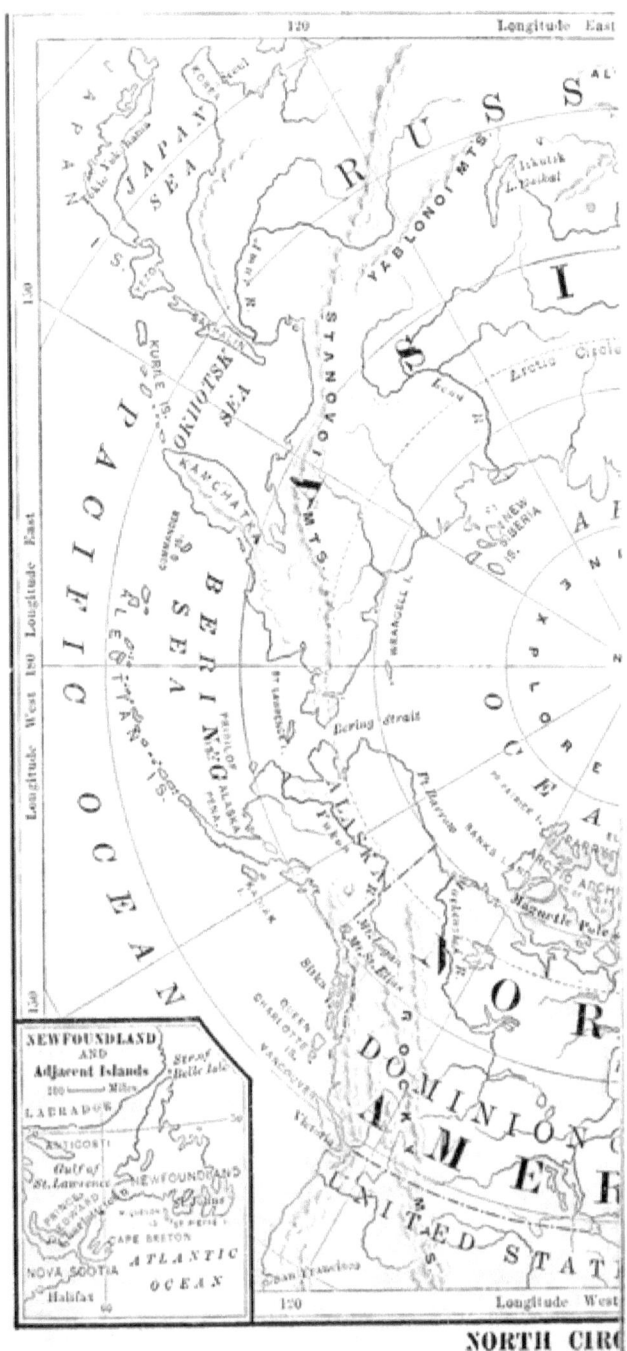

NORTH CIRC
Including Greenland, Iceland, Spitzbergen, Nova Zembla, Kurile

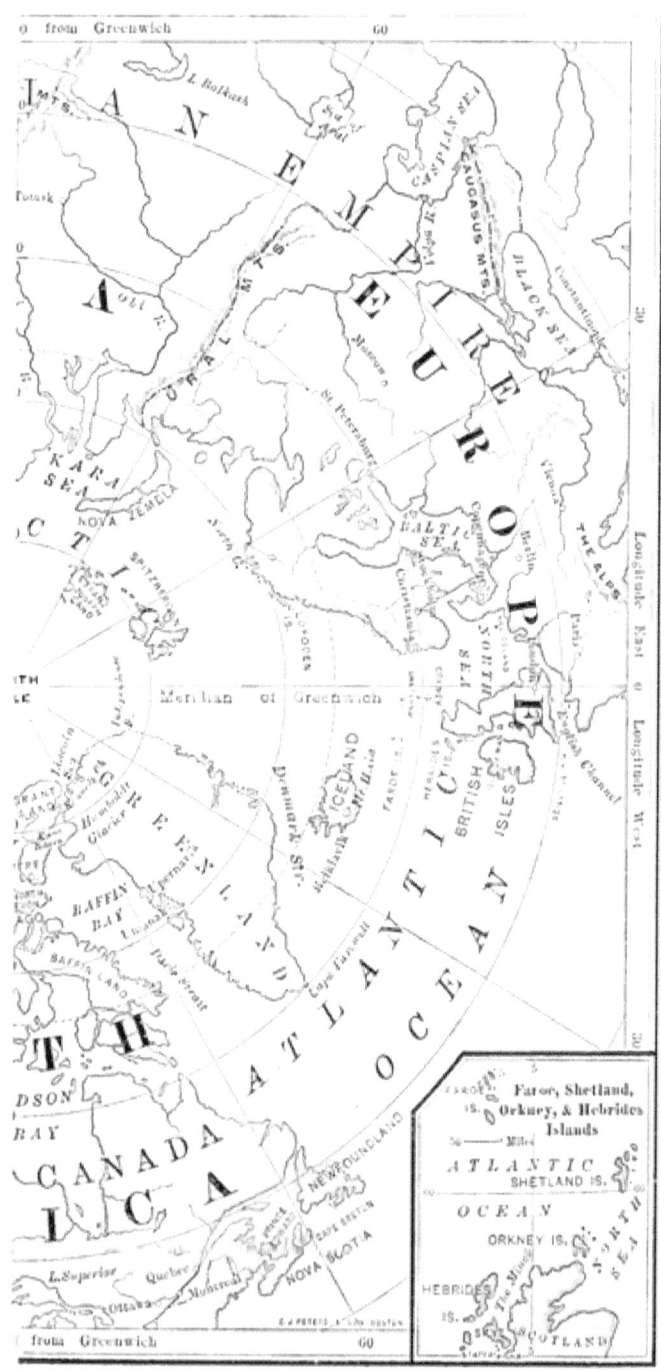

...MPOLAR MAP

...nd Aleutian Islands, Arctic Archipelago, Hebrides, Newfoundland,

AUSTRALIA AND THE ISLANDS OF THE SEA.

IN GREENLAND WATERS.

fiords, most of which have been followed to their heads. Many of them stretch several miles into the interior, and are ended by glacier prolongations of the "inland ice." These are known as "ice fiords."

For the purpose of ascertaining the character of the northern shore, Lieutenant R. E. Peary with one attendant, in the summer of 1892, undertook "The Great White Journey" over the "inland ice." He started from Redcliffe on the western coast, in latitude seventy-seven and a half, and traveled along the "inland ice" toward the northeast.

The journey was begun on the first day of May, and, after traveling for fifty-seven days over a barren waste of ice and snow, he reached "a strange new land lying red-brown in the sunlight, and dotted with snowdrifts here and there." A journey of four more days brought him to a cliff three thousand five hundred feet high, now known as Navy Cliff. It stands in latitude eighty-one and a half, and longitude thirty-five, and marks the northeastern extremity of Greenland. At its foot lies Independence Bay, so named by Lieutenant Peary because discovered on the fourth of July. This bay opens into the Arctic Ocean.

"It was almost impossible," he says, "for us to believe that we were standing upon the northern shore of Greenland, as we gazed from the summit of this bronze cliff, with the most brilliant sunshine all about us, with yellow poppies growing at our feet, and a herd of musk oxen in the valley behind us. Down in that same valley, I had found an old friend, a dandelion in bloom, and had seen the bullet-like flight, and heard the energetic buzz, of the bumble bee."

The summer season in Greenland is very short, not exceeding four months, during two of which the sun is always above the horizon. It is characterized by a rapid growth of vegetation. In the north and northwest, grass and soft moss, studded with thousands of flowers, quickly cover the ground. Farther to the south there are tangled growths of junipers, whortleberry, crakeberry, and willows, while the grassy sod is decorated with plants in bloom, among which are the dandelion, bluebell, crowfoot, and cochleria. The angelica grows beside the streams, to the height of three feet. The stem of this plant is used by the natives as food, as is also a kind of cress called scurvy grass.

No attempt is made in any part of Greenland to raise anything more than the ordinary garden vegetables, such as lettuce, radishes, and cabbage.

The civil organization of Greenland is very simple. The northern and northeastern parts are given up to England, America, and Germany, by right of discovery. The western coast is claimed by Denmark. For purposes of government and trade, the latter is divided into two political divisions called inspectorates. The southern inspectorate extends nearly to the sixty-seventh degree of latitude, and the northern comprises the rest of the Danish territory.

Each inspectorate is governed by an inspector, whose authority is absolute throughout his jurisdiction. There is no appeal from his decision, except to the Government Board at Copenhagen. The residence of the southern inspector is at the capital city, Godthaab. The capital of the northern inspectorate is Godhavn, on Disco Island.

Each inspectorate is divided into districts. The southern contains seven. The northern has five, of which Upernavik, at the very verge of human exist-

THE GOVERNOR'S HOME, GREENLAND.

ence, is the farthest north, and, strangely enough, bears a name which signifies "the summer place." Each district is presided over by a governor.

The districts are divided into outposts, each one of which is ruled by a Dane or a half-breed. His principal business is to keep the Government accounts, dispose of its stores, and gather products for its profit. These stores, consisting of wheat, coffee, sugar, tobacco, and firewood, are distributed among the outposts. In a similar manner the native products, consisting of stock fish (the cod, dried without salt), eider down, furs, seal skin, and blubber, are collected ready for shipment to Denmark. Cryolite, found in quantity in Greenland only, is at present the only mineral exported. It has been discovered only in one spot, Ivigtut, on the shore of Arsut Fiord.

The river system of Greenland is unlike that of countries with which we are familiar, and we must give it special attention.

Can you imagine a country the center of which is one vast unbroken sheet of water? Can you see rivers flowing from this lake in every direction to the sea? Greenland is like that, only the lake is a frozen one, and the rivers are frozen streams.

The interior of Greenland is not habitable, for it is covered by a great mass of ice. This is called the "inland ice," and it is estimated that its average thickness is at least five hundred feet.

What becomes of this great quantity of ice? It flows to the sea, and we call the name of these frozen rivers glaciers. The rate of flow depends upon the steepness of descent. It has been calculated that the average movement is from five to eight inches daily.

In the Alps the glacier never reaches the foot of the mountain. Long before that, it has changed into a river of water. But in Greenland the glacier never melts. It reaches the ocean in all the glory of its cold and crystal hardness. In its progress down the valley into the fiord, it must necessarily adapt itself to every inequality of the bank. This is not done without serious resistance. Tons of earth, sand, and rocks are torn up and pushed aside when the glacier spreads itself into the side valleys. This resistance accounts for the fact that a glacier, like a river, flows swifter in the center than at the sides.

Many of the Greenland glaciers are of wonderful

A GREENLAND GLACIER.

extent. The Great Humboldt Glacier, lying at the head of Smith Sound, and discovered by Dr. Kane, is sixty miles wide. Its front is in the water and it is washed by the waves like any other coast line. Below the surface of the water, this wall of ice extends downward to the bottom, and in places the depth is over two thousand feet. Another glacier, twenty miles wide, is to be seen in the fiord of Aukpadlartok, near which Upernavik is situated.

An iceberg is a detached portion of a glacier. When it is about to break loose, a loud report is heard, quickly followed by another louder than the first. The detached mass now plunges forward. The front sinks while the inner side rises, and volumes of water, lifted with the sudden motion, pour from its sides into the agitated sea.

Imagine a piece of ice, a third of a mile deep, a mile long, and half a mile wide, hurled away into the water and set in motion by the impetus of the act. One side dips down almost out of sight, the other rises and then falls again with irresistible force; and this process goes on for hours, until the great mass finally comes to rest. Such an exhibition of power is nowhere else to be witnessed on the face of the earth.

Not all of the icebergs are separated from glaciers in this manner. Instead of falling into the sea, the enormous masses of ice are propelled inch by inch, and year by year, until, reaching water which can sustain their weight, they are quietly floated away.

CHAPTER X.

LIFE IN AN IGLOO.

THE hut of the Esquimaux is called an "igloo." It is built of stones and turf. In order to effect an entrance, one must go down on his hands and knees and creep through a sort of tunnel from six to twenty feet long.

This tunnel is very low, straight, and level until it reaches the inner part of the chamber, when it rises abruptly by a small hole, through which, with some squeezing, you enter the true apartment. Over this entrance is a rude window, covered with scraped seal intestine. A smoke hole opens through the roof.

AN OLD GREENLAND RUIN.

A platform, one and a half feet from the floor, about four feet wide in the middle and two and a half at the sides, runs all around the walls of the igloo, except that part of the floor in which is the aperture for entrance. The middle of this platform, for about five feet, is the bed. The ends of it, on either side of the doorway, are devoted to the stoves, in which chunks of blubber are burned.

Above each stove hangs a soapstone pan containing

snow, to be melted into water for drinking purposes. Above these pans are racks on which the inmates hang their wet mittens, stockings, and bird-skin shirts. It not unfrequently happens that insects fall from these into the drinking water. But no notice is taken of this, for the igloos are exceedingly filthy and alive with vermin.

The men and women dress very much alike. The body is covered with two garments. One is made of bird skin, and worn with the feathers next to the body. The other is made of seal skin, and is worn with the fur on the outside. These garments, fashioned just alike, are made to fit the figure. They are cut short at the hips, and are pointed at the back and front. A close-fitting hood is sewed to the neck of each garment for outdoor use. An extra breadth is sewed into the back of the woman's outer garment, so as to form a sort of pouch. In this she carries her baby until it is large enough to walk.

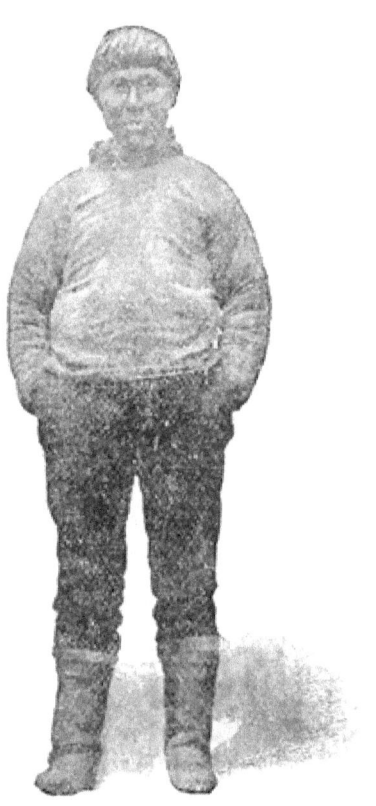

A NATIVE GREENLANDER.

The men wear seal-skin, dog-skin, or bear-skin trowsers, reaching below the knee. Their stockings are made of the fur of the Arctic hare. The trowsers of the women are made of fox skin or seal skin and are little more than trunks. Their stockings are long, and are made of reindeer fur. Their boots are equally long, and are made of tanned seal skin.

The only arms the men carry are knives, which they conceal in their boots. Their lances, which are formidable weapons, are lashed to their sledges.

These sledges, or sleds, are made up of small fragments of porous bone, strongly knit together by thongs of hide. The runners are made of highly polished ivory obtained from the tusks of the walrus. The sledge is drawn by two or more dogs. Each dog is fastened to it by a single line, and all are guided and controlled by the voice of the master or by his whip.

The Esquimaux visit one another in the winter time, as this is the best season for traveling. At such times, the igloos are crowded to the utmost, as many as fifteen persons being stowed away in one six feet wide and fifteen feet long. With no ventilation to speak of, with the blubber burning in the stoves, and with the natural heat thrown off by the bodies, the temperature often rises to ninety degrees, while on the outside it is thirty or forty below zero.

The walrus is the staple food of the Esquimaux throughout the year. In the winter time, a chunk of raw meat, frozen solid, is brought into the igloo and thrown upon the floor in a convenient corner. From this the hungry ones help themselves.

The season for hunting the walrus opens in March and continues into the fall. The natives attack him with the spear, when they find him lying upon the ice. If he is in the water, they assail him with line and harpoon. In the latter case, the attack often becomes a regular battle, the male gallantly fronting the assault and charging the hunters with furious bravery. It often happens that the male, the female, and the calf are all killed in one of these contests.

When a walrus is secured, the igloos— those poor, miserable dens— become scenes of life and activity. Stacks

UMANAK CHURCH.

of jointed meat are piled upon the ice. Women are stretching the hide for sole leather. Men are cutting out harpoon lines. Tusky walrus heads stare at you from the snow bank, where they are stowed away for their ivory. The dogs are tethered to the ice. And the children, each armed with a curved walrus rib, are playing bat and ball among the drifts.

The Greenlanders are never idle, and never lose a day when it is possible to hunt. When prevented by storms, they work at stowing away the carcasses of previous hunts. The excavation made for this purpose is called a "cache." The jointed meat is stacked inside and covered with heavy stones. Sometimes the flesh of eight or ten walruses is stored away in a single cache.

It would seem that what has been gained during a season of plenty would be sufficient to put the Esquimaux beyond want during the following winter; yet it often happens that they suffer from hunger. The true cause of this scarcity is excessive eating. Their law is that all shall share with all. If one settlement falls short, all the members of it migrate to the neighboring village, and thus the tax on the latter place is great.

The seal is prized as food as well as for his skin. Lying by the side of their breathing holes, seals fall an easy prey to the hunter. The natives resort to strategy to secure them. They erect a white screen on a sledge, which the hunter pushes in front of him, and behind which he hides until he comes near them.

Other animals sought for are the fox, the hare, and the polar bear. The latter has been killed in such large numbers that it is now nearly extinct. During the summer time, the natives vary their diet by catching birds. They have the sandpiper, the grouse, the plover, and the auk, besides sea fowls of different kinds.

When the matron of the igloo wishes a bird supper, she calls a boy and sends him in search of little auks. These birds breed in large numbers in the rubbish under the edge of the cliffs. The boy climbs the cliff and, with a purse net of seal skin at the end of a narwhal's tusk, in a few minutes catches all he can carry.

Of the sea fowl, the lumme and eider duck are of the

most importance. The lumme is about the size of a canvasback duck. It selects for a summer home the ledges close to the water. Some of these shelves are not more than a foot wide; others are three feet or more. Some are not more than ten feet long, while others measure several rods. But on all of them, birds are sitting, bolt upright, packed close together and facing outward. They make no nest, and the female lays but one egg. This, by means of her bill, she stands on its end and then sits down on it, as if it were a stool.

Eider ducks are to be found in the largest numbers in Duck Islands, a hundred miles north of Upernavik. These islands are covered with innumerable pools of snow water, which furnish moisture for the growth of large quantities of moss. At length the water evaporates, leaving the moss dry. In this, the ducks build their nests, lining them with the delicate down which grows upon their breasts. Each bird with her bill plucks out a good handful, leaving the feathers intact. When she goes away from her nest, she covers her eggs with this warm material.

People from farther south make descents upon these islands and carry away the nest linings, which, when cleaned, become the valuable eider down of commerce. The same down plucked from the breast even an instant after death is worthless, as it loses the wonderful elasticity which gives it such great value.

The only vegetable dish of the natives is a mixture of sour grass and little purple flowers which grow everywhere in the summer time. They pour a little water

UMÁNAK VILLAGE AND FIORD.

over them and stew them for fifteen minutes. They never wash them before cooking, asserting that a little sand is good for the stomach. The flavor resembles that of our rhubarb. This dish is eaten only by the women and children. On the other hand, the men eat the eggs of different birds, but will not allow the women or children to do so.

Some of their social customs are very peculiar. The old practice of carrying off the bride by force is one which they abandon reluctantly, even when converted.

They have their prophet, or powwow as he is called among our western Indians. He acts as a sort of general counselor. He prescribes, or powwows, in sickness or in case of wounds. He declares the proper penances of grief. These are sometimes very oppressive. The bereaved husband may be required to abstain from hunting seal or walrus for a year. But more frequently he is denied some luxury of food, as the rabbit or a choice part of the walrus.

The inmates of the igloo are a merry, happy people. They are generous to a fault and never hesitate to sacrifice their own meal to the necessities of a guest. They never borrow trouble about the future. They seem to have no care beyond that of procuring enough to eat and to wear.

CHAPTER XI.

A PEN PICTURE OF ICELAND.

YEARS ago, so say the wise men, mighty volcanic eruptions brought Iceland up from the bottom of the sea, and, ever since, fire and water have been contending for its possession.

It lies in the northern part of the Atlantic Ocean on the confines of the Arctic Ocean. Its northern coast reaches nearly to the Arctic Circle. It is six hundred miles from Norway, five hundred from Scotland, and two hundred and fifty from Greenland. It has an area of forty thousand square miles, about equal to that of the state of Ohio.

Its coasts are very much broken by bays, or fiords. The southern shore is flat and sandy and has few good harbors. The remaining part of the coast is rocky and precipitous; but in places the rocks have been rent asunder, and fiords stretch far into the interior. Lofty ridges of rock running out into the ocean separate them from one another. In some places these ridges assume a most magnificent appearance, attaining an elevation of two to four thousand feet.

We find the Icelandic dwellings along these fiords. Their shores afford the best pasturage for cattle. Their waters are a favorite retreat for fish, especially the cod. They are not affected by storms, as is the ocean, and in them the fisherman carries on his business with more safety. They also resemble canals, and, where there is a fiord, the settlements extend far

AUSTRALIA AND THE ISLANDS OF THE SEA. 113

AN ICE GIANT.

inland; while in its absence only a narrow strip of country along the seashore is inhabited.

The principal bay on the western coast is the Faxa Fiord, at the southeastern extremity of which stands the chief town of Iceland, called Reikiavik. The view of this bay from the sea is exceedingly grand. It has a width of fifty-six miles between its two extreme points, one of which runs down into a rocky ridge of pumice, while the other towers to the height of five thousand feet and is crowned with everlasting snow. The intervening semicircle is crowded with the peaks of scores of noble mountains, between whose base and the sea stretches a greenish slope, one part of which is covered with the houses that make up the town of Reikiavik.

The effects of light and shade in Iceland are extremely pure, and the contrasts of color most surprising. The atmosphere is clearer, the light more vivid, and the air more bracing than in other countries. One mountain shines forth in a blaze of gold against another of darkest purple, while up against the azure sky rise peaks of glittering whiteness.

On approaching Iceland, the attention of the traveler is arrested first by the *jokuls*. The word *jokul* means "ice" or "an icy mountain." The mode of their formation closely resembles that of the glaciers of Greenland. The *jokuls* appear long before the shore comes in sight, one of them being visible at a distance of one hundred and forty miles.

Most of them are found in two parallel chains, which cross the island from northeast to southwest. They are separated by a deep valley. The highest summits reach six thousand feet.

Mount Hecla, of which we shall speak again later, belongs to neither chain, but stands between them at their western termination and commands a view of both. Other mountains of this class are located in the northern part of the island. Another, called Sneefield, stands not far from Taxa Fiord. On account of its isolated position and lofty height, it is one of the most magnificent elevations on the island.

Between these two mountain chains lies the great desert of Iceland. Containing, as it does, many volcanoes, its surface has become one great black field. Wide chasms and immense masses of rock interrupt the progress of the traveler everywhere; and, owing to the magnetic influence of some of the rocks, the needle of the compass is rendered useless as a guide. There are no birds, no beasts, and scarcely a plant to relieve the monotony of the scene.

There are two classes of rivers in Iceland, distinguished by their color. Those which issue from the *jokuls* have a whitish color on account of the clay or pumice which they carry in solution. The rest of the rivers are like those of other lands. On account of their rapid flow, none of them are navigable, and they are characterized by sublime waterfalls. Some small streams, as the Cataract River, form almost a continuous succession of cascades, the water escaping from one dark pool merely to plunge into another.

The rivers which rise in the *jokuls*, called *jokul* rivers, are often flooded, and travelers passing around the coast experience much difficulty in crossing them, as they are not bridged and there are few ferryboats. The only river of any considerable size on the west coast is the White River. This rapid *jokul* stream is forty-six miles long, and two or three hundred feet broad.

The northern side of the island has a great many streams, of which the largest is but eighty-five miles long. On the eastern coast the Bridge River, fifty-six miles long, is the most remarkable. As this is the only river in Iceland spanned by a bridge, it is called Bridge River.

The usual way of crossing rivers that cannot be forded or ferried is more hazardous. From the edge of the precipice on either side, two ropes are suspended on which a wooden box is hung. This is large enough to contain a man and the ordinary load of a horse. The traveler climbs into the box and pulls himself over by means of a rope. Owing to the looseness of the main ropes, the box passes so swiftly until it reaches the center of the stream that it threatens, by the sudden stop it makes, to throw its contents into the river below. When this method of crossing the river is employed, the horses are first made to swim across a little farther up stream. If they fail to reach a certain point formed by the projection of a rock, they are hurled over a dreadful cataract and are seen no more.

Iceland has but few lakes. The largest one is but thirty-six miles in circumference, and the next in size, the Thingvalla Lake, is but twenty-five.

The climate of Iceland is not as severe as its high latitude would indicate. In the southern part the average temperature for the summer is fifty-three degrees, and for the winter is minus twenty-nine.

No cereals are grown; but in some places a kind of wild oats is found. Potatoes, carrots, turnips, and cabbage are cultivated. The only tree is the wild birch, which seldom attains a height of over twelve feet.

The only wild quadruped in Iceland is the fox. Seals abound on the coast, where sea fowls are also numerous. Swans frequent the lakes. Fish are abundant on the coasts, and salmon and trout in the rivers.

Iceland is subject to the King of Denmark, who shares the legislative power with the Althing, an assembly of thirty-six members, thirty of whom are elected by the people and six appointed by the king. The Althing meets at Reikiavik every second year.

The secretary for Iceland, who resides in Copenhagen, is responsible to the king and the Althing for the maintenance of the constitution. The king appoints a Governor General, who resides in Reikiavik and conducts the government on the responsibility of this secretary. Besides the governor general there are two amtmands, or under-governors, one for the south and west, the other for the north and east. Under these are sheriffs, each of whom has an assistant. Below the sheriffs are committees of from three to five members, who administer the poor laws and look after the general welfare of the people.

Surely some strange fascination chains the Icelander to his home. There are, in all, thirty known volcanoes on the island, and eight of them have been active within a century. Pasture lands have been devastated, homes have been ruined, and innumerable lives of cattle, horses, and people have been lost. And still to the Icelander there is no clime like the "Maid of the North."

Hecla, one of the most famous volcanoes, is situated in the southwestern part of the island, thirty miles from the coast. It is about five thousand feet high, and has three peaks a little elevated above its body. The craters form hollows in the sides of these, and, together with many fissures, are generally filled with snow. The crater of the principal peak does not much exceed one hundred feet in depth.

Since the year 900, there have been forty-three eruptions of this famous volcano. The latest occurred in 1845, and lasted over half a year. The torrent of lava, two miles from the crater, was a mile wide and fifty feet deep. The beautiful and fertile plain which once surrounded Hecla was buried beneath great heaps of cinders, pumice, sand, and ashes. For ten miles around, no grass nor any kind of plant can grow. The ruined walls of farm houses and inclosures, still seen amid the windings of the torrents, tell the mournful tale of prosperous days passed away forever.

The most violent eruption of Hecla occurred in 1766. First a huge pillar of black sand mounted slowly into the heavens, accompanied by subterranean thunders. Then a circle of flame inclosed the crater, and countless masses of red-hot rock and pumice were hurled incredible distances. One boulder six feet in circumference was thrown twenty miles. Sand, to the depth of four inches, covered the ground for a circuit of one hundred and fifty miles. Clouds of ashes turned daylight into darkness. The people living in the Orkney Islands, which are but a short distance from Scotland, were badly frightened by what they thought were showers of black snow. After this had continued for four days, lava began to flow, and later an immense column of water shot up to the height of several hundred feet, accompanied by dire underground reports heard at a distance of fifty miles.

But, striking as have been the eruptions of Hecla, those of Skapta Jokul have been infinitely more terrible. This volcano occupies the center of an unexplored desert four hundred square miles in extent. The most noted eruption occurred in 1783. The preceding winter and spring had been unusually mild. Near the latter part of May, a bluish fog began to hover over the desert. In June this was accompanied by a great trembling of the ground. On the eighth day of the month, immense columns of smoke hung over the hill country. On the tenth, countless pillars of fire were seen dancing and gleaming amid the icy hollows of the mountain. On the same day the river Skapta, one of the largest on the island, after discharging a vast quantity of fetid water mixed with sand, suddenly disappeared.

Two days afterward, a stream of lava came rolling down the bed of the dried-up river. It filled it from bank to bank, though the channel was of great depth and two hundred feet broad; and shortly afterwards it overflowed a low country, tearing up the turf before it and pouring into a great lake, " whose affrighted waters flew screaming and hissing into the air." Having completely filled the basin of the lake, the flood poured onward by two different channels. While this flood was marching onward by the course marked out by the Skapta River, a similar one followed a river flowing in the opposite direction and rushed onward with even greater fury and velocity.

Geysers, or spouting springs, are found in every part of Iceland. But the larger number are found in places where the volcanic agencies are apparently dying out, this being their last manifestation of power. There are two kinds of geysers. One has jets of clear water, the other sends up puffs of scalding vapor through a soft mud or clay.

The three geysers which attract the most attention are the Great Geyser, the Little Geyser, and the Strokr, or "Churn." They are situated about forty miles east of Thingvalla. The Great Geyser does not display its powers oftener than once in two or three days. The first indication that something unusual is about to take place is a subterranean noise, as of artillery, which shakes the ground for a considerable distance around. Suddenly the fountain seems to explode. The water rushes up the pipe with amazing velocity, and is projected by irregular jets into the atmosphere. An immense amount of steam rushes out with the water, sometimes hiding the column entirely from view. The first jets do not usually exceed twenty or thirty feet. These are followed by one which shoots upward perhaps fifty feet, and this by others of lesser altitude. Then, as if to form a fitting climax, the geyser gathers all its strength and sends up a last magnificent column of water, ten feet in diameter, to the height of ninety feet or more. The eruption seldom lasts more than ten minutes, when, the force being exhausted, the waters fall with a sullen roar within the tube and leave the basin dry, sometimes for several hours.

A GEYSER.

By far the most interesting of the geysers is the Strokr. The Great Geyser cannot be forced into action, and, unless parties have leisure to stay two or three days to await its pleasure, they may not witness an eruption at all. It would not perform for Prince Napoleon nor for the king of Denmark, who visited it at the time of the Millennium. Truly the Great Geyser is no "respecter of persons." But obliging Strokr may be induced, by artificial means, to display its powers at any time. It differs from the other geysers in having no basin; and therefore it is possible to approach close to the pipe, which is about six feet in diameter. The boiling water rises to within twelve feet of the top, where it remains bubbling and splashing, with an occasional emission of steam.

In order to provoke an eruption, a large number of sods must be collected and thrown into the funnel. After the irritation from this has been endured for thirty or forty minutes, a rumbling, angry sound is heard; then, with a roar, the black mass is upheaved. A column of water, as large as the opening and consisting of innumerable jets, shoots into the air to the height of forty or fifty feet, carrying along with it the whirling masses of sods. Many of the sods and much of the water fall back into the opening, only to be ejected again and again. The greatest height attained is over a hundred feet. After the eruption has lasted about ten minutes, the water gradually subsides and remains boiling at its accustomed depth.

One of Iceland's great chieftains was named Snorre Sturleson. He did two things which have made his name famous. He wrote a book about the kings of Norway, and he built in Iceland the famous bath which for more than six centuries has survived the ravages of time. This grand specimen of his ingenuity forms a nobler monument than any of his most zealous admirers could have erected to his memory.

It is perfectly circular in form, and fifteen feet in diameter. It is constructed of hewn stones, which exactly fit one another and have been joined together by a fine cement. The floor is paved with stone of the same kind, and a stone bench, capable of seating thirty persons, runs round the inside of the bath.

The water is supplied from a hot spouting fountain, five hundred feet to the north. It is carried by an underground aqueduct, constructed of stones cemented together in the same way as those that form the bath. On reaching the basin, the water is admitted through a small aperture, which is closed up with a stone when a sufficient amount has been received. There is another opening at the bottom of the bath, by means of which the water is allowed to run away, and thus the bath is kept perfectly clean.

CHAPTER XII.

THE CAPITAL, THE COUNCIL, AND THE PEOPLE.

REIKIAVIK, with a population of four thousand, is the capital of Iceland.

Of the two principal streets of Reikiavik, one stretches along the shore and is built up on one side only. It is occupied altogether by merchants. Their stores, which resemble those of our country towns, are much crowded with a great variety of merchandise. The other street strikes off at the west end of the town, and runs back into the interior toward a little lake. It contains the houses of the bishop and some other officials. At the east end of the town, back of the merchants' street and

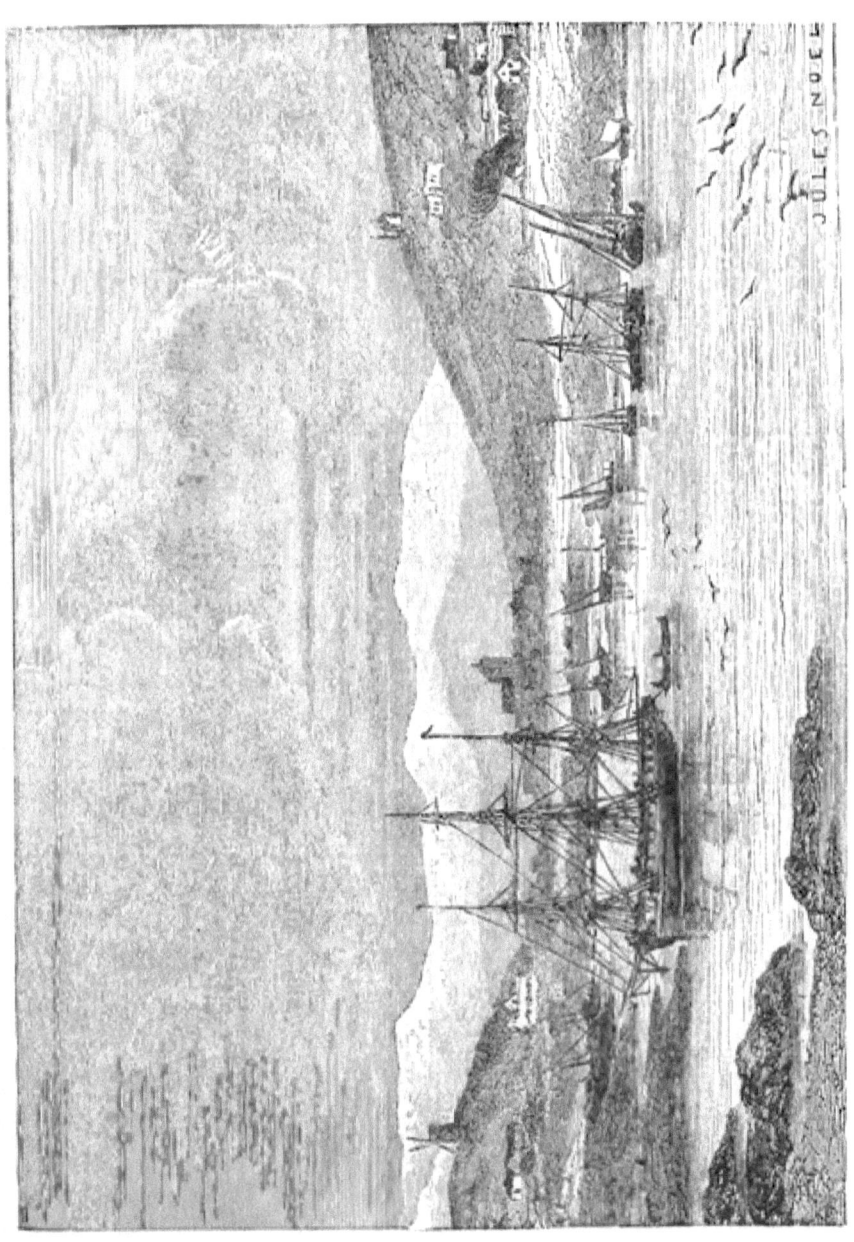

running parallel with it, is a street on which fronts the house of the governor.

The church, standing by itself on a gentle rise of green, is a short distance southwest of the governor's house. It is built of lava blocks, brick, and stucco. It is much larger than the ordinary church building, and is capable of seating about twelve hundred people.

The jail, or house of correction, is one of the most prominent buildings in the town. It stands on the rising ground at the end of the governor's house, and has never had an occupant, which certainly speaks well for the descendants of the vikings. Crime and theft are unknown in Iceland. Soldiers and policemen are not needed. Even Reikiavik, corrupted as it is by its foreign population, employs but one policeman in winter, and two in summer.

The dwelling houses of Reikiavik are nearly all built of wood, and have storehouses and gardens attached to them. Their outside appearance is very neat, and their inside arrangement is both pleasing and convenient. The streets are level, and black with volcanic sand. They are comparatively wide and clean.

While we are in Reikiavik we must visit the valley of Thingvalla, forty miles to the east. The people of Iceland regard this place as almost sacred; since here, for more than nine hundred years, the national council, or Althing, was accustomed to meet and deliberate upon matters of public interest. Thingvalla means the "plains of the council."

Iceland was first settled by a band of Irish monks about 795 to 800 A.D. In the year 874 two cousins

from Norway landed on its shores. They were so well
pleased with the country, and circulated so good a report of it, that settlers from northern European countries poured in rapidly. These were not from the dregs
of society, but came from the better classes. They
formed a government resembling our republic. The
highest officer was called the *lagmann*. He was the
supreme judge of the island and the president of the
Althing. At first he held the office for life, but later
the term was limited. The republic continued for three
hundred and thirty-two years, and down to 1262 was
the only free republic in the world. During its existence, thirty-one persons were chosen to this office of
lagmann. Several of these served two terms each.

The existence of the republic was marked by unequaled literary and political vigor. But in 1262 it
came to a violent end, on account of its own chieftains
intriguing against the liberties of its people. At that
time it took the oath of allegiance to the king of Norway, and in 1380 became a province of Denmark.

With the loss of self-government, the people seemed
to lose their political enthusiasm and mental power.
Up to this time, literature had held an important place.
While Europe was sunk in intellectual darkness and
engaged in fearful wars, the historic events, not only
of Iceland but of other countries, were rescued from
oblivion by the native poets of Iceland. These historical poems were recited in public and private, and
were well known among the people. Beside being
committed to memory, they were engraved in runic
characters; and, after the introduction of Christianity,

in Roman letters also. As these poets wandered everywhere, and were always received with honor, they brought back to Europe the recollection of important events which would otherwise have been forgotten.

When Iceland commemorated its millennium in 1874, the principal exercises were held in Thingvalla, and

GREAT CHASM WORN BY A GLACIER.

the king of Denmark and all other foreign visitors journeyed thither to assist in the celebration.

A great chasm separates the Thingvalla from the plain which must be traversed in order to reach it. This chasm is called by a difficult Icelandic name which means the "Chasm of All Men." Behind us lies the lava-covered barren plateau; in front of us is a beautiful, gay, sunlit plain, sunk to a level lower by a hundred feet, and stretching away ten miles to the eastward, where it is terminated by the corresponding chasm called the "Chasm of the Ravens." This chasm is about one hundred and eighty feet deep, and as many wide.

But how shall we get into the valley? A natural pathway, accidentally formed in the face of the cliff, leads across the bottom and up the other side of the chasm into the plain of Thingvalla.

Near the center of the valley are a church and a parsonage, and not far from these, to the northwest, is the most famous spot in the whole plain. It is called the "Mount of Laws." By some strange freak of nature, as the subsiding plain cracked and shivered into thousands of fissures, an irregular oval area, about three hundred and fifty feet long by fifty wide, was left almost entirely surrounded by a crevice so deep and broad as to be utterly impassable. This fissure, filled to within sixty feet of the top with bright green water, is in places forty fathoms deep, while at other points no bottom can be found at all. A narrow causeway at one extremity of this oval area connects it with the adjoining plain and permits access to its interior. At one point alone it is barely possible to leap the chasm; and an ancient worthy, pursued by his enemies, did actually perform this dangerous feat. But, as falling short one inch would entail certain drowning, it would be unwise for any of us to make the attempt.

It was this fortified spot that the founders of the Icelandic constitution chose for the meetings of their Althing. The meetings were held in the open air in the last half of June, until 1690, at which time a house, that is now in ruins, was built for the purpose. In 1800 the place of meeting was transferred to Reikiavik.

At the time of the assembling of the ancient Althing, crowds of people came from all over the island. The president sat near the center of the Mount of Laws, and the judges sat round him on banks of earth which are still visible. An armed guard defended the narrow causeway. The people crowded as near as the terrible chasm would permit. The old laws were read, and new ones were enacted. Persons charged with crime were tried, and either acquitted or sentenced to immediate punishment.

At the time of its millennial celebration in 1874, the Thingvalla presented a picture such as had never been witnessed there before. Tents large and small crowded every available space. Flags of every nation were flying over the great pavilion, while the flag of free Iceland — a white falcon on a blue ground — floated from the Mount of Laws.

It was a great event. A song of welcome to the king of Denmark was sung, a genuine Icelandic dinner was given, and the usual toasts were delivered. Later in the day, when the king rode away up through the rift, the great crowd of people assembled on both sides of the road, in order to give him one more farewell cheer. Guessing their intention, the king graciously dismounted and walked, shaking hands with many of the people and bowing to all. On his ascending the pass which leads out of the rift, the people burst into their last farewell cheer, which lasted till he was out of sight. Thus appropriately ended the ceremony at Thingvalla.

A farmhouse of the modern Icelander consists of a number of small cottages joined together. Sometimes the walls are composed of driftwood, but usually they consist of immense blocks of lava laid one upon another. The holes or cracks are stopped up with moss or earth. Some of these houses have the usual sort of rafters, but the majority of them have whale ribs instead. These are covered with brushwood, on top of which turf is heaped. This turf bears a good crop of grass, which is carefully cut for hay.

The houses have no chimneys, and a fire is never kept in any room except the kitchen, even in the coldest weather. The smoke passes out through a hole in the roof. The only windows are small pieces of glass or thin skin, four inches square, which are placed in the roof. No attention is given to ventilation, and the atmosphere of the houses is almost unendurable to a foreigner. The natives' sense of smell is deadened by the universal habit of taking snuff.

The Icelanders are descendants of the ancient Norwegians. They have mixed, especially along the coast, with Danes and Swedes. They are of moderate size, with yellow hair and blue eyes, quiet in disposition, polite, and exceedingly hospitable. Their piety is also very marked. The feebleness of their constitutions is due to poor food and want of proper care and exercise while young. The head is moderately large, and the countenance open, but possessed of a dreamy look, due to the prominence of the eyeballs. The cheek bones are too high to look well. Poor teeth are unknown, and there is not a dentist on the island. A corpulent

THOR, THE NORSE GOD OF THUNDER.

person is seldom seen in Iceland. The women are pale and sallow, owing to the imperfectly lighted and ventilated houses and the long winter nights. The men have long bodies and short legs. The universal manner of traveling is on horseback.

The ancient Icelanders were worshipers of the gods Thor and Odin. In the year 1000, when the national council met at Thingvalla, advocates of Christianity proposed its adoption as the national religion. The discussion was a very excited one, and when it was at its height, a subterranean peal of thunder shook the ground. "Hark!" cried the orator of the heathen party, "hear how angry is Odin that we should even consider the subject of a new religion; his fires will consume us, and justly." For some moments, it looked as if the new religion had received a fatal blow. But a quick-witted chieftain, who favored it, changed the tide of opinion by asking, "With whom, then, were the gods angry, when the plain upon which we stand was melted?" This argument had the desired effect. Christianity was adopted as the national religion.

At first their religious beliefs were few and simple, but subsequently they adopted the doctrines of the Catholic Church. A few centuries later, Catholicism gave way to Protestantism; and since then the people have remained strict Lutherans.

The everyday dress of the Icelandic peasant resembles that of a common sailor. The short jacket and wide trowsers are fashioned of homemade cloth, and are black, gray, or blue in color. They wear woolen stockings and have either short boots or shoes, made of untanned leather and without heels.

The everyday costume of the women is very simple and becoming. The dress is made of woolen stuff, and

AUSTRALIA AND THE ISLANDS OF THE SEA.

ODIN, THE CHIEF GOD IN NORSE MYTHOLOGY.

is worn with long sleeves and an apron. The headdress is a flat round piece of cloth fastened on with pins and adorned with a long tassel of black silk.

The Sunday dress is quite richly ornamented. The black or red bodice, the seams of which are covered with strips of velvet, is fastened in front with silver clasps. A high velvet ruff is worn around the neck. Over this is a black jacket with silver buttons. A cloak lined with velvet and fastened with silver clasps is worn outside of this. The stockings and shoes resemble those of the men. But the helmetlike headdress is the most remarkable article of the toilet. It is made of white linen stiffened with pins, and usually stands from fifteen to twenty inches high. Near the head it is round, but higher up it curves first backward and then forward. It is bound on by a colored handkerchief wound several times around the head. On important occasions it is decorated with gold or silver.

The people have few amusements, and their taste for music has nearly died out. But they love to read, and have a passion for poetry and history. In the southern part of Iceland the shortest winter day is but four hours long, while in the northern part they have one week during which the sun never rises at all. On long winter evenings, all the members of the family and the servants gather in the sitting room and busy themselves with some sort of work, as knitting, spinning, or preparing shoe soles. One member of the family, previously selected, places himself near the lamp and reads aloud from some volume of history or poetry.

There are but few schools in Iceland, and the children are taught at home by their parents. The pastor of the church usually tests their progress by three or four examinations in the course of the year. But, notwithstanding their lack of advantages, all the people are well read, and, with few exceptions, write a legible and beautiful hand.

There are in reality only two seasons in Iceland, — winter and summer. In the winter the family rise about seven o'clock. The women prepare the meals, which are very simple. Stockfish, which is the cod or haddock dried without salt, butter made without salt and allowed to sour, and sour whey, form the customary dishes for breakfast and supper. The dinner is the same varied with sago soup, curds, Iceland moss, and occasionally mutton. Besides cooking, the women knit, spin, and sew.

The men take care of the cattle and sheep, make horseshoes, prepare leather, and, when nothing else is at hand, help the women about the knitting.

The summer ushers in a far greater range of employment. The fishing season opens on the third of February and continues till the twelfth of May. Early in the morning the men betake themselves to their boats and stay all day. On returning to the land they give half the fish to the owner of the boat, whether he has been with the company or not. The fish are then split and dried on the rocks or in open sheds. When the fishing season is over, the men prepare turf for fuel. It is cut from the ground in blocks and placed in small heaps to protect it from the rain.

But the busiest season begins in July. The people

then turn their attention to the interior; for at that time the hay harvest commences. Much of their comfort depends upon this crop, as, without it, their cattle could not survive the winter. The men use short scythes about two feet long and two inches broad. The women attend to drying and raking it into heaps. It is then made into bundles, which are carried home either by the men, or on the backs of horses, one bundle being secured on each side. The better hay is given to the cattle, while the coarser hay, cut from the marshes, is reserved for the sheep.

The hay harvest being over, the men go in search of the sheep, which, during the summer months, are turned loose to wander at will over the mountains. Sheep in Iceland are never sheared. The wool is pulled off instead, so as to avoid cutting the long hair, which is the principal protection against rain.

During two or three weeks in the summer, when the men are fishing, or have gone to distant towns for purposes of trade, the Iceland moss is gathered. This work is done by the women, two or three going from each farm. They travel on horseback, carry food and tents with them, form large companies, and take two or three men along to protect them from the robbers whom they never see, but whom they believe to exist in the uninhabited interior. The short period of time which the women spend in this way, wandering about, amid the romantic scenery of their wild island home, is one of the happiest of their lives, and they look forward to it with the greatest expectations.

CHAPTER XIII.

THE FAROES, SHETLANDS, ORKNEYS, AND HEBRIDES.

The Faroe Islands, twenty-four in number, are in the Atlantic Ocean, three hundred miles southeast of Iceland and two hundred northwest of the Shetland Islands. The area of the group is five hundred square miles, and the population thirteen thousand. The coasts, which are steep and lofty, are broken by deep inlets, whirlpools, and rapids. There are no large valleys or streams, but small lakes of fresh water are numerous.

The Faroese belong to the same stock as the Icelanders, though they are not so intellectually inclined. They are governed by a Danish bailiff and a director of the police, and are represented in the Danish legislature by a deputy appointed by the king.

The agricultural products are small, owing to the rocky character of the soil and the shortness of the summer, which lasts merely through July and August. The only grain that can be ripened is barley.

Fishing is an important industry. When a school of dolphins is in sight, the news is communicated by signal fires, and the boats, to the number of several hundred, quickly surround the prey, driving them into shallow water, where they are speedily dispatched. The land is well adapted for the raising of sheep, cattle, and ponies.

The chief town is Thorshavn, situated on the rocky hills surrounding two bays separated by a peninsula.

A NATIVE OF THE FAROE ISLANDS.

The character of the ground has caused the houses to be placed in utter confusion, which makes it very difficult to find the way from one point to another. The streets are nothing but steep, irregular lanes paved with stones, and so narrow as often to admit of people going only in single file. The refuse from the houses is thrown into the streets, and the odors of fish and oil predominate everywhere.

The houses are small, miserable, wooden buildings, with sod roofs, and tarred to preserve them from dampness. The fronts and projecting corners are decorated with strings of fish hung up to dry.

Let us enter one of the shops, a fair representative of its class. It stands at the end of a dark, poorly paved, winding alley. In one corner, the men are drinking; in another, women are making trifling purchases over which they are chatting with evident satisfaction. The room is crowded with a great variety of articles. Candies, pins, snuff, nails, kegs of fish, and "fire-water" are all stored here awaiting prospective buyers.

The people are characterized by ruddy complexions, abundant light-colored hair, blue eyes, tall stature, and stalwart forms. Their dress is like that of the Norwegians. The men wear woolen breeches of their own manufacture, buttoned below the knee. Their upper garments are like those of a northern fisherman. They wear long, woolen stockings and seal-skin shoes, and over these they pull wooden clogs for protection against the dampness of the pavement. The dress of the women is not peculiar, with the exception of the headdress, which consists of a black silk

HOY EXPRESS, ORKNEY ISLANDS.

handkerchief tied behind, with a point toward the forehead.

As in Iceland, all the people are Lutherans; but the altar, the burning candles, and the tones, attitude, and dress of the clergymen remind one of the Catholic Church service.

The Shetland and Orkney islands are in the North Sea, and form a county of Scotland. The Orkneys are separated from the mainland by Pentland Firth, and the Shetlands lie fifty miles northeast of them. There are sixty-seven islands in the Orkney group, and nearly a hundred in the other, and altogether they contain a little more than nine hundred square miles.

The people of these islands, both in language and customs, bear traces of the old Scandinavians and the Norse vikings who settled there long before the historic period. Their life is uneventful, there being scarcely any excitement except that arising from perils at sea. They are in fairly comfortable circumstances, and extreme want seems to be unknown.

Kirkwall, the principal town in the Orkney group, is a place of great antiquity. The streets, though steep and narrow, are well paved, and the houses have a comfortable though quaint appearance. The great point of interest here is the cathedral of St. Magnus, which is more than seven hundred years old. It is one of the best specimens of Gothic architecture in existence. It is built of red sandstone, and was begun by Ronald in memory of his uncle. It is two hundred and twenty-six feet long and fifty-six feet wide, the cross or transept being ninety-two by twenty-eight feet; it is seventy-one feet high inside, and one hundred and forty to the top of the present spire. The cross is the oldest part, and contains four massive Gothic pillars twenty-four feet in circumference, spanned by five arches, the central spire resting upon these; and the next six pillars are perhaps even older.

STROMNESS, ORKNEY ISLANDS.

Its windows, doors, arches, and colonnades are all worthy of close examination. In the choir is the famous Gothic rose window three hundred and fifty years old; it consists of four arches, separated by three stone divisions surmounted by the twelve-leaved rose.

The three bells of the cathedral are nearly as old as the window. The principal door is on the west side, and still shows traces of elaborate carvings. The interior is simple and grand. The aisles and floor contain several strangely sculptured stones, which mark the resting place of Norse celebrities. The steeple was destroyed by lightning over three hundred years ago, and has never been rebuilt.

The Mound of Maeshowe, about nine miles from Kirkwall, is one of the most important antiquarian discoveries in Great Britain. It is a circular mound of earth thirty-six feet high and ninety feet in diameter, surrounded by a shallow trench forty feet wide. It contains a central chamber fifteen feet square and thirteen feet high, from which branch off three cells, one each to the north, east, and south. On the west side is the door opening into a passage fifty-four feet long, formed of large stone slabs set on edge. The age of the mound is not known, but the most probable opinion is, that it was built as a place of burial for noted personages by the Celts or Picts, as early as the eighth or ninth centuries. The walls are covered with inscriptions and with figures of animals, one of the latter being a winged dragon pierced by a sword.

Stromness, a seaport on the western coast of Mainland, thirteen miles from Kirkwall, is a most picturesque locality.

The chief town of the Shetland Islands is Lerwick, near the middle of Mainland, the largest island of the group. The houses are crowded together on the hillside. Almost every store is engaged in the sale of hosiery, veils, and shawls, for which the islands are famous. The fabric is so delicate, and the colors and

144   THE WORLD AND ITS PEOPLE.

PONIES, SHETLAND ISLANDS.

patterns are so pretty, that it is hard to resist the temptation of buying some of the bewitching drapery.

One of the finest buildings is the Anderson Institute, presented to the county by Mr. Arthur Anderson, a native of the Shetlands. It consists of an upper school and an elementary one, both of which are well attended, the instruction being of a very efficient character. The Widows' Asylum was also erected by Mr. Anderson for the benefit of the widows of Shetland sailors and fishermen. The Shetlanders are excellent sailors, and many of them hold responsible positions as officers on ocean steamships of the highest grade.

The Shetland ponies, those favorites with the boys and girls, are to be found here, feeding in the pastures or patiently plodding over the roads with heavy burdens on their backs. They are very small, rough-coated on account of exposure and want of care, but very strong and docile.

The Orkney and Shetland islands form one sheriffdom, but the sheriff has a substitute in each group. The County of Orkney and Shetland, as it is called, returns one member to Parliament, and Kirkwall is included in the Wick district, which returns one member. The population of the Orkneys is thirty-two thousand, and that of the Shetlands twenty-nine thousand.

Hebrides is a name sometimes applied collectively to all the islands on the west coast of Scotland. Those inhabited number about one hundred and twenty, and the entire area is estimated at about three thousand square miles. They are divided into two groups, the

Outer and the Inner Hebrides, and the total population is about one hundred thousand. Sheep are raised extensively, and fishing is one of the best paying industries.

Lewis, with Harris, the most northern and the largest of the Outer Hebrides, is a rugged, bare island, including many low, swampy tracts. Much of the surface is

A CROFT IN THE HEBRIDES.

covered with peat and with the remains of ancient forests. In olden times the Druids inhabited the island, and many of their ruined fortresses and edifices remain to this day.

Skye, the next in size after Lewis, and the most northern of the Inner Hebrides, is noted for its grand and picturesque scenery. In some places the coast presents magnificent basaltic formations far exceeding the

A SKYE OCTOGENARIAN AND HIS GRANDSON.

Giant's Causeway in grandeur. Over these cliffs descend many remarkable waterfalls, and their bases are frequently worn into deep caves, some of which are of historical interest. There are many beautiful inland lakes, one of which has been made famous by Sir Walter Scott in his "The Lord of the Isles."

Staffa is a small basaltic island of the Inner Hebrides, especially noted as the site of Fingal's Cave. Iona, another island of this group, was an ancient seat of the Druids. The cathedral, which is now in ruins, was founded in the thirteenth century.

Enjoying the benefit of the Gulf Stream, the climate of the Hebrides is peculiarly mild. Snow seldom lies long on the shores or low grounds, and in sheltered spots tender plants are not nipped by winter frosts. Drizzling rains are frequent, and the islands are often enveloped in mist.

In recent years many large estates have passed from old families of note into the hands of opulent modern proprietors, by whom extensive improvements have been made. The greatest improvement of all, however, has been the work of a Glasgow firm, by whom has been established an extraordinary system of steam navigation in connection with the Hebrides, calculated to bring them within the sphere of trade and the reach of tourists. By opening up remote tracts, formerly reached only with extreme difficulty, this system may be said to be gradually altering the character of the islands and giving them a new value.

AUSTRALIA AND THE ISLANDS OF THE SEA.

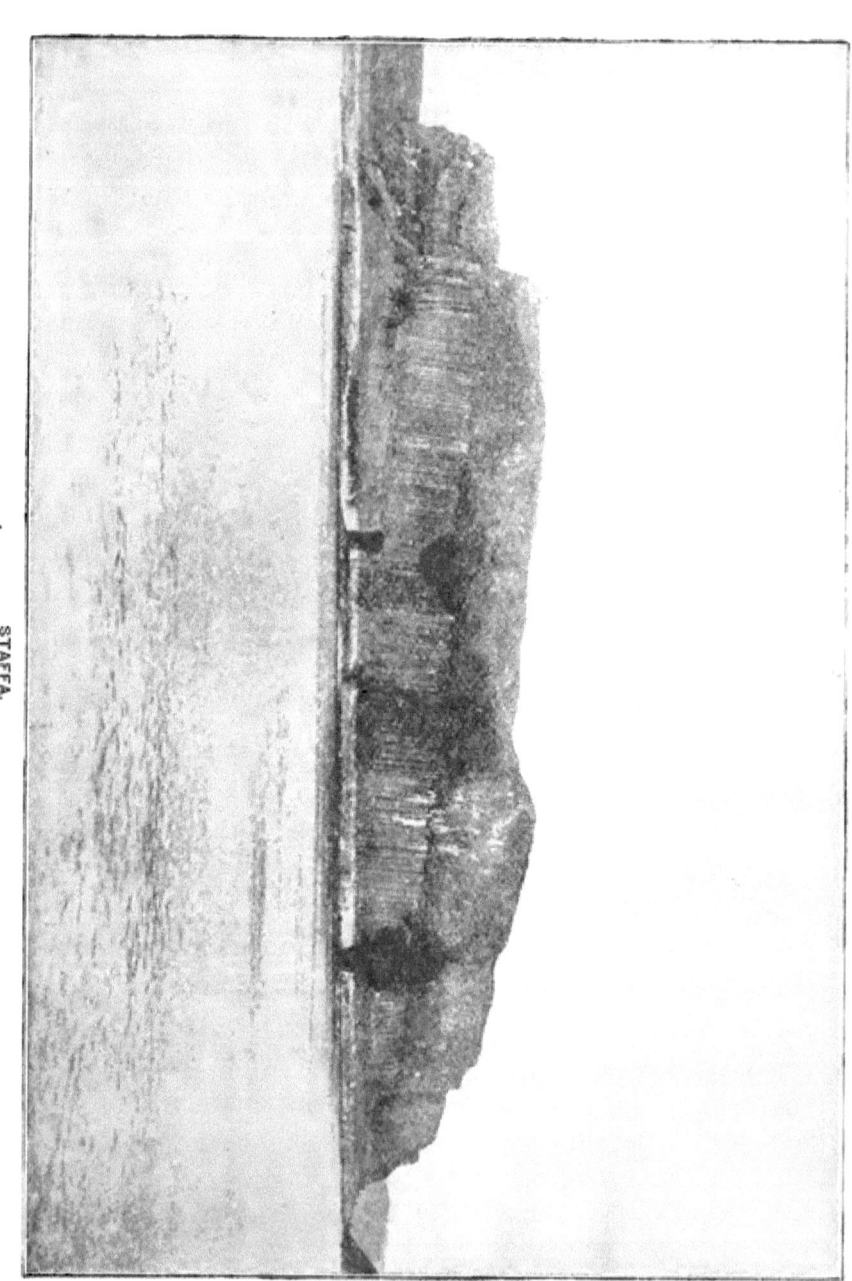

STAFFA.

CHAPTER XIV.

NOVA ZEMBLA AND OTHER ISLANDS OF THE NORTH.

Nova Zembla is a name applied to two large islands of the Arctic Ocean belonging to Russia. They are separated from the mainland on the east by the Sea of Kara, and from each other by a strait. So narrow is this strait, and so sharp are its windings, that vessels are reported as having sailed some ten or fifteen miles into it, when, seeing land close ahead, with no apparent outlet in the right direction, the captains have come to the conclusion that they were running into some deep inlet, and have sailed out again in order to search farther for the strait they were actually in.

The shape of the islands is that of an elongated crescent about five hundred miles long with an average width of sixty miles. The largest part of the interior has never been explored, and the north coast is very imperfectly known. The formation of the land on the east coast is very different from that on the west. On the east, low undulating plains take the place of noble hills, deep valleys, picturesque glaciers, and somber-looking ravines, for which the west coast is so conspicuous. Both, however, possess many excellent harbors.

A noticeable feature of the coast washed by the Kara Sea is that, where the land terminates in a bold cape, there is generally a rocky islet a little distance away, which has doubtless been detached from the mainland. These isolated spots are preferred by the sea birds as places in which to make their nests, because, being inaccessible to foxes, the eggs and young birds are secure from the depredations of these thieving animals.

The whole territory is wild and desolate in the extreme. The coast swarms with seals, various kinds of fish, and vast numbers of waterfowl. The interior, which is partly covered with stunted shrubs, short grass, and moss, is frequented by white bears, reindeer, ermines, and Arctic foxes.

The shores are literally covered with driftwood. No party of men, who, from shipwreck or any other cause, have to spend the winter there need suffer from cold, provided of course a stock of fuel is procured before the winter's snow covers the land.

There are no permanent inhabitants, but the islands are visited by Russian hunters and fishers. All along the southwest shore there are ruined huts, old fire-places, foxtraps, and, occasionally, circlets of stone about ten feet in diameter. The former doubtless owe their existence to the Russians, while the latter are, very likely, the remains of old Samoyede encampments. These nomadic tribes, bearing a strong resemblance to the Esquimaux, pass a great deal of their time in southern Nova Zembla. Originally they inhabited the whole vast Siberian plain; but, for many hundred years the Mongolians have forced themselves in among them. Their chief seat at present is the territory lying between the Obi and Yenisei rivers.

New Siberia is a group of islands in the Arctic Ocean, lying north of Siberia. They are comprised between 73° and 76° of north latitude, near the mouth

A SPITZBERGEN GLACIER.

of the Lena River, consisting of numerous small islands and three large ones from sixty to one hundred miles long by twenty to forty broad. They are completely barren, and present in their soil and subsoil alternate layers of sand and ice in which are imbedded some curious vegetable and animal fossil remains. They belong to Siberia.

Spitzbergen is a group of islands in the Arctic Ocean, midway between Greenland and Nova Zembla. The latitude of the island farthest north is 80°. This archipelago is classed among European islands, and is claimed by Russia as one of its dependencies. There are three large islands and many small ones. Near its northern limit is a group of seven islands called the Seven Sisters.

Very little is known of the interior of these islands, but the coasts have often been explored. On approaching them, they present a grand, though desolate, picture. An endless number of terribly cold heights rise one behind another, and in many places jagged, precipitous rocks crowd down to the very water's edge. Glaciers are everywhere present, and frequently extend along the seacoast twenty miles or more without intermission. Here and there in these frozen streams may be seen a dark and forbidding rock rising a thousand feet into the air. In fact, one traveler has described one of these islands as " a large tract of mountainous snow-covered heights, planted in a bed of glaciers." Many of these mountain chains bristle with granite peaks which have an altitude of four thousand feet.

NORDENSKJOLD IN THE ARCTIC SEAS.

The climate is intensely cold, and even during the three warmest months the mean temperature on the west coast is only 30° 50′. Vegetation is necessarily confined to a few plants of rapid growth. These grow only to the height of three or four inches, and, for the most part, spring up, flower, and seed in a month or six weeks. They produce nothing upon which human beings could manage to subsist. The lichens which grow on a level with the sea, give the land a sort of yellowish appearance. Higher up, the rising plateau, during the summer time, is covered "with masses of stonecrop, the brightest of yellow in patches, together with great clusters of the most brilliant orange. Here and there the stones are covered with a sort of light green, encircled by different shades of dark blue moss, and many of these stones are themselves of the deepest red, on whose tops are growing quantities of flowers of a sere autumnal magenta, the whole making a very varied picture in coloring."

Winter sets in in September, and for four months the sun remains below the horizon, but at so short a distance from it that the darkness is relieved for about six hours by a faint twilight. An effect similar to this is also produced by the unusual brightness of the moon and stars, and still more by the remarkable brilliancy of the aurora borealis.

These dreary lands are uninhabited by man, but their shores are frequently visited by English, Dutch, and Norwegian whalers, for the numerous whales, white bears, and other animals on the coasts. Spitzbergen is said to be a wonderful country for reindeer. So, each year many ships of from ten to sixty tons register leave the coast of Norway for the islands, expecting to return partly laden with reindeer meat. They also collect floe seals, eider ducks' eggs and nests, white whales, and sharks. If the season is favorable, they also capture walruses and white bears.

The Lofoden Islands form a group lying northwest of Norway, between 67° and 69° north latitude. They have a length of one hundred and thirty miles and an area of 1560 square miles. The population numbers twenty thousand. They are divided by the Raftsund into two sections. To the west and south lie eight islands which form the Lofoden proper; to the north and east lie six others.

The islands are lofty and precipitous, and are composed mostly of granite and gneiss. The highest peaks are found in the islands of Lofoden proper, and reach more than three thousand feet in height. Their appearance is wildly romantic and extraordinary. In some places they assume the shape of lofty cones, while in others they appear like the gigantic walls of some venerable Gothic ruin, topped with innumerable turrets.

The channels separating the islands are narrow and tortuous and generally of great depth. They are remarkable for the strength of their tidal currents, particularly the Raftsund and the once famous Maelstrom. The more ancient the description of the latter, the more exciting it is, since it is the more exaggerated. One writer says: "When the stream is most boisterous and its fury heightened by a storm, it is dangerous to come within seven miles of it; boats, ships, and yachts having been carried away by not guarding against it before they were within its reach. It likewise happens frequently, that whales come too near the stream, and are overpowered by its violence; and then it is impossible to describe their howlings and bellowings in their fruitless struggles to disengage themselves. A bear, once attempting to swim from Lofoden to Mosköe, with a design of preying upon the sheep at pasture in the island, afforded the like spectacle to the people; the stream caught him, and bore him down, while he roared terribly, so as to be heard on shore. In the year 1645, early in the morning of Sexagesima Sunday, it raged with such noise and impetuosity, that on the island of Mosköe the very stones of the houses fell to the ground."

The situation of the Maelstrom is nearly at the extremity of the Lofoden Islands. Two large islands of the group, together with a chain of innumerable smaller ones, inclose a part of the ocean for several miles. In the midst of these is the Mosköe, a lofty uninhabited rock. "The whirlpool is simply caused by the rushing of the ocean, as the tide rises or falls, between this chain of islands, which impedes its course." The situation of the surrounding islands causes the Maelstrom to form a large circle; and the great inequalities of its bottom, which from a few fathoms deepens suddenly, increase the violence of the current.

A recent writer describes it thus: "With respect to the Maelstrom, there is, in reality, no more danger than is attached to the Pentland Races, between the Orkney

Islands. From the irregularity of the bottom, and the sea being confined within the Lofodens, a very rapid course is formed at certain periods, through the channel of the islands; and as the passages all run in a direct line from the sea, they receive, particularly with certain winds, a very heavy swell, which, meeting the current, naturally creates a considerable vortex, and with the sea beating against the rocks, causes an impetuous noise, like the roar of a cataract, which sound is peculiar to the whole Norway coast. When I crossed it, I observed the fishermen in their small boats in the middle of the Maelstrom with their long sea lines overboard, quietly following their daily labors, which will be rather at variance with the usual reports concerning it. The inhabitants of the Lofodens, who call it simply by the name of the ström, know very little and think less about it."

The climate of these islands is not extremely rigorous when compared with the rest of Norway. In summer time there are only patches of snow on the hills, the snow limit being three thousand feet. The pasturage is sufficiently good in places to admit of the rearing of cattle, but the growth of cereals, chiefly barley, which matures in ninety days, is insignificant. A few potatoes are planted. No wood is yielded.

The great characteristic industry of these islands, and an important source of national wealth, is the cod and herring fishery, which is carried on along the east coast from January to April. It employs about eighteen thousand men from all parts of Norway. The annual take of cod alone amounts to an average of twenty million. The fish are dried during the early summer and shipped to Spain, Holland, Belgium, and Sweden. Other industries arise out of the cod fishery, chief of which is the manufacture of cod liver oil.

The Arctic Archipelago is an irregular group of islands northeast of North America, extending to Greenland. Some of the principal islands are Baffin Land, Melville Land, Grinnell Land, and Prince Albert Land. While for human habitation the regions are the most desolate that can be imagined, there is an extraordinary abundance of the lower forms of animal life. For centuries men have visited these islands only for the purpose of gathering their living products or exploring their shores. Traces of human habitation, in a distant age, are to be found in many places. At a still remoter period forests abounded, and Barrows Straits were the habitat of the coral and the sponge.

A very large portion of the area included by the Arctic Ocean is still unexplored, but almost every year diminishes the extent of the unknown. The nearest approach to the pole has been made up the West Greenland channel.

CHAPTER XV.

NEWFOUNDLAND, CAPE BRETON, AND PRINCE EDWARD ISLANDS.

NEWFOUNDLAND, which is a British possession, lies on the eastern coast of North America, directly across the Gulf of St. Lawrence. Its southern extremity approaches within fifty miles of Cape Breton Island. Its figure resembles that of an equilateral triangle. Its greatest length is from Cape Ray to Cape Norman, and measures three hundred and seventeen miles. Its greatest breadth is three hundred and sixteen miles, and it has an area of forty-three thousand square miles. Two large peninsulas project from the mainland. One of these points north, and is long and narrow. The other, Avalon, on which the capital is situated, extends to the southeast, and is almost severed from the island, the connecting isthmus being in one place but three miles wide.

The shores present a rocky aspect, but the line of cliffs, two hundred to three hundred feet high, is broken by magnificent bays running forty to fifty miles inland; so that, though the coast line measures but a thousand miles from headland to headland, the actual length is twice that distance.

Newfoundland has an unusually large number of lakes and ponds, of which the largest is Grand Lake, containing one hundred and ninety-two square miles. As yet, the shores of the great lakes and the valleys through which flow noble streams are absolute solitudes.

The climate is more temperate than that of the adjoining continent. The thermometer seldom falls below zero in winter, or rises above seventy degrees in summer. The Arctic current exerts a chilling influence on the east coast, but, as a compensation, it brings the enormous wealth of commercial fishes and seals, which has rendered the Newfoundland fisheries the most important in the world. They constitute the grand staple industry of the island, whose trade depends mainly upon the exportation of fish and oil. Codfish are more numerous here than anywhere else in the world. They are taken along the coast of the island, on the Banks, and along the shore of Labrador. Fishing has been carried on here for nearly four hundred years, and yet the supply appears to be as abundant as ever.

The cod begin to appear about the first of June. Their arrival is heralded by the capelin, a beautiful little fish about seven inches long. As these press in on the shore, the greedy cod follow, devouring the prey by thousands. The capelin is the best bait for the fisherman, and its stay of six or seven weeks is his richest harvest time. The seal industry ranks next to that of catching cod, but the salmon, herring, and lobster are also valuable fisheries.

Among the wild animals indigenous to the island are the reindeer, the wolf, the black bear, and the fox. Birds are very numerous, and nearly all of them are migratory. There are but few fine specimens of the "Newfoundland dog" now to be found in the island from which it derived its name.

The government of Newfoundland is vested in a

A FISHERMAN'S CAMP, NEWFOUNDLAND.

Governor, appointed by the Crown, and holding his office for six years; an Executive Council, chosen by the party commanding a majority in the House of Assembly, and consisting of seven members; a Legislative Council of fifteen members, nominated by the Governor in council, and holding office for life; and a House of Assembly of thirty-six members, elected every four years by a vote of the people.

St. John's is the capital. The approach to its harbor is striking and picturesque. In a lofty, rock-bound coast, we see a narrow opening guarded on each side by imposing hills. We enter, and awe mingles with admiration, as we gaze upon great cliffs of red sandstone piled in irregular masses upon a foundation of gray slate rock. On the right is Signal Hill, over five hundred feet high, upon which stands the "Block House" for signaling approaching vessels. On the left side is a hill rising still higher by a hundred feet. From its base a rocky promontory juts out, and on its summit stands the Fort Amherst Lighthouse.

The Narrows, leading to the harbor, are half a mile long, and we must traverse two thirds of the distance before the city comes in sight. The channel is very deep, and vessels of the largest size can enter at all periods of the tide.

St. John's is built on the north side of the harbor, on the gentle slope of a hill. There are three principal streets running parallel with the harbor throughout the entire length of the city, and these are intersected by a number of cross streets.

On the hill back of the city stands the Roman Catholic

cathedral. It is richly ornamented with statuary and paintings, and over the gateway and near the entrance are some fine pieces of sculpture. Close beside the cathedral are the Episcopal residence, the Catholic college, and the Presentation convent and schools.

The Church of England cathedral ranks among the finest ecclesiastical edifices in British America. It is of the pointed Gothic style of architecture. Inside and out, it is beautifully finished, and its lofty pointed windows are filled with fine examples of stained glass.

St. John's has an abundant supply of the purest water; it is obtained from Windsor Lake, four and a half miles distant and lying five hundred feet above the city. The pressure is so great that water from the hydrants may be thrown over the highest buildings. In case of fire no engines are needed.

Among the public buildings, the Government House and the Colonial Building are the most important. Both are built upon the plateau stretching inland from the sloping declivity on which the main portion of the city stands. The former is a plain, spacious building with no architectural beauty, but commodious and comfortable in the interior. The Colonial Building was built of white limestone imported from Cork. It has a stone portico, supported by six massive Ionic pillars. It contains chambers for the two branches of the legislature, and, with one exception, all of the government offices. The city has a population of about thirty thousand.

The people of Newfoundland are descendants of the English and Irish. Reared in one of the healthiest climates in the world, with plenty of outdoor exercise, they are as fine a race physically as can be found. Owing to the stress of circumstances, their intellectual development has not been greatly promoted by educational advantages; but those who go to other countries for the higher education frequently carry off the first honors at school or college.

They are an orderly and law-abiding people, and serious crime is very rare. Their kindness and hospitality to strangers visiting the country are well known. Benevolence is also a universal characteristic. And when, through the failure of the precarious fisheries, distress occurs, the fishermen help one another to the full extent of their means.

Cape Breton Island, belonging to British America, lies northeast of Nova Scotia, and is separated from it by a channel fifteen miles wide. It is triangular in shape, having a length of one hundred and ten miles, and an extreme breadth of eighty-seven. The island is nearly divided into two parts by a large irregular seawater lake, connected with the ocean by two channels which are separated from each other by a long narrow island. The existence of this lake makes every part of Cape Breton accessible by water, although the area is a little more than three thousand square miles.

The two natural divisions thus created are in striking contrast. The northern one is high, bold, and steep; while that to the south is low, intersected by numerous inlets, and rises gradually from its interior shore until it presents abrupt cliffs toward the Atlantic Ocean.

There are several lakes of fresh water on the island, of which Ainslie is the largest. There are also numerous rivers, but none of them are navigable. Salt springs are found on the coast. The climate is varied, but not so rigorous as that on the adjoining continent. Corn and other grains may be raised.

The forests of Cape Breton furnish large quantities of pine, oak, birch, beech, maple, and ash. Shipbuilding constitutes an important and lucrative branch of business in the island. Granite, limestone, salt, and coal are found — the latter in great abundance and of a superior quality. There are also rich deposits of the best iron ore.

Cape Breton has long been noted for its fisheries. During the time of its occupancy by the French, not less than six hundred vessels were engaged in the trade at a time. Cod, salmon, mackerel, shad, and whitefish are found in great abundance.

The island forms a colony under the government of Nova Scotia and sends two members to its Legislative Assembly. The population, made up principally of the descendants of Scotch, French, and Irish, numbers more than eighty-five thousand.

Sydney was formerly the capital of Cape Breton. It is situated in the east part of the island, at the head of an excellent harbor which has a safe and secure entrance. A lighthouse has been erected on a low point of land at the south side of this entrance, showing a fixed light one hundred and sixty feet above the sea.

The growth of the town during its century of existence has been exceedingly sluggish. But the development of the coal mines, three miles above its lighthouse, has brought about a great change; so that Sydney is now classed with the active mercantile communities of Nova Scotia, and has direct railway connection with the rest of the continent. The coal fields referred to are estimated to contain two hundred and fifty miles of workable coal. The thickness of the vein worked is six feet. The coal is transported three miles by railway to a wharf where it is taken on board of vessels. At a distance of fifteen miles from Sydney are the Bridgeport mines, where the coal seam is nine feet in thickness.

But we must not leave Cape Breton without a visit to Louisburg, which at one time held the fortunes of France at the portals of the Gulf of St. Lawrence. It had formerly a finely built stone fortress. The harbor was defended by a high wall and a ditch eighty feet wide, a battery on Goat Island, and one called the "royal battery" farther down the harbor. These fortifications, built in thirty years and costing more than five and a half millions of dollars, were destroyed by the British in less than three months and at a cost of $50,000.

No large city stands upon this historic ground. Nothing greets the eye but a few scattered houses, a deserted fort, and the boundless sea. At the northeast entrance of the harbor is a rocky promontory called the Lighthouse Point, upon which the lighthouse is built. It is a tall, wooden building, painted white, and has a fixed light. More than a hundred and fifty years have passed since the French built the first lighthouse on this spot. A short distance east of the lighthouse a mound of earth represents the battery which in Wolfe's time did so much execution on the works at Goat Island about a third of a mile to the south.

We pass by the little northeast harbor, which forms so safe a haven, and soon reach the present village of Louisburg, consisting of thirty or more whitewashed or painted houses, a canning factory, and two or three churches. Shops occupy the roadside and the vicinity of the wharves. The ruins of the royal battery are visible to the west, and it is easy to trace the line of the works. Following the contour of the fortifications, we come to the old burying ground where, near the middle of the eighteenth century, hundreds of soldiers from England, New England, and France found a last resting place.

Prince Edward Island lies between 46° and 47° north latitude on the south side of the Gulf of St. Lawrence. It is separated from Nova Scotia on the south, and New Brunswick on the south and west, by Northumberland Strait, which has a varying width of nine to thirty miles. The greatest length of the island is one hundred and fifty miles, and its average breadth thirty-four. Its area is 2000 square miles. It is altogether irregular in form, but its northern outline resembles a crescent, the two horns being North and East capes. In no place does the land rise higher than five hundred feet, although the surface is undulating.

The island is well watered. The Dunk is a fine salmon and trout stream. Many oysters and lobsters are taken. By the disintegration of the soft, red sandstone, a bright, red, loamy soil of great fertility is produced. To this the province owes its remarkable productiveness as an agricultural district. Charlottetown and Georgetown are the chief harbors.

The gently rolling surface of the island, its rich fields, and its pretty homesteads embowered in green, give variety and beauty to the landscape. The climate is much milder than that of the adjacent provinces. Vegetation develops rapidly, and agriculture is extensively prosecuted.

The forests have been much reduced by lumbering operations, fires, and the need of the people, though many trees still remain, — chiefly beech, birch, pine, maple, poplar, spruce, and fir. Shipbuilding is carried on, but not so extensively as in former years.

The fisheries are exceedingly valuable, particularly those on the north coast. The chief kinds of fish are mackerel, haddock, cod, hake, and herring. Wild ducks, teal, wild geese, partridges, pigeons, and snipe are abundant. There are two hundred and sixty species of birds. Of wild animals, the most important are bears, which are seen only occasionally, lynxes, foxes, muskrats, hares, and squirrels. In the summer and autumn, large numbers of seals frequent the shores.

Prince Edward Island returns five members to the Canadian House of Commons, and four senators are appointed to the Canadian Senate by the Crown.

The population, numbering about one hundred and ten thousand, is of mixed origin. A large proportion are emigrants from Great Britain, and the rest are

QUEEN'S SQUARE GARDENS, CHARLOTTETOWN, P. E. I.

natives of the country, descendants of the French Acadians, Scotch, English, and Irish settlers, and of the loyalists who went to the island at the close of the Revolution. There are less than three hundred Indians. The religion is Church of England and Roman Catholic.

Charlottetown, the capital, has a population of about twelve thousand. It is the county town of Queen's County. Summerside, with a population of three thousand, is the county town of Prince County, and Georgetown is the county town of King's County. Princeton is the chief summer resort.

Anticosti is a barren island belonging to British America. It is situated in the Gulf of St. Lawrence, between 49° and 50° north latitude. It is 135 miles long by 40 miles broad. Most of the coast is dangerous, but lighthouses have been built at different points, and there are also provision posts for shipwrecked sailors. The lighthouse keepers and other officials are the only inhabitants of the island.

Miquelon consists of two islands off the south coast of Newfoundland, forming, with the adjacent island of St. Pierre, a colony belonging to France, with an area of ninety-one square miles. The united population of Great and Little Miquelon, as they are called, is over five hundred. They make fishing their sole occupation.

St. Pierre lies southeast of Miquelon, from which it is separated by a narrow channel. It has, together with one or two smaller islands belonging to the St. Pierre group, a population of nearly six thousand. The surface of these islands is rocky, and the vegetation scanty. The chief industry is cod fishing.

CHAPTER XVI.

THE BERMUDAS AND THE BAHAMAS.

NEARLY six hundred miles southeast of Cape Hatteras, off the coast of North Carolina, lies a group of islands occupying an area about eighteen miles long by six wide. They number as many as there are days in a year, and lie in the form of the letter J. Three hundred and sixty of them are small, being nothing but rocky islets. Of the remaining five, the largest is Long Island, or Great Bermuda, and on this the capital, Hamilton, is situated. With a single exception, these larger islands are connected with one another by bridges. The group is surrounded on all sides but the east by formidable coral reefs, nearly all under water, and extending in some places ten miles from the islands.

The Bermudas belong to England, and, with the exception of Gibraltar and Malta, are her most strongly fortified hold. Indeed, this is the rendezvous for the British fleet in this part of the world, and here are stored up vast quantities of arms and ammunition. In Godet's history it is said that, "Bermuda, conjointly with

THE LAND OF WHITE HOUSES.

Halifax, holds in check the whole Atlantic coast of the United States, upon which nature has bestowed no equivalent for naval purposes; and also controls the West Indies, the Gulf of Mexico, and the south coasts of the United States." Strangers are not allowed inside the forts, but there is no law against their climbing the heights and making all the outside observations that they wish.

This is a land of white houses. No other color is to be seen. They are all built of the native white stone of coral formation, which underlies every foot of soil. When first quarried, this stone is so soft that it may be cut with a knife, but it hardens with exposure to the air. When a Bermudan wishes to build himself a house, all he has to do is to buy a piece of land, scrape off a foot or two of soil, and behold! there lies his quarry ready to his hand.

By means of a saw, the stone is cut into pieces two feet long by one foot in breadth and in thickness. Then it is piled up so as to admit of the free circulation of the air. The place excavated forms the cellar, already walled and floored. When the blocks of stone are dry, the builder proceeds with the erection of his house. Thin, flat slabs of the same material form the roof. The houses, even including the roof, are frequently whitewashed on the outside, and contrast strongly with the deep-green verdure by which they are surrounded. There are no shanties, as there are in the rest of the world; and, though there is no great accumulation of wealth, extreme poverty appears to be unknown.

The islands are very fertile, and with ordinary cultivation will yield two crops of potatoes in a year. No climate in the world is better adapted for beets, potatoes, onions, and tomatoes. Of barley, oats, and corn, two and sometimes three crops may be raised in a year. Tropical fruits, and also those of more northern latitudes, are to be found. There are strawberries and peaches, oranges and lemons, bananas and mulberries.

One of the conspicuous trees of the island is the flaming star, which has great star-shaped flowers of fiery red. Another is the monkey tree. No one knows why it received such a name, unless it is because no monkey could possibly climb it, its massive trunk being thickly set with short, sharp thorns. The oleander grows everywhere, and the great straggling bushes are so covered with bright blossoms as to give a decided character to the landscape.

There are but few birds that make their home in these islands throughout the entire year. One of these is the bluebird. Another is the scarlet grosbeak, noted for the brilliancy of his plumage and the sweetness of his song. Besides these there are the ground doves — tiny creatures clad in quiet gray and as demure as their color.

The population, consisting of about fifteen thousand people, is composed of whites, free blacks, and mulattoes. All classes seem to lack the energy which is so characteristic of the people of the United States. The work is done mostly by the negroes, and they can live well by working three days in the week. Working seems to be the exception, and doing nothing the rule, in this favored clime. It is said that when the south wind blows, everybody feels lazy,—and the south wind is very prevalent.

The government is vested in a Governor, an Executive Council of six members, and a Legislative Council of nine members—all appointed by the Crown, and a House of Assembly of thirty-six members, returned by the nine parishes.

The lighthouse on Gibbs Hill is the pride of the Bermudas. It is on the southern point of Long Island, and six miles from Hamilton. Let us make a visit to this famous light. Driving down Front Street, we pass the Parliament House, the Public Library, and Pembroke Hall with its group of royal palms. Then, rounding the harbor, the way leads through Paget and Warwick streets into Southampton, past fine country mansions and cozy cottages, with here and there a glimpse of the sea.

When we leave the main road to ascend the hill, we pass a ruined house which looks canny and unreal amid the splendid verdure. But we press steadily up the hill, which is next to the highest point on the islands, and, when we have reached the top, we are only two hundred and forty-five feet above the water level.

The lighthouse is a massive tower of stone, filled in with concrete, and is one hundred and thirty feet high. From the deck of a ship, forty feet above the water, the light may be seen thirty-three miles away. It is a revolving one, and is among the largest and most powerful in the world.

Although the tower is so lofty, the ascent is not difficult. The view from the gallery is magnificent beyond description. We can see all the islands of the group, and what specks they are in the middle of the great waste of waters! The exquisite coloring, the ethereal softness of the ever-changing tints of sea and sky, the purple of the reefs fading into the palest amethyst, — all this must be seen to be appreciated.

To the east, south, and west lies the boundless expanse of ocean. To the north is the Great Sound, studded with innumerable islands and skirted by the fair, green shores of the larger islands dotted with white houses half hidden in the foliage. And away beyond it all, the mysterious glory of the mighty waves blends with the still more mysterious glory of the sky.

The Bahamas form a group of about five hundred islands and rocky islets, lying northeast of Cuba and east of the coast of Florida. They constitute the most northern division of the West Indies Islands. The Gulf Stream passes between them and the mainland. They have an entire length of about six hundred miles, extending from the Grand Bahama in latitude 27° 30′ to Mouchoir Bank in latitude 21°. They belong to Great Britain.

The discovery and early history of the Bahamas is of especial interest to the American people. San Salvador, or Cat Island, of this group, was the first land discovered by Columbus on his earliest voyage, in 1492. At this period the larger of the islands were densely inhabited by a mild and inoffensive race of Indians.

AVENUE OF PALMS IN THE BAHAMAS.

They were of fine form, and many of them had handsome features. Their hair was coarse, and they wore it cut short, except a little at the back of the head which was left long and never cut. They were in the habit of painting the body, or only a part of it, white, black, red, or any other color that suited their fancy. They were quick, intelligent, of good demeanor, and were kindly disposed toward the white men.

The later treatment of this people by the Spaniards was utterly barbarous. "Their lands and goods were first taken from them. Their persons were next seized, under the text that 'the heathen are given as an inheritance.' The Spaniards with appalling atrocity proceeded to act towards these unfortunates as if they did not belong to the human race. It was one unspeakable outrage, one unutterable ruin, without discrimination of age or sex. They who died not under the lash in a tropical sun, died in the darkness of the mine." In fourteen years the inhabitants of the Bahamas, numbering about forty thousand persons, were totally exterminated.

The islands remained uninhabited for nearly one hundred and fifty years, when they were colonized by the English, who were afterward expelled by the Spanish. Subsequently, a change of masters occurred again and again; but, finally, the Bahamas were ceded to Great Britain in 1783.

They extend from Great Bahama to the Caicos group, a distance of about six hundred miles. The principal islands are Great Bahama, Great and Little Abaco, Andros, New Providence, San Salvador, Harbor, Watling, Long, and Crooked Islands. The entire area is about fifty-five hundred square miles, and the population forty-eight thousand. Nassau, on the island of New Providence, is the capital. The legislature consists of a Governor and Council appointed by the crown, and a House of Assembly. Education is under the management of a board of education.

AVENUE OF SPANISH LAURELS.

Generally speaking, the islands are long and narrow, and present a flat appearance. Their soil is well adapted to the growth of various kinds of fruit. Of the whole group not more than twelve or fourteen are inhabited, and some of the largest are altogether uninhabited or but thinly peopled; while others again are mostly unexplored. Though generally sterile, some of the islands produce oranges, limes, lemons, esculent vegetables, and maize for the consumption of the inhabitants, and some cotton for exportation. The wild vegetation consists of mahogany, lignum-vitæ, pigeon, alum, and dyewoods, with an entangled underbrush. In the more southern islands there are salt ponds of great value, the cultivation of which is increasing constantly.

The city of Nassau is built on the north shore of the

SHORE ROAD, NASSAU.

island of New Providence and has a population of about eleven thousand, one fifth of whom are white. The principal part of the city was built many years ago, and many of the streets are named after members of the royal family in England, as George, Frederick, and Cumberland streets.

The harbor of Nassau is a good one, its natural breakwater being formed by Hog Island, which lies about half a mile from shore. The chief entrance is at the west end, where the water is deep enough to admit vessels drawing seventeen feet of water. The town is built on sloping ground, rising to an elevation of about ninety feet and fronting the harbor. Each house has its own garden, in which grow all sorts of creepers laden with blossoms of every color, besides a wealth of roses, jasmine, hibiscus, and double oleanders. The streets are bordered by stately palms, graceful bananas, and tall cocoanut trees, beside countless others which grow only in tropical climes.

Bay Street, which is the principal business street, runs along the edge of the harbor. Starting from this one, streets run up to the top of the hill where the Government House, the Royal Victoria Hotel, and other notable buildings are situated. In a small space, near the center of Bay Street, is a park devoted to the court of justice and other public buildings.

The white people live in the city proper, the negro population living apart in the suburbs, chief of which are Delancy Town, Bain's, and Grant's Town. Still farther away are Fox Hill and Adelaide, both of which were settled in the first place by rescued African slaves. The market of Nassau is largely supplied with vegetables and fruit by the women of these places, who travel into the city every morning, carrying their products neatly arranged in baskets or trays upon their heads. Children often accompany their mothers, and carry palmetto thatch or leaves which are split into narrow pieces and woven into hats.

There are many places in New Providence worth visiting. About seven miles southwest of Nassau are

DONKEY EXPRESS, BAHAMAS.

two small lakes, Killarney and Cunningham, which are separated by the Blue Hills range. The surface of each is dotted with beautiful little mangrove islands. Their water is shallow and brackish, and rises and falls with the tide. This peculiarity is noticeable in nearly all the ponds and lakes in the Bahama Islands. There is no stagnant water here.

The Mermaid's Pool, of fresh water, in the southern part of New Providence, about half a mile from the coast, is situated in a perfectly level plain and has no banks. It is one hundred and fifty feet in diameter and sixty-five in depth. The water comes "to the very brim," and "it has a depth of forty feet at the very edge, which is the more remarkable as the adjacent sea is so shallow that it would be necessary to go five miles from the shore before a depth equal to that of the pool is reached."

But the most remarkable lake is known as "Waterloo, or the Lake of Fire." It is an artificial lake, within a short distance of Nassau, and is one thousand feet long by three hundred broad. It was constructed for the purpose of storing turtles. The bed is cut out of coral rock, and it is connected with the sea by a narrow ditch. When the gate is open, the water in the lake rises and falls with the tide. It is a phosphorescent lake, and "the phosphorescence is so powerful that the effect of it is unsurpassed in any other part of the world." The changing of the water never destroys the phosphorescence. No adequate explanation of the phenomenon has ever been made. The best time to visit this lake is at night. The light caused by the dip

A NATIVE HUT, GRANT'S TOWN.

of the oars is sufficient to enable one to read coarse print. "Whenever a boat travels through the water, there is of course a cutting of water at the bow, and an eddy left just behind the stern. At Waterloo, that cut water and eddy are of flaming fire. The lake is full of fish, and as the boat moves along frightened fish dart about on all sides, leaving fiery trails behind them. Now and then a turtle is disturbed, and, as he moves along, he looks like a revolving sun. As the more distant fish move about, they form little vapory clouds of fire, flashing and darting about on the surface like northern lights."

The Blue Hills reach an altitude of nearly one hundred and twenty feet. They are noted for the many caves found in them, which were doubtless the final resort for the unfortunate Indians when pursued by the Spaniards and their bloodhounds.

The sponge fishery is the most important industry of Nassau, and a large number of men and vessels are engaged in it. All the sponges of the Bahamas are taken to the Nassau market, which is a large, open building, long and narrow, and with no side walls. On the arrival of a vessel her cargo is sorted into piles three or four feet high. Each pile is labeled as belonging to a certain owner. Several vessels arrive every day. At nine in the morning the market is opened, and the sponge dealers assemble and look over the different piles, estimating and setting down the value of each. These estimates are handed to a clerk, who at the end of the day announces the highest bidder on each lot.

The Bahamas enjoy an extremely fine climate, serene

and temperate. Frost and extreme heat are unknown. There is no snow, hail, or northwest wind. For many years they have been popular as a health resort, and invalids from all parts of the world flock thither.

CHAPTER XVII.

THE WEST INDIES — CUBA.

THE West Indies form an extensive system of islands in the Atlantic Ocean, stretching from the Strait of Florida in North America, with a semicircular sweep, to the Gulf of Venezuela on the north coast of South America. On the north and east lies the Atlantic Ocean, on the south the Caribbean Sea, while on the west are the Caribbean Sea and the Gulf of Mexico.

They are divided into three distinct groups: the Lesser Antilles, the Greater Antilles, and the Bahama Islands. We have learned about the Bahamas in the preceding chapter. The islands composing the first-named division form the most southerly of these groups. They are arranged in the form of a crescent, with the convex side facing the east. They are divided into the Windward Islands and the Leeward Islands, the former terminating on the north with the Virgin Islands. The Greater Antilles comprise the four largest and finest islands in the archipelago, — Cuba, Haiti, Porto Rico, and Jamaica, — with the small islands adjacent. The Bahama Islands form the most northern portion of the system, and are the most numerous. The whole area of the archipelago does not exceed ninety-five thousand square miles.

The Antilles are generally considered to be part of a mountain range which at one time connected North and South America. Some of the Lesser Antilles are flat, but generally the islands of the West Indies are bold, with a single mountain or group of mountains near the center, sloping on all sides to the sea. Volcanic action is confined to the smaller islands. The most considerable eruptions of modern times (1812) have been those of St. Vincent; but more remotely San Domingo and Jamaica were the scenes of some of the most tremendous earthquakes on record.

The climate in the Antilles is extremely hot; but the length of the nights, the sea breezes, and the elevation of the land tend to modify the influence of the sun. Violent hurricanes occur frequently, generally between June and October.

On account of their rich and varied products, the West Indies hold an important place in the commercial world. The principal exports are coffee and sugar, both of which have been introduced there by man. The first West India sugar was produced in Haiti. In the early part of the sixteenth century the Spaniards had sugar presses in operation. Near the latter end of the same century, coffee was introduced from Ceylon and the Isle of Bourbon. Tobacco of a superior quality is also exported in large quantities.

At the time of their discovery, the more southern islands were occupied by a fierce, warlike tribe of

A CUBAN SUGAR PLANTATION.

Indians called Caribs: the northern ones were inhabited by a more gentle race. With the exception of a few hundreds in Trinidad, both tribes are now extinct.

Cuba is the largest and most westerly of the West Indies, and lies at the entrance to the Gulf of Mexico. It is nearly eight hundred miles long and from twenty-seven to ninety miles broad, with an area of about forty-six thousand square miles, including its coast islands. It belongs to Spain, and is the most important of her American possessions.

Cuba was discovered by Columbus during his first voyage. On October 28, 1492, he landed on its north coast. Several attempts to bestow a Spanish name on the island have been made, but it has always returned to the original Indian name of Cuba.

The surface attains its greatest height on the southeastern coast, rising in some places to an altitude of eight thousand feet. Another mountain ridge runs through the central part of the island. A rugged, hilly district lies on the southwestern coast. The remaining part of the country is undulating, and consists of well-watered plains covered with luxuriant forests or fertile plantations. There are a few extensive tracts of marsh land, particularly on the southern coast. The shores are generally low and are lined with dangerous reefs and shallows, but in many places there are deep and excellent harbors.

The rivers in Cuba flow north and south; they are all short, the longest not having a course of more than seventy miles.

Cuba is a warm country, the average yearly temperature at the extreme northern point being 77°, and at the southern, 80°. The year is divided into two seasons, — a hot and wet season, lasting from May to October, and a cool and dry one.

There are vast forests of hard wood, such as mahogany, cedar, ebony, and rosewood, suitable for manufactures, shipbuilding, and cabinet work. The orange, the wild lime, the palm, and many other tropical fruit trees are to be found here. The cocoanut tree belongs to the palm family, and displays its fruit beautifully in clusters at the top. The cocoanut is eaten at an earlier stage of its growth in Cuba than by people at the north.

Another tree which holds the attention of the foreigner is the ceiba, or silk cotton, tree. Nearly every estate has one, on some favorable spot, as an ornament. It is good neither as timber nor fuel, and the cotton it yields is very scanty in amount. There is one on the Santa Ana Estate which towers to the height of a hundred feet, and for sixty-five feet is a smooth cylinder without knot or limb. Six feet from the ground the circumference of the trunk is twenty-seven and a half feet, and near the base, where it spreads itself in the direction of its principal roots, the trunk measures forty-six and a half feet. Were nothing to be seen but this smooth, white shaft, it would still be an object of beauty ; but, at the height mentioned above, it stretches forth its branches and forms a top worthy, in beauty and grandeur, of the trunk below. By actual measurement its diameter has been found to be one hundred and sixty-five feet. From these widely extended limbs, vines, which grow on them, run downward to the ground, where they lie like coils of rope. When one of these vines is cut, it yields a sweet, milky juice, which proves a delightful beverage.

The plantain is one of the most useful plants growing in Cuba. It constitutes about three fourths of the subsistence of the black population of the island, and is also used to a great extent by the whites. It will grow in almost any kind of soil.

Cuba is divided into six provinces, each having a capital of the same name. These provinces are subdivided into districts, each presided over by a mayor, having under him local judges. The island sends as representatives to the Spanish Cortes sixteen senators and thirty deputies. The chief executive is the Governor General, appointed by the Crown of Spain for a term of three to five years, at an annual salary of $50,000. He is both civil and military commander. All state officers, from the highest to the lowest, are Spaniards and come directly from Spain.

The population of Cuba is composed of coolies, negroes, Spaniards, and creoles, or native descendants of the French and Spanish. The two last-mentioned classes dislike each other heartily. The reason for this is found in their abnormal political relations. Nearly all of the thousand Spaniards who go to Cuba are government officials, employés, and soldiers, whose business seems to be to make all they can for the mother country, and, in the meantime, to grow rich themselves. As a rule, after the Spaniard has accom-

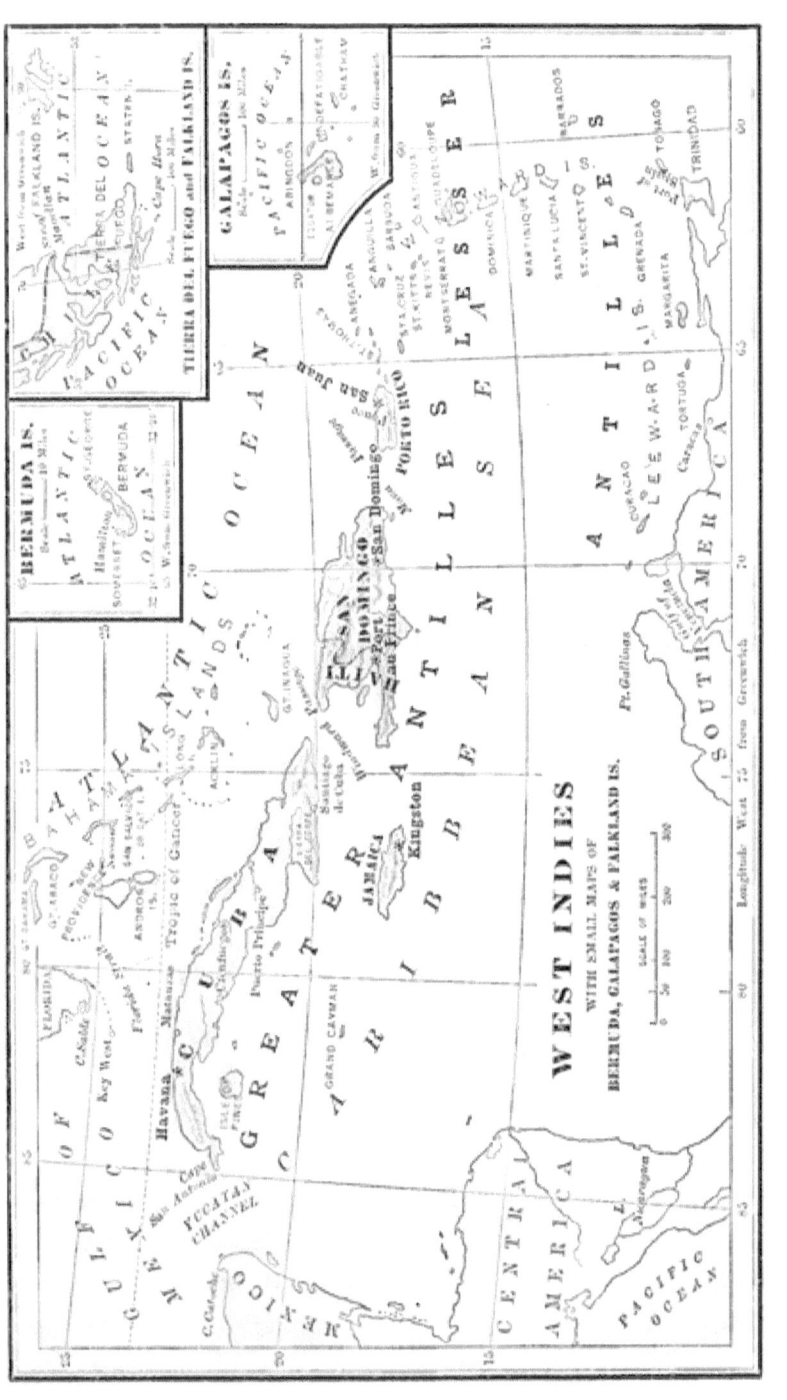

plished these objects, he goes home. The Cuban stands no chance except in the industrial or commercial line. There is no opportunity for him in the liberal professions or in the public service. He cannot take any part in public affairs. He cannot worship as he pleases. He has few rights worth mentioning, and he is grievously taxed. He cannot engage in any sort of business without buying official permission.

There have been six considerable uprisings against Spain since 1829, one of which lasted for ten years. The present revolution began in February, 1895, and has extended throughout the island. General Weyler, commander in chief of the Spanish forces, is carrying on a savage sort of warfare, which seems to have for its object the total extermination of the Cubans.

The Cubans are making a valiant stand for right and freedom. While sustaining some great losses, they have achieved some wonderful victories. They are fighting for a principle, and they stand side by side, as men only can when their purpose is honorable and their cause justifiable.

Havana is the capital of Cuba and the most important city on the island. Its harbor is the beautiful Bay of Havana, which nowhere exceeds a mile and a half in width. It is one of the finest harbors in the world, being deep enough for the largest vessels, and capacious enough to accommodate a thousand ships of war. The entrance to the bay is by a channel half a mile long, and so narrow that only a single vessel can pass at a time. This channel is fortified throughout its whole length; and its mouth, about a quarter of a mile wide,

A CASINO NEAR HAVANA.

is guarded by two strong castles, the Punta on the west and the Morro on the east. The far-famed Morro does not suggest the idea of a castle so much as that of a palace, so delicate is its beauty. Its walls are of a light golden brown and it is built upon a ridge of rock curiously worn and seamed by the action of the water.

After the firing of the sunset gun, no vessel may pass the Morro, but must turn aside and anchor outside the harbor for the night. But the bay is fatal as well as fair. Except when stirred by the north wind, its waters lie perfectly quiet and it becomes almost like a stagnant pool. This gives rise to fevers, which every year carry off many strong and healthy seamen.

The streets of Havana, though regularly laid out, are narrow and poorly paved. The houses are generally built close upon them, and awnings are frequently stretched across the entire street. It is barely possible for two vehicles to pass abreast, and blockades are common.

The walls of the houses are often two or three feet in thickness, are built of an irregular mixture of stones and mortar, and are painted. The colors employed are dazzling in their brilliancy and variety. One house has walls of light green with pink trimmings. Its neighbor may be blue with salmon trimmings. Gray and orange, lilac and yellow, or any conceivable combination of colors, may be seen; and this seems in keeping with the tropical surroundings, which suggest and almost demand color.

The private houses are usually but one story high; this, however, is generally twenty feet. The roofs are commonly tiled, sometimes shingled, and some of the more ancient are thatched with palm leaves. You enter from the street into a large square room, part of which accommodates the volante, or two-wheeled carriage commonly used in Cuba, the remaining portion serving as an entry to the rest of the house. The parlor also fronts on the street. It has two monstrous windows, very wide, and fifteen feet from the top to the bottom. There is no glass in the windows, an iron or a wooden grating taking its place. A heavy wooden shutter, containing a single pane of glass, is placed on the inside for use on rainy days and at night. As these windows reach almost to the floor, everything within is open to inspection from the street.

The door which opens into this room is opposite one of the windows, and is large enough to accommodate the passage of an ordinary load of hay. These immense openings appear odd to strangers, but they enable the occupants of the houses to obtain a fine current of air. Through this door you pass into a court open to the sky, at the right and left of which are sleeping rooms, and in front of which is the kitchen. The floors are often made of brightly colored tiles, but those made of plaster are also common; and, though cool, they necessarily supply a sufficient amount of lime dust to keep the furniture well covered.

A strange custom is observed in the parlors of all the houses. Rows of chairs, four or five in each line, are placed facing each other and running at right angles with the street; and upon these the members of the family and their company are always seated in the evening. As there are no curtains, and as screens are seldom interposed, passers-by may look in as they walk, and see what each lady wears, and who her callers are.

The volante (which has been superseded to some extent in the larger cities by carriages of modern style) is worthy of a description. It consists of an enormous pair of wheels, not less than six feet in diameter, with an axle of corresponding size, to which is fastened a pair of long curved shafts, eight yards in length. Forward of the wheels and between the shafts is suspended, by means of leathern straps, a phaeton-shaped body, the top and dashboard of which nearly meet. Into the shafts, three or four feet from the dashboard, a single horse is harnessed. There is a great deal of leather and plate about his harness, and on his back is placed a heavy saddle, which enables him to support the cumbrous vehicle that he is expected to draw. To a whippletree at the left side, a second horse is fastened by a pair of traces long enough to allow him to keep about half his length ahead of the other horse. On him is mounted a negro with a brightly colored jacket, decorated hat, long boots, large silver-plated spurs, and a heavy leathern whip. He leads the other horse by a short rein, and by dint of shouting at him, cracking his whip, and employing less gentle means, he keeps him going at a brisk pace. It often happens that there is but one horse. In that case he serves as carriage and as saddle horse at the same time.

Ordinarily the volante has but one seat, which may be occupied by either one person or two persons. It is much used by both gentlemen and ladies. No woman, except

198 THE WORLD AND ITS PEOPLE.

PORT OF SANTIAGO DE CUBA.

a negress, ever walks in public in Havana. When the ladies wish to go out to do their shopping, and in the evening, they always go in a volante. They do not alight and enter the shop, but the obliging clerk carries his goods outdoors for inspection.

The more common method of shopping, however, is to have the goods sent home. No matter how trivial or how expensive the article desired, the mistress calls a negress and gives to her a writing, setting forth the nature, quality, and quantity of the article she needs. The negress departs, and speedily returns with a large assortment of the goods required. Usually she carries the bundle of goods on her head. These are taken to the lady's room, where, with the assistance of the children, several servants, and all the unemployed occupants of the house, they are examined and the selection made. Time is never taken into account, and usually the obliging servant trots back and forth several times before the bargain is concluded. The amount and value of goods thus intrusted to servants is often very surprising.

There are several places of interest in Havana which one should not fail to visit. The public parks and promenades are said to surpass those of most cities in the Old World. One of these is the governor's square, called the Plaza de Armas. It is handsomely laid out with walks and ornamented with a few palm and cocoa trees. The inclosure is surrounded by a thick row of very old banyan trees, whose dark glossy foliage makes the densest shade to be found in all Cuba. On the south side of the square stands the palace of the

Spanish Governor General. It is built of yellowish stone and is in the form of a hollow square. It is two stories in height, and the upper one only is used as a residence by the Governor General. The upper floor projects far over the lower one and is supported by a row of stone pillars, making a pleasing colonnade along the front. The lower floor is devoted to numerous public offices. An arched way leads into the court, upon which open the windows of the interior.

On the north side of the square is a beautiful arch of marble which leads to the barracks. A little further east is a small but elegant chapel, recently built to commemorate the first mass celebrated on the island by Columbus. It has a front inclosure and a beautiful gateway, but the effect of the latter is impaired by contrast with that of the more towering arch which leads up to the barracks.

The next point of interest is the cathedral, in which lie the remains of the great Genoese, Christopher Columbus. It is a plain old-fashioned building on the outside, with a tower at each angle of the front, but inside it is sumptuous. The floor is of variegated marble, and the walls are beautifully frescoed. There are no seats nor screens. Delicate masonry of variously colored stone is everywhere to be seen, while tall pillars lend a majesty to the whole. The altar is made of porphyry, and a little to the left is a white tablet, showing where the remains of Columbus rest, inurned in the chancel wall.

The great prison of Cuba is a large building of yellow stone, standing near the fort of the Punta. It is one of the striking objects as you enter the harbor. It looks more like a palace than a jail on the outside, but inside it is full of all uncleanness. It has none of the modern improvements of English and American prisons.

The general elementary education of the people of Cuba is in a low condition. The people in the country do not live near enough together to admit of the successful operation of public schools, though free schools were established in 1822, and attendance on them was made obligatory in 1880. The richer classes of people send their children to Havana or out of the country to be educated.

There was once a large number of coolies in Cuba. These were natives of China, and were brought to Cuba by men regularly engaged in the business. The importer received four hundred dollars a head from the purchaser, who might then enforce from each coolie eight years of labor, for which he bound himself to pay four dollars a month to the coolie. They were more intelligent than the negroes and were put to higher labor. They worked under the eye of a taskmaster, but they would not submit to the indignity of being whipped. If one of them was flogged, somebody usually had to die for it, either the coolie himself, the perpetrator of the indignity, or some one else, according to their strange ideas of vicarious punishment. Yet their labor was considered so valuable that there was no difficulty in disposing of all who were brought. Of late coolies have not been imported, and their numbers have become very few on the island. In 1886, slavery was absolutely abolished in Cuba.

The great sugar estates of Cuba lie in the "upper district," the region of the famous "red earth." Many of these properties yield princely revenues, in times of peace, but on account of the prolonged insurrection of 1895-97, and the prevailing state of war throughout the island, the sugar crop has fallen to a very low figure. The plantations are all worked by gangs of negroes. Each large plantation is a village within itself, containing church, dwellings, hospital, workshops, storehouses, and waterworks.

The owner of the estate usually lives in a mansion not far removed from the sugarhouse, the avenue leading up to which is generally shaded by rows of stately palms or orange trees.

The negro quarter is a quadrangular structure, looking like a high wall, with no exterior opening other than a massive archway closed by an iron gate. The mayoral who carries the key admits us into a large court covered with a meager growth of coarse grass.

Near the center is a stone fireplace and a large boiler, where the cooking is done for the entire tenantry. Around the inside of the wall is a hollow square of two story dwellings, the second floor being reached by means of an outside staircase. Each room serves as a home to a limited family. A bed of rude plank with a blanket on it, a stool or two, several pots and pans, three or four coarse garments hanging on the wall, — that is all. Surely the negro's life differs little from that of the beast of the field. During the daytime the quarters are deserted, the adults being at work and the children being cared for elsewhere.

Next comes the hospital. Its exterior is similar to that of the negro quarters. On entering the court forty or fifty children may be seen at play in very scant attire. One side of the court is occupied by the nursery, where all the babes of the plantation are gathered and attended to by girls eight years old and upward. Standing near the hospital is a little chapel, where religious services are held occasionally by the priests of the neighboring village.

The sugarhouse is near at hand. It is a vast building, from one hundred and eighty to two hundred feet in length, and about half as broad. It is supported on stone pillars and is pierced by a tall chimney. In this building the sugar making goes on without cessation during the grinding season.

The cane, fresh from the fields, is brought to one end of the building, where it is passed through three heavy horizontal rollers. From these it emerges crushed and nearly dry, and is carried off to be dried perfectly, and afterward used as fuel for the furnaces.

The juice falls into a receiver below the rollers. After being boiled and skimmed in three successive boilers, it is poured into large, open, shallow vats and left to cool. After this, it is shoveled into barrels with pierced heads. These barrels are then conveyed to a room in which the floor is composed of narrow strips of plank with cracks between. The barrels are placed with the pierced ends downward and the drainage falls into an immense copper tank below, and constitutes the molasses of commerce. The sugar left in the barrels forms the larger part of our imported sugar, the refining being a separate business done for the most part in the United States.

But the most delightful place of all to visit in Cuba is the coffee plantation. The coffee plant needs to grow in the shade. Therefore the owner of an estate upon which he designs to raise coffee, first plants it with the fruit or shade trees which he prefers, and it becomes a vast grove of cocoa, mango, or cedar. These groves are divided into sections by shady, winding paths and into squares by broad avenues of palms. There are also narrower alleys of orange, mango, or other tropical trees. Interspersed everywhere are flowering shrubs and vines, — the oleander, lemon, lime, and hundreds of others. The cactus family is also largely represented, and of this the night-blooming cereus is the most beautiful. Humming birds, butterflies, and countless insects flit everywhere.

The Cubans call a coffee plantation "Paradise"; and a lovelier, more peaceful abode it would be difficult to find. The coffee plant is an evergreen shrub, growing to the height of sixteen feet or more; but it is kept pruned down to five or six feet, for convenience in picking. It has snowy, fragrant blossoms and a round fruit like a cherry, of changeful hues of green, white, yellow, and red.

The coffee berries ripen mostly from August to December. The berry is then red and about as large as a cherry. The coffee of commerce is the seed of this fruit, and two are contained in each, having their flat surfaces together. The ripe berries are picked carefully by hand and spread on large wooden frames

AUSTRALIA AND THE ISLANDS OF THE SEA. 205

PLAZA, CIENFUEGOS.

called driers. They are exposed to the sun by day and protected from the dew at night for about three weeks.

They are then cracked open by means of a wooden wheel moving in a circular trough which is kept filled with the dried fruit. Then they are passed through a fanning mill, which clears them of the dried pulp and also separates the larger from the smaller grains, which, with the dirt, fall through into a receiver and are picked out afterwards by the negroes, who spread them on long tables for the purpose. The coffee is then put into bags, and is ready for market.

Another beautiful sight is an orange grove in the fruit season. Acres of trees with ripe oranges, sometimes with blossoms and oranges on the same branch, give a luscious appearance, while the air is full of rich fragrance. The tobacco fields are not so picturesque, and the plants take away the fertility of the soil. The use of guano fertilizers has also caused the tobacco to deteriorate, except in certain localities.

Santiago de Cuba, with a population of 70,000, is the capital of the eastern department, and has a fine harbor. It was for several years the capital of the island. Cienfuegos, a seaport on the southern coast, has a population of over 40,000.

Near Matanzas, there is a great variety of scenery, and the famed Umori Valley, between high cliffs, forms a most delightful region. Large bamboo groves stretch along the banks of streams; the uplands, with banana fields, orange orchards, and luxuriant foliage, make a beautiful picture, with the blue sea stretching away off to the dim horizon.

CHAPTER XVIII.

HAITI.

HAITI is a rich and beautiful island fifty-three miles southeast of Cuba. It is irregular in form, being deeply indented with bays and inlets. The largest of these is the Samana Bay on the eastern coast, the distance between whose extreme capes is seventeen miles. It has an average breadth of twelve miles, and is fifty miles long. The channel by which it is entered is narrow and difficult, but the harbor is a safe and commodious one.

The length of the island from east to west is four hundred miles; its greatest breadth is one hundred and fifty miles. Including its coast islands it is about as large as Scotland with its adjacent islands.

It is intersected from east to west by three chains of mountains, more or less connected with each other by offsets. Extensive plains and savannas lie between them. The loftiest peak of these mountains is a little more than seven thousand feet high. They are richly and heavily timbered, and most of them are understood to be susceptible of cultivation almost to their tops.

All the streams of Haiti of any importance originate in these mountains, and flow either east, west, or south. No river of any consequence flows north. Few countries are as well watered as Haiti, for what the rivers lack in size they make up in number.

Few countries have greater mineral wealth than Haiti. Gold, silver, copper, jasper, marble, jet, and agate are among the most abundant, and are found in and about the mountain ranges. Rock salt, sulphur, and saltpeter may be procured with but little labor.

The soil is of every color and variety. In one place we find a rich vegetable mold; in another, a mixture of this with pebbles or sand; and in still another, a

CUTTING SUGAR CANE, HAITI, W. I.

light spongy loam. The color of the soil also varies; in some places it is red, in others of a bluish tint or a lava color, in others yellow, though still retaining its productive qualities; but generally it is black and from six inches to ten feet in depth.

It is exceedingly productive, surpassing anything found elsewhere in the West Indies. Sugar cane grows the year round so thick and fast, that by the time the laborer has cut over a ten-acre field, it is ready to cut again where he began. In truth, the stalk, though never reaching the height of Jack's renowned bean stalk, actually measures from eighteen to twenty-four feet. Stalks having a diameter of five inches have occasionally been found. Once planted, no further care is required until the time for cutting, and as it sprouts again as soon as cut, no replanting is necessary oftener than once in ten years.

Corn is cultivated as easily. A hole is made in the ground, and into this the grains are dropped. With no further care, the stalks grow to the height of from eight to fourteen feet, and bear from three to five ears each. All other crops grow with equal rapidity and strength. It is said that in some places the melon, the pumpkin, and the squash ripen in six weeks from the seed. Ginger is produced in great abundance. Indigo grows spontaneously, and yields two crops a year. Oranges, citrons, bananas, plantains, pineapples, and other tropical fruits are not excelled — perhaps not equaled — in any other country in the world.

Haiti was discovered by Columbus on his second voyage to America. It was inhabited at the time by a peaceful tribe of Indians, who treated Columbus and his followers with great kindness. Later they revealed to the Spaniards the rich gold fields of San Domingo. The Spaniards, with base ingratitude, enslaved the Indians and compelled them to work in the mines, and in about fifty years the tribe was entirely exterminated. This remorseless cruelty to the Indians is a foul blot on Spanish rule in the West Indies.

The extirpation of the Indians was the ruin of their destroyers. To replace them, negroes were imported, and Haiti became the seat of the first negro slavery in America. But in three centuries, in spite of a great expenditure of money and the sacrifice of soldiers, sailors, and planters, the Spaniards were entirely vanquished by their slaves.

In 1697 the western part of the island was ceded to France, and, a hundred years later, the eastern part also. In the latter part of the eighteenth century a war of races began, resulting in the supremacy of the blacks. The negroes were then emancipated by the French, and have been free ever since. But they desired political liberty as well, and in 1801 the whole island was declared independent, with the famous Toussaint L'Ouverture as President for life.

Napoleon, wishing to reduce the colony to subjection, sent troops to Haiti, and the negroes were forced to retire to the mountains. Toussaint was taken captive and carried to France. On reaching that country he was hurried into Normandy, where, in a dismal, damp cell, without the presence of a single friend, he expired in 1803. Thus perished, without trial or even examination, a grand man, who, though the leader of his own race, had shown abundant mercy to the whites in a country where their enormities had provoked hatred.

Haiti was not fortunate in the rulers who succeeded this noted man. The negro who followed him in command had himself proclaimed Emperor, but so cruel and tyrannical was his rule that in five years he was assassinated. Several rival chiefs then contended for leadership. The result was the crowning of a certain Christophe, under the title of Henry I. After displaying all the cruelty and savagery of the worst potentate of Africa, he committed suicide in 1820.

Sixteen years previous to this time, all the remaining whites had been massacred or driven from the country. The blacks took possession of their vast estates, and their leaders built for themselves beautiful dwellings and palaces.

The ruins of one of these palaces remain to this day, forming one of the chief attractions of Cap Haitien on the northern coast. It was a palace erected at the command of Christophe; it stood on the brow of a hill, in a long, beautiful valley, completely surrounded by mountains; it crowned the knoll with broad terraces and esplanades, and contained suites of rooms grand enough to satisfy the most extravagant taste. There was a throne room where the king held his receptions, and a chapel where he and his family went through forms of worship. From the terraces, beautiful views were obtained. Rivulets, whose flow was broken by numerous cascades, came hurrying down the mountain sides. There was no end to the fruits and flowers produced in the royal gardens. But the palace was long since ruined by earthquakes, and the king and his nobility are no more.

The modern Haitian is still fond of display, and spends most of his money for "regimentals," so as to make as fine an appearance as possible before his humbler neighbors.

The island is at present divided into two rival

republics, — Haiti, including the western third with Port-au-Prince as its capital city, and San Domingo, comprising the remaining portion, the capital of which bears the same name. The Haitians in some parts of the island are generally regarded as very low in the scale of civilization.

"It is a great mistake, however," says a recent writer, "to think that the Haitians as a whole are a barbarous, uncivilized nation. The trouble in Haiti is largely geographical: in the north, the mulatto element prevails; in the south, the blacks are in the majority. The Haitians, as a nation, are an intellectual people, except in the interior mountain fastnesses, where ignorance and superstition prevail. It would be as unfair to judge the United States by the actions of the Sioux Indians as to class the Haitians of the coast with those in the mountain fastnesses. Around the ports you will find a great deal of refinement and education, and much of the chivalry of the French nation. The newspapers that caricature the Haitians as a people are simply doing so through ignorance."

Haiti, under the administration of President Hyppolite since 1890, has shown marked progress both in her internal affairs and her relations with the civilized world.

The inhabitants of the other part of the island, San Domingo, are more enlightened than those of Haiti; and yet they seem utterly unable to appreciate the blessings of their island home. At one time they were united with the republic of Haiti; but they had so much trouble that they were compelled to separate again; yet they are always hankering for union with a stronger state.

Columbus thought Haiti the most beautiful place on earth. It is to be hoped that the time will come when it will be more accessible to civilized people.

The legal rights of the white race in Haiti are very few. They cannot possess real estate; they cannot hold mortgages for a longer time than nine years; they cannot become citizens. Consequently they cannot vote nor hold political positions. They can be wholesale merchants, artists, mechanics, professors, teachers, clerks, engineers, and the lessees of estates; but the retail trade, the bar, the bench, military honors, and civil distinctions are not open to their attainment. In social life and in the legal callings for which they are qualified, however, they are treated with due regard and courtesy. "Exemplary conduct on their part always enables them to overcome the social disadvantages attaching to their unfortunate color!"

CHAPTER XIX.

JAMAICA.

JAMAICA belongs to Great Britain, and is its principal possession in the West Indies. It lies ninety miles south of Cuba, and is about as large as Connecticut. Its coast line is five hundred miles long, and is indented with a great number of excellent harbors, of

KINGSTON, JAMAICA

which Kingston is the most important. This harbor is a landlocked basin, available for the largest ships, and inclosed on the south by a long tongue of land, at the extremity of which is Port Royal. The entrance and the harbor itself are defended by several large forts.

Kingston, the capital city and chief seaport of Jamaica, is on the north side of the harbor. It stands on a gentle slope and is regularly laid out, its houses being mostly two stories in height and furnished with verandas. It is inclosed on the north by a lofty ridge of mountains, the intermediate space being taken up with country residences and sugar estates.

The public buildings of Kingston possess little architectural interest. The Victoria Market and the public landing at the foot of King Street form a very fine market place. Here stands a statue of Rodney, the great English naval commander who at one time saved Jamaica from falling into the hands of the French.

Markets in Kingston are open several hours every day, but there are two full market days a week. All provisions are brought from the country on the backs of donkeys, or in carts drawn by mules. The quality of the air is such that meat and fish may be carried long distances, notwithstanding the heat, without spoiling. All kinds of tropical fruits abound, and oranges of a flavor unknown in the north may be bought for ten cents a hundred.

Ice never forms in Jamaica, but artificial ice may be obtained in the city for a cent a pound. Instead of being distributed from carts, the ice is wrapped in cocoanut trash and carried on the backs of donkeys.

The general appearance of the country is extremely beautiful. On the north are gently rolling hills covered with groves of a brilliant verdure, and separated from one another by vales which exhibit the most exquisite scenery. On the south are abrupt precipices and inaccessible cliffs, the general effect of which is heightened by the large number of streams which pour from every valley, and often precipitate themselves from the overhanging rocks into the ocean.

The form of the coasts presents the outline of a turtle, the mountain ridges by which it is traversed in all directions representing the back. The principal chain is the Blue Mountains, running east and west and reaching in some places an elevation of eight thousand feet. The valleys are all narrow, not more than a twentieth part of the island being level ground.

The soil is not so fertile as it is in some other of the West Indies; but the usual tropical products are raised, sugar cane being the chief. Pimento, peculiar to Jamaica, is native, and furnishes our allspice. The rainy seasons are from May to August and from October to November.

Jamaica is divided into three counties, and subdivided into twenty-one parishes. The government is vested in a Governor and a Privy Council of twelve members, appointed by the Crown, and a Legislative Assembly of forty-five members, two elected by each parish and one member by each of the three principal towns.

The quadrupeds, birds, and fishes are like those of Cuba and Hayti; but there is a rat known as the Sir

Charles Price rat, which is not found on the other islands. Sir Charles Price owned at one time an estate on the island, which was very much infested with native rats. With a great deal of trouble he imported a very large, strong species for the purpose of killing the others. The newcomers succeeded so well that in a short time the native rats on the estate were exterminated; then they gave their attention to the cats and soon had the better of them. Now the species has increased so prodigiously that its members are a greater nuisance to the island than all the others put together.

But by far the most interesting animal in Jamaica is a kind of crab which inhabits a shell like a snail's. Its shell is so small in proportion to its limbs that the way in which it contrives to fold the latter under instantly, upon the slightest alarm, is curious and interesting. These crabs inhabit the mountains, but regularly, once a year, they travel in large troops down to the seaside. They are seldom used as food except for soup. They grow as large as a man's fist. Occasionally one will be found alone; but, as they generally form themselves into armies, and move in a straight line to the sea, the soldier crab found by himself may be looked upon as a deserter.

The dwelling houses of Jamaica are more frequently two stories high than one, this always being the case in the lowlands, where the ground floor is liable to be damp. The upper story is used to live in, and the lower one is given up to storerooms, open cellars, and harness and carriage rooms. A veranda extends along the front, from which you descend into a driveway overgrown with short turf and bordered with myrtle and orange trees. Every house has its flower garden, in which roses, violets, heliotrope, and numerous tropical plants are grown.

A main hall extends from the front door through the middle of the house. Near the front it opens, right and left, into a dining room and a library. All the rooms are large, and those belonging to the more affluent classes are floored throughout with mahogany.

Back of the house a thatched cottage of two stories, called a bungalow, is generally built, having the lower floor devoted to storerooms, closets, a bathroom, and sometimes a study, and the upper one to bedrooms.

A Jamaica kitchen is a novelty in its way. Instead of a stove or range, there is a huge embankment of rough brick along one side of the room. On top of this are holes in which the fires are built. On the embankment stands a sort of large two-barred gridiron on legs two feet high. This holds the pots and pans. Sometimes a chimney ascends out of the open hole above the embankment, but not always. There is also a vast brick oven in the kitchen; and when it is used a great fire of wood must be built under it. The pots and pans used for cooking are similar to ours; but there is a kind of red bowl of earthenware, called by the African name, yabba, round and varying in diameter from three inches to three feet. It has handles on two sides, and, though usually wobbly on its base, is a great favorite with the black cook, by whom it is much used.

The servants, all of whom except the housekeeper are usually colored people, are paid all the way from

AUSTRALIA AND THE ISLANDS OF THE SEA. 219

COOLIES PREPARING RICE, JAMAICA.

one dollar to two and a half dollars a week, and out of this they have to board themselves. Their fare consists almost wholly of yams, salt fish, and hot water sweetened with brown sugar; so that their living costs them but little. The yam, when properly prepared, is delicious. It is an ungainly root, one or two feet long and as thick as a man's arm.

In common with the other West Indies, slavery was introduced into Jamaica at an early date, and continued until 1834. At present, negroes are in the majority; out of a population of six hundred thousand, only about twenty thousand are white people.

There is no established church on the island; but the Church of England, the Baptists, the Methodists, the Presbyterians, and the Roman Catholics embrace most of the church members.

The negroes are growing more enterprising all the time, and cannot now be described as idle. They cultivate their gardens and fields with care, and produce enough sugar, coffee, and rice to enable them to buy a considerable number of imported articles. Extreme poverty is unknown among them, and they are a law-abiding and inoffensive community.

CHAPTER XX.

PORTO RICO.

THIS island was discovered by Columbus on his second voyage to America in November, 1493. Leaving the Virgin Islands, he sailed along its southern shore, coasting in and out of its harbors fringed with tropical trees, and finally landed in a place which he called Aquadilla, a name signifying "the watering-place." Here he watered his ships, and here a large volume of water is still sent forth.

Porto Rico is rectangular in form, being about ninety miles long and thirty-six broad. The interior, with the exception of a few extensive savannas, is one vast expanse of rounded hills, covered with such rich soil that they may be cultivated to their summits.

A mountain chain traverses the island from east to west, but its highest point is less than four thousand feet above the level of the sea. Numerous caves are to be found here, and in these the Indians formerly lived. There are many rivers, both large and small, and hot springs are occasionally found. The country is well adapted to grazing purposes, and is famous for its fine cattle, horses, and sheep.

The population numbers about eight hundred thousand, of whom fully half are white people. Porto Rico is one of the most thickly populated regions in the New World, having about two hundred and sixteen inhabitants to the square mile. Ponce, on the southern coast, is the largest town. It is near the center of the sugar district.

San Juan, the capital, is situated on an island on the north coast, and is connected with the mainland by a bridge and a causeway. An excellent highroad leads through the center of the country to Ponce. But a line of railroad, which has been projected, will soon connect all the coast cities and send shorter lines out into the country. The capital is compactly built and, on the side farthest from the mainland, is terminated by a fortress. It is surrounded by a wall from fifty to one hundred feet high. The houses are all stone, with iron balconies, and are painted every color except white. There are no window sashes with glass, but the window openings are usually provided with shutters. The houses have no chimneys.

Wooden houses are not allowed in the city proper, but may be built along the wharves and along a broad concrete walk, which skirts the outside of the city wall and is lined with seats and adorned with rude statues. Between the walk and the wall is an ornamental garden of flowers and trees. Through these may be obtained glimpses of the wall, cold and gray, from which project, at regular intervals, antique sentry boxes.

When the gates fronting the sea are closed, there is but one way of entering the city, and that is through an arched entrance where a road leads out into the country. At first the way lies through an open pasture, and there it skirts the shore of the bay, where it is thickly bordered with cocoa palms. Here and there is a village full of shops and drinking booths, and much frequented by the city people on afternoons and Sundays. The road passes on through another broad waste, and then the bridge is reached, the shore at this place being thickly bordered with mangroves.

The streets and houses of San Juan are dirty, and crowded with a somewhat thriftless population. Yellow fever makes its yearly ravages, and foreigners prefer to

live in the immediate suburbs, where there are many fruit and shade trees and where the air is pure.

Porto Rico belongs to Spain, and is ruled by a Captain General, the same as Cuba. On account of the foreign soldiery and officials, a discontent, similar to that which exists in Cuba, is prevalent. The social life is thoroughly foreign and Spanish, and presents all the gentle breeding and true courtesy of Spanish noblemen of the Old World.

The fort that guards the harbor is called the Morro, and is not unlike the one of the same name at Havana. Within its walls are a chapel, houses, and barracks, deep dungeons, covered ways, and ancient-looking guns. There are also a beacon light and a signal station. But by far the most interesting structure is a building occupied at present by the Royal Engineers. It is called the Casa Blanca, and was built as a residence by Ponce de Leon, the discoverer of Florida.

Toward the bay, the Casa Blanca is protected by an ancient wall backed by a garden of tropical plants, brought into prominence by a double row of cocoa palms. The garden and the windows which look out over the water command a fine view of the bay and the harbor. Immediately below is the gray old wall of the city, while beyond the water of the bay lies the palm-fringed shore of the mainland, with its never-ending rows of hills melting away into the distance.

After the subjugation of Porto Rico, Ponce de Leon had leisure to listen to the wonderful stories told by his Indian servants about the mysterious island in the north that concealed in its deep forest the wonderful Fountain of Youth. And doubtless it was while sitting in this same ancient castle that he planned the voyage that has made his name famous.

The market is situated on a hill near the ocean side of the city. The court is paved with great stones, and in it booths are erected containing various sorts of meat, vegetables, and country produce. An occasional parrot is to be seen, but by far the most common bird displayed for sale is the gamecock. Each one has the feathers shaven from his back and plucked from his head, neck, and tail. Here, as in Cuba, the pit is much frequented, and over these disgraceful fights much money is lost and won.

It is remarkable that, though the soil is so fertile, there are scarcely any flowers on the island. When the Spaniards came to make a settlement, the astonished Indians saw, for the first time, the horse, the cow, and the sheep. As their largest animal was no larger than a raccoon, their surprise may be imagined. The horses especially excited their admiration; but they shrank from them in fear.

Porto Rico is rich in unique antiquities, one of which is both curious and common. It consists of a stone collar, in shape like a horse collar and elaborately carved. It is supposed to have been made for use after death. Each Indian, with no other tools than stone knives and chisels, spent the greater part of his life in carving out this peculiar collar. When he died, it was placed upon his breast in the grave, "to keep him in place forever, so that the devil could not take him away."

CHAPTER XXI.

TRINIDAD.

TRINIDAD is the largest and the most southern of the Lesser Antilles, and belongs to the Windward Islands. It is square in shape, with long, projecting capes on each corner except the southeast. It is separated from South America by a shallow body of water called the Gulf of Paria. There are two entrances to this gulf, called respectively the Dragon's Mouth and the Serpent's Mouth.

Columbus was the discoverer of Trinidad, and gave it that name because the first sight of land was of three mountain peaks. Sir Walter Raleigh afterward visited the island in search of gold. It is said he tarred his ship with pitch from its famous lake.

The island belonged alternately to the Spanish and French, until the beginning of the present century, when it fell into the hands of the English. It then formed a Crown colony, the public affairs being administered by a Governor, assisted by an Executive and a Legislative Council. The island of Tobago was annexed to Trinidad in 1889. The laws were a mixture of Spanish and English; and neither coroners' inquests nor trial by jury were established.

Approached from the north, Trinidad appears like an immense ridge of rocks. Its east and south shores are also rocky and high. But on the side next the Gulf of Paria it presents a series of hills, valleys, and plains, covered with a verdure that never decays. The mountain chains run from east to west, attaining a height of about three thousand feet. The plains are watered by numerous streams, which generally terminate toward the Gulf of Paria in extensive swamps.

The cultivated land is a mere fringe around the edge of the forests. In the valleys are built the country houses of the merchants and the cabins of the black peasantry. The latter resemble great boxes very loosely nailed together, and are usually set up on stones a foot or more from the ground, so as to admit of a free circulation of air under the floor.

There are in all about two hundred and thirty-eight thousand people in Trinidad, and twenty thousand in Tobago, of whom ten thousand are coolies, twenty-five thousand whites and mulattoes, and the rest negroes.

On landing at the Port of Spain, as the capital city of the island is called, one finds a well-built, foreign-looking place, most of whose buildings are constructed of stone found in the neighborhood. The streets are long, wide, well paved, and densely shaded. Nearly every house has a garden containing coffee plants, palms, and other tropical trees.

Strange as it may seem, there are no sanitary arrangements, and the city depends on the abundant rainfall and those natural scavengers, the crows, to keep things clean. Of these filthy but necessary birds, there are hundreds, and when they have gorged themselves with refuse, they perch upon the roofs of the houses. In this island, as in others, they are protected by law.

Outside of the city is a park, where the better class of business people live. Their houses are built so as to admit all the wind there is, and to exclude the sunshine.

The residence of the Governor stands at the foot of a mountain in a fine situation. It was built recently, and no expense was spared to make it a handsome, commodious building. In one place on the lawn stands

TRUNK OF A SILK COTTON TREE.

an immense silk cotton tree, whose umbrella-shaped top measures about a hundred and fifty feet in diameter.

Adjoining the Government House are the Botanical Gardens. Plants, which with us are familiar only in conservatories, are here expanded into mammoth giants; and, besides these, there are scores of others which have not even a puny representative in colder climates. Palms of every known species, from the cabbage palm towering up into the sky, to the fan palm of the desert, grow in the greatest luxuriance. Many of the trees have flowers similar to those of the pea, and hang their seeds in pods. But the grandest among them all is the sacred tree of Burma. At a distance it resembles the horse-chestnut in form, but in place of the white flowers it is covered with pendant bunches of crimson blossoms.

Dispersed among these royal beauties are spice, orange, coffee, and cocoa trees, besides shrubs, vines, and plants of innumerable sorts. The prettiest of the spices are the nutmegs. They have a little glen all to themselves, and load the surrounding air with their fragrance. Only one other place beside Trinidad has nutmeg trees of so large a size. They grow here to the height of thirty or forty feet. Their leaves are a dark and brilliant green, resembling those of the orange, but extremely delicate and thin. The lowest branches reach to the ground and the whole tree forms a sort of bower, in which, during a tropical shower, one may find a safe retreat. Flies and moths seem drawn to the tree by the fragrance, and beautiful butterflies often hover around. One visitor to the garden saw a pair which for beauty surpassed any he had ever witnessed. They were of a dark blue, shot with green like the color of a peacock's neck, and as large as a bat. He asked a black boy to catch one for him; but the boy promptly replied, " That sort no let catchee, massa."

Countless vines and creepers are found in the garden. In one place stands a gigantic dead cedar completely covered with a fig vine. Years ago this parasite began to twine itself about the stem, choking out the natural life and spreading itself over every twig and limb, until at last the lifeless limbs were completely covered with a verdure not their own.

At the farther end of the garden is the old Government House, made famous by the presence of Charles Kingsley as the guest of the Governor, Sir Arthur Gordon. The house is a long wooden building surrounded by verandas. It commands views of the park, through arches formed by tall bamboos, which shoot up into the air for nearly a hundred feet, where they meet forming frames for the landscape. Kingsley took especial pleasure in these bamboos, as he had never seen anything like them before. Visitors are still shown the room in which he used to write, and the long gallery where he was accustomed to walk up and down.

The principal animals in the island are a species of small deer, opossums, porcupines, lizards, ant-bears, sloths, and monkeys in great variety. The latter class is very interesting. They invariably travel in the tops of the trees, and each company is led by the oldest of its number, who is exceedingly sly. They keep up a sort of grunting or barking while traveling, and while feeding make a strange, low, chattering sound.

Between the dogs and the monkeys there is a mutual dislike, and the latter lose no opportunity for annoying the former. They approach a house, when they can see no one around, and, climbing into a safe position, sit and make faces at the dog, which becomes frantic with rage in his efforts to reach them.

The wonder of Trinidad is a lake, the like of which can be seen nowhere else in the world. We may well forego the pleasure of a trip to the picturesque Blue Basin for the purpose of seeing a lake in which the sky is never reflected. Running down from the Port of Spain, some thirty-six miles toward the south, we come to a peninsula whose flat top is somewhat higher than the lowlands on either side. As we near the shore, we see that the beach and the long slope beyond are black. We land, and after walking for a little more than a mile find ourselves standing on the verge of the Pitch Lake, which lies not in a depression but at the top of a rise. On two sides the ground slopes gently away, and on the other two it rises very slightly. A group of islands, some twenty yards wide, is scattered about the center of the lake, which is a mile and a half in circumference; and though several attempts have been made to find out its depth, no bottom has yet been discovered.

What a strange looking lake it is! Some one has likened it to a black glacier, for the pitch has overflowed and is still overflowing, but very slowly. We walk out upon this pitch, which at the sides is quite hard; but after proceeding a short distance we are stopped by a channel of clear water. On looking around, we observe that the whole lake is intersected with channels similar to this one.

Charles Kingsley has compared it to a "crowd of mushrooms of all shapes, from ten to fifty feet across, close together, side by side, their tops being kept at exactly the same level, their rounded rims being squeezed tight against each other." Now conceive water being poured over these so as to fill the open spaces. " Thus would each mushroom represent, tolerably well, one of the innumerable flat asphalt bosses, which seem to have sprung up, each from a separate center."

Scattered all over the lake are occasional sticks of wood, five or six inches in diameter and several feet in

CABBAGE PALMS, TRINIDAD.

length. No one knows how to account for their presence. They seem to come up from below, and on reaching the surface of the lake usually stand in an upright position and look like stumps of trees protruding through the pitch; but their parvenu character is curiously betrayed by a ragged cap of pitch which invariably covers the top and hangs down like hounds' ears on either side.

The small islands, which are said to change their number and position, are covered with a growth of scrub, holly, and cocoa palm. Beyond them is that part of the lake where the pitch still oozes up in a liquid state. The old proverb, that one cannot touch pitch without being defiled, does not hold true here. It is so mixed with earthy matter that it may be molded into balls or sticks, leaving nothing but clean gray mud and water on the hands. It may be kneaded for an hour before the mud is sufficiently driven out of it to make it sticky.

CHAPTER XXII.

THE LESSER ANTILLES.

BARBADOS is the most eastern of the Caribbees, or Lesser Antilles. Bridgetown, its capital, is situated in the southwest corner of the island, near the thirteenth degree of north latitude. The island is twenty-one miles long, fifteen broad, and has an area of one hundred and sixty-six square miles. Navigation is rendered dangerous by the neighboring coral reefs.

It has belonged to Great Britain since 1625. The local government consists of a Governor in chief, assisted by a Council. The Governor is invested with the chief civil and military authority. The Council is composed of twelve members, appointed by the sovereign. The House of Assembly consists of twenty-four delegates, elected annually, two for each parish. Churches and schools are numerous, as are also charitable and benevolent institutions. There are several literary and agricultural societies and a number of weekly newspapers.

With the exception of Hong Kong and Malta, Barbados is said to be the most densely populated island in the world. The population is one hundred and eighty-seven thousand, which gives over one thousand individuals to each square mile, or nearly twice that of England.

Barbados is considered one of the healthiest islands in the West Indies. Its climate is especially adapted to make it one of the most agreeable and advantageous winter residences for invalids. There are but two seasons in the year, — the wet and the dry, or the hot and the cool. The former lasts from the beginning of June to the end of October; the latter covers the remaining months. During the dry season the northeast trade wind blows steadily, and the climate is extremely pleasant.

The first glimpse of Barbados from the deck of a vessel is sure to be disappointing. The view of Bridgetown harbor consists for the most part of a low, flat shore, lined with warehouses, above which tower, here and there, a few scattered palm trees. Farther inland the surface is much diversified, presenting, on a small scale, a succession of hills and valleys, table-lands, cliffs, gorges, and ravines, some of the latter presenting perpendicular walls of one hundred and fifty feet.

The productive soil of Barbados is of a reddish-brown color on the higher table-land; in the lowlands it is black and somewhat reddish in places where it is shallow. The black mold is best suited to sugar raising; over forty thousand acres are planted in sugar cane. All the native woods have been cut down to make way for farming operations.

Fruit trees flourish in abundance. The breadfruit tree, the bread nut, the lemon, the orange, mango, golden apple, and many others, overshadow the little huts that

BREADFRUIT, BARBADOS.

dot the steep slopes and perch upon jutting rocks, diversifying the pervading greenness by their variously tinted foliage and many-colored fruits. The steep hillsides, which are unfit for the growth of sugar cane, are usually occupied by the black people, who grow tiny patches of arrowroot and fruit to the great improvement of the landscape.

Caves abound in Barbados, as in all other places of

coral or limestone formation. The most remarkable one is called the "Animal Flower Cave." It has attained great celebrity, not from its size, but on account of its beautiful inhabitants, a species of zoöphyte. It is situated at North Point, at the northern extremity of the island. For a considerable distance in this place the shore is precipitous, the cliffs descending at many points into deep water. These exposed to the fury of wind and wave are worn into deep caverns, one of which is the Animal Flower Cave.

The entrance is in the face of a steep cliff forty feet high and is reached by crossing a ridge of rock called the "Saddle." The crossing must be made during the interval elapsing between the retreat of one wave and the approach of the next. On reaching the inside of the cave, the ground is found to slope upward and all danger is passed.

The cave consists of several connected rooms. The most attractive chamber is called the "Carpet Room," on account of the soft and beautiful mosaic of marine algæ with which it is covered. Near the center is a large circular basin, in the bottom of which is a huge stone covered by salt water of wonderful clearness.

At first sight the visitor will probably see some stems, resembling those of aquatic plants, projecting from the stone and floating in the water. But if he keeps still, and leaves the water undisturbed, the bulbous end of a stem will suddenly flash open, displaying a lovely flower of a pale yellow color, resembling single marigolds with many petals. If an attempt is made to pluck a flower it closes instantly, its neighbors follow its example, the stem contracts, and the whole is withdrawn into the crevice of the rock, to await the restoration of quiet again. The seeming petals are but the arms or feelers of the animal, which suddenly contract and inclose those particles which come within their reach, and are suitable for the creature's food. Similar animals are found in considerable numbers on the reefs, but they lack the brilliant coloring of their brethren in the cave.

St. Vincent, one of the British West Indies, is one hundred miles west of Barbados. It has an area of one hundred and thirty-two square miles, and a population of forty-one thousand. Kingstown, at the southwest extremity of the island, is the capital. In the northwest is a volcano, of which a tremendous eruption occurred in 1812. It has a height of three thousand feet; its crater is three miles in circumference and five hundred feet deep. The climate of St. Vincent is humid but not unhealthy. The principal products are sugar, rum, molasses, arrowroot, and cotton.

Another of the Lesser Antilles is called Curaçao, and belongs to the Dutch. It has an area of two hundred and ten square miles and a population of 28,000.

Martinique, one of the French West Indies, has several good harbors, the best of which is Port Royal on the southwest side. The principal town is St. Pierre on the northwest. The administration is under a Governor and a Privy Council aided by a General Council. The population numbers one hundred and ninety thousand. The Empress Josephine, first wife of Napoleon, was born in Martinique.

There are six extinct volcanoes on the island. The loftiest summit is Mount Pelée, which rises to the height of 4450 feet. The mountain slopes are for the most part covered with primeval forests. Numerous rivulets flow from the heights. The fertile valleys produce sugar, coffee, cocoa, and cotton.

Nevis, one of the Lesser Antilles, belongs to Great Britain, and has an area of fifty square miles. Long ago, in its better days, it was the "Bath and Saratoga of the Caribbees." At one time the population numbered twenty thousand; now it is less than twelve thousand. Landing at the wharf, and taking the left-hand road, you pass St. Paul's church and school. The road at the right passes a tiny square, the post office, and a hotel. About a third of a mile farther on, you reach a fine sulphur bath and the ruins of a superb stone building, erected in 1803 at a cost of £40,000 and sold a few years ago for £40. Nevis was the birthplace of a man whose name is known to every school boy in the United States, — Alexander Hamilton, the great orator, good soldier, and talented lawyer.

St. Christopher or, as it is generally called, St. Kitts, and Nevis have an Executive and Legislative Council in common. Basse-Terre, the capital of St. Kitts, has a population of 7000.

Antigua belongs to the Leeward Group of the West Indies, and is owned by Great Britain. It is about forty miles from Nevis. It has an area of one hundred and eight square miles, and a population, including the small neighboring islands of Barbuda and Redonda, of thirty-seven thousand. St. John is the chief town. Ships come to anchor about two miles from the city, since the harbor is barred by a coral reef only fifteen feet under water. Spacious leper and insane hospitals are located north of this harbor; but, aside from leprosy, Antigua is regarded as one of the healthiest islands in the West Indies. The finest building is a large English cathedral, rebuilt in 1845 at a cost of £40,000. It stands on high ground back of the town. It is built with double walls, as a protection against earthquakes, and has two sightly towers.

The island is of coral formation, comparatively low and undulating. The primeval forests disappeared long ago, but this low land contains petrified forests consisting of nearly every sort of tree now growing on the Caribbee Islands. Beautiful specimens of cedar, mangrove, palm, and many others may be obtained in the valley of petrifaction not far from St. John. The climate is remarkably dry. Sugar and molasses are the chief exports.

Montserrat has an area of thirty-two square miles, and a population of twelve thousand. Plymouth is the capital. Much of its surface is mountainous and barren. The remainder is under excellent cultivation. Sugar and cotton are the chief products. Rum and molasses are also exported in considerable quantities.

This island was discovered by Columbus in 1493.

He named it Montserrat because of its fancied resemblance to a mountain of that name in Spain. The white population of the island is small and is constantly decreasing. The inhabitants are chiefly negro-Irish. They nearly all have Irish names and speak a dialect of Irish, English, and negro, in which the Irish predominates. The island belongs to Great Britain.

Guadeloupe has an area of five hundred and eighty-three thousand square miles, and a population of one hundred and sixty-seven thousand. It belongs to France, and is one of her principal island colonies. It is separated by an arm of the sea into two distinct islands. The western portion is the larger, and forms Guadeloupe proper, or Basse-Terre; it is of volcanic origin, and is traversed from north to south by a range of hills having a medium altitude of 2296 feet. The culminating points are an active volcano, La Souffrière, 5108 feet high, and three extinct volcanoes.

The smaller island, Grande-Terre, is flat, nowhere rising higher than 115 feet above the sea. Both islands are watered by a number of small streams, running in deeply cut channels, which become dry in summer. The atmosphere is remarkably humid, and the climate hot and unhealthy. Hurricanes are frequent and very destructive. The mountainous parts are covered with fine forests. Mangroves and manchineel trees grow on the marshy coasts. The chief articles of export are sugar, coffee, dye and cabinet woods, rum, cotton, wool, annotto, hides, copper, and tobacco.

Basse-Terre is the capital; Pointe-à-Pitre, with

seventeen thousand population, is the largest town, and has an excellent harbor.

Dominica, a British island of the Leeward Group, has an area of two hundred and ninety-one thousand square miles, and a population of twenty-eight thousand. The language spoken is a mixture of English and French.

On approaching Dominica from the sea, it presents a striking appearance. It is of volcanic origin, and the most rugged and elevated of the Lesser Antilles. The highest point reaches an altitude of 5314 feet. The island was named Dominica by Columbus because he discovered it on Sunday. It is said that when the Queen questioned him as to its general appearance, he, for an answer, crushed a piece of paper in his hand and threw it down upon the table. Nevertheless, the mountains are interspersed with beautiful and fertile valleys, through each of which flow one or more rivers.

In former times this island was inhabited by Caribs, a warlike race of Indians. A few of their descendants are still to be found here and in St. Vincent.

Roseau, the capital, has a beautiful location near the center of the western coast. The land slopes rapidly from the shore, and at but a short distance there are no soundings; vessels anchor close to the rocks, or alongside jetties built upon piles.

Palms and other tropical trees are to be seen everywhere, softening, by their glossy leaves and strange fruits, the roughness of the prevailing architecture. The market occupies a square in the south end of the town, and on Saturdays it is the center of attraction. Then it is always filled with country people from near and far away, each of whom carries a tray of breadfruit or a bunch of plantains. Near the market is an old fort which seems "an attractive, innocent, sunny sort of place to spend one's time in; but to the observer of this calm scene it is not easy to realize the desperate battles which have been fought for the possession of it, nor to picture the gallant lives that have been laid down under the walls of this crumbling castle. These cliffs had echoed the roar of Rodney's guns on the day which saved the British Empire, and the island on which we are gazing was England's Gettysburg."

CHAPTER XXIII.

CAPE VERD ISLANDS AND ST. HELENA.

The Cape Verd Islands lie three hundred and twenty miles west of Cape Verd, on the west coast of Africa. They are ten in number, and have an area of nearly seventeen hundred square miles. The population numbers one hundred and eleven thousand, and only one person out of every twenty is white.

The surface of the islands is mountainous, some of the peaks attaining a considerable height. The volcano of Fogo is over nine thousand feet high. The soil is of many kinds, and is for the most part fertile. There are but few trees and little water, which lack gives rise to frequent distress. The climate is very hot.

The chief vegetables raised are maize, rice, and French beans. Coffee, which was introduced in the latter part of the eighteenth century, has proved a great success. The cotton shrub is native, and indigo grows wild. There are many tropical fruits.

Cattle are extensively reared, and dried and salted provisions form a large part of the exports. Asses and mules are the only beasts of burden. Fowls are so abundant in most of the islands that they are sold for the merest trifle. Amber is found on all of the coasts, which are frequented by large numbers of turtles.

The natives are a quiet, docile race, but extremely indolent, and their houses are very filthy. They are nearly all engaged in agriculture and the preparation of salt. There are only a few schools in the archipelago, and the religion is Roman Catholic.

St. Helena lies in the South Atlantic Ocean, twelve hundred miles west of the west coast of South Africa and eighteen hundred miles from the east coast of Brazil. Being in the former direct line of the great ocean thoroughfare from Europe to the East, it became a most important halting station for vessels making that long voyage. It has an area of nearly forty-seven square miles.

When seen from a distance, it has the appearance of a lofty, pyramidal mass of dark gray color, rising abruptly from the water and presenting no sign of vegetation. On nearer approach, the precipitous and almost inaccessible coasts become still more striking, particularly on the north, where they rise almost perpendicularly to the height of from six hundred to

twelve hundred feet. A number of openings in these precipices form the mouths of narrow valleys leading gradually to a central plateau, and on the shore of each, where a landing might be effected, the British government has erected small forts or other military works for the purpose of making the island a secure prison.

Jamestown, the residence of its principal authorities, is situated in one of these ravines on the northwest coast. It has an excellent harbor of twelve fathoms of water and is defended by strong batteries. It contains the governor's residence, called "The Castle," three churches, six schools, and several very fine buildings, beside twenty-nine shops of fair size. There is a government garden above the castle, and a botanical garden above the infantry barracks.

The central plateau of the island is traversed by a limestone ridge, dividing it into two unequal portions and attaining, in Diana's Peak near the center, a height of twenty-seven hundred feet, the greatest elevation in St. Helena. The portion lying south of the ridge is the more rugged of the two, and consists of a succession of hills and peaks, several of which assume curious and fantastic shapes.

In this part is situated the craterlike district known as Sandy Bay. There is little doubt that this great amphitheater was once a volcanic crater. Crossing it from side to side in parallel lines are great dikes of harder material. The great peaks called the "Asses' Ears" look as if they had been built up of so many distinct prisms. Lot and Lot's Wife are both formed of strangely contorted columnar basalt. Along the coast, in this same part of the island, there stretches a wall of the same material, which rises to the height of from fifty to one hundred feet. The isolated portion of this forms what is known as the Chimney, a remarkable column sixty-four feet high.

All kinds of vegetables are raised here. Of fruits there are peaches, pears, plums, figs, limes, lemons, all kinds of apples, and many kinds of berries. The prickly pear, a large cactus, bears a luscious fruit about three inches long, which is considered a great delicacy, especially among the poorer classes. Fowl and fish are abundant, but fresh meat is hard to obtain.

NAPOLEON'S TOMB, ST. HELENA.

Closely linked with the name St. Helena is that of the great emperor, Napoleon Bonaparte. Banished from Europe, he was carried to this rock-girt island, where he spent the last five years of his eventful life in solitude. The house in which he lived and died has become famous and is visited yearly by many people. It is called Old House Longwood, and is a neat, plain, but not large, structure. A new house was in process of construction at the time of the emperor's death.

Many interesting places are pointed out on this island. Our attention is arrested by a signboard bearing these words, — "The road to Napoleon's Tomb." We take this path, and, after walking about three quarters of a mile, reach the gate in the hedge of privet which almost surrounds the tomb land. Passing this gate we notice a bed of rushes just below the road, and a little farther on is the house of the keeper.

In two minutes after leaving the house we are at the tomb. It is surrounded by a neat iron railing, fifteen Norfolk Island pines, eighteen cypress trees, and a young weeping willow, an offshoot of the older tree blown down several years ago. At the left is a little well, into which trickles the water of Napoleon's favorite spring. We inscribe our name in the visitor's book, and take our way once more toward the Old House Longwood.

After proceeding some distance we come to a cottage, just beyond which is Wood End Gate, so called on account of its being situated at the end of the "Great Wood" of native gum trees which existed here at the discovery of the island. Near this entrance are the police constable's quarters. Walking up the avenue, we pass the Magnetic Observatory, now used as a boarding house, and the New House Longwood, and are at the gate leading to Old House Longwood. This is opened for us, and we are politely conducted to the room where the bust of the great conqueror stands in the very place where he breathed his last.

Neat flower and vegetable gardens are seen in the inclosure, which is surrounded with privet. At the back of the house is the emperor's fish pond, and a few yards beyond is the signal station, from which every ship coming to St. Helena is descried, and telegrams are sent to all parts of the island.

CHAPTER XXIV.

THE AZORES.

The Azores, or Western Islands, are in the north Atlantic near latitude 38° and west longitude 28°. They belong to Portugal, by which they were colonized, and were named the Azores from *açor*, or *azor*, a hawk. They are nine in number, and are arranged in three groups. St. Michael, in the most southern group, is the largest of all the islands, being fifty miles long and five to twelve miles broad. Ponta Delgada is its chief town. Horta is the capital of the island of Fayal.

They are all of volcanic origin, and present a rugged though picturesque appearance, being lofty, precipitous, and generally of a conical form. The highest point is Mount Pico, seven thousand six hundred feet high, on an island of the same name in the central group. Angra, on an island not far from Pico, is the capital of the Azores, and has the only good harbor in the archipelago.

The combined area of all the islands is nearly one thousand square miles, and the population about two hundred and seventy thousand. The climate, though humid, is delightful, and, combined with the natural fertility of the soil, brings every variety of vegetable product to perfection. Coffee, sugar cane, tobacco, and corn are cultivated with the best success. Lupine, which grows to a great size, is one of the most valuable

ST. MICHAEL, AZORES.

productions. The seeds of this plant, soaked in sea water to rid them of their bitterness, form a favorite food of the lower classes. Wine, brandy, lemons, and oranges are exported in large quantities.

Between two and three hundred sailing vessels and forty steamers are busy in transporting oranges. The fruit is carefully picked from the trees by boys and placed in baskets, which women take on their heads and empty in the midst of large groups of boys and men. Small boys near by are kept busy smoothing out corn husks to be used as wrappers. The oranges are wrapped singly and passed to the packers, who place them carefully in the boxes. From ten to fifty fresh juicy oranges may be purchased for a single cent.

When the Azores were discovered, they were totally uninhabited and without animals of any kind except birds, which were numerous and of many varieties.

Modern improvements have no place here. Flax is much cultivated, but, in preparing it for the loom, a spindle and distaff are generally used instead of a spinning wheel. The wheels in use are of the crudest kind. Wheat is trodden out by oxen on a large threshing floor. Butter is made by shaking the milk in an earthen vessel or burying it in the ground in a leather bag. Plows are made of wood, the share only being shod with iron.

The common cart is an unwieldy, two-wheeled vehicle with high, woven, wicker sides, resembling the ancient Roman chariot. The wheels are made of solid wood bound with iron, and are firmly attached to a wooden axle, and the whole revolves together. The peasant dislikes to grease these axles, maintaining that the noise frightens witches away and makes the oxen work better. Thus, moving vans squeak along the highways, making a noise worse than that of howling dogs.

The houses are of every style of architecture and are built of lava blocks, the roofs being covered with tiles.

Nearly all are whitewashed on the outside. The stores are generally without windows, two or three large open doors supplying their places. Strange signs are often

PREPARING YARN FOR THE LOOM.

displayed. A strip of cloth tied to a stick indicates a dry-goods store; a bunch of onions, a grocery. Some of the streets have very curious names. We hear of a

252   THE WORLD AND ITS PEOPLE.

FAYALESE COSTUMES, AZORES.

"John the Baptist Street," and a "Virgin Mary Street," and a "Street of the Good God."

As regards dress, there is a great variety of costumes.

The rich people dress as do those of European countries, but among the poor many national peculiarities exist. Every woman has a capote, and wears it on the street. It is a blue cloth coat, made long enough to reach nearly to the ground. To the neck is attached a stiff hood of the same material, which, on account of its great size, makes the head appear all out of proportion to the body.

The corresponding curiosity in the men's apparel is a high-peaked hat of blue cloth lined with serge. The visor, which is crescent-shaped, projects six or eight inches over the forehead. From the back of the hat, a large cape falls over the shoulders and fastens under the chin.

The better class of people are intelligent and refined; a system of free schools is carried on by the government. The condition of the lower classes is wretched in the extreme. Poor and ignorant, oppressed by church and state, many of them annually seek to escape to the United States and Brazil. But passports are not granted to those desiring emigration, unless they give bonds to the amount of three hundred dollars to return and serve in the army when conscripted, and this the most of them are unable to do. As a result many of them try to escape clandestinely, and "stealing Portuguese," as assisting these people to escape is called, was at one time a large and paying business.

Horses and carriages are very scarce, and all traveling is done on the backs of donkeys. The saddle used consists of a thick pad of matting or straw; over this a wooden frame, somewhat resembling a sawhorse, is strapped, and over all is a soft pillow or a strip of carpeting. There are no stirrups, and the bridle is but a piece of rope, at one end tied round the donkey's neck, and at the other to one of the saddle horns. The donkey is driven by a boy or man who runs along behind. When he wants the donkey to go faster he uses a goad or his voice; and a long drawn out "Ye-e-e," accompanied by a vigorous pull at the tail, is a signal for the poor beast to stop.

RETURNING FROM MARKET.

The Azores are overrun with beggars. On Saturday, "Beggar's Day," they literally swarm in the streets and importune you on every corner. They have little modesty, and make a great display of their deformities and ailments in order to excite more sympathy. Able-bodied vagabonds are arrested, and either transported or employed on public works.

CHAPTER XXV.

THE CANARY AND MADEIRA ISLANDS.

About sixty miles from the west coast of Northern Africa is a group of seven islands and several islets, known as the Canary Islands. They have an area of about three thousand square miles. The capital is Santa Cruz, situated on the northeast coast of Teneriffe, the largest island of the group.

The coasts of these islands are rocky and abrupt. Their formation is as singular as it is interesting, consisting of a continuous series of volcanic mountains, which rise from the coast in a circular form around a principal crater. The greater part of them are deeply indented, and in the form of a cone reversed. The surface of the ground is volcanic, presenting a succession of mountains and plains, extinct craters and fertile valleys. There are no rivers, but numerous torrents.

The tropical heat is moderated by the Atlantic breezes. Winter is almost unknown along the coasts. In October, the hottest month, the thermometer ranges from seventy-eight to eighty-seven degrees; and in January, the coldest, from sixty to sixty-six near the sea. The islands lie between twenty-seven and twenty-nine degrees north latitude.

They abound in caves, which, being cool in summer and sheltered in winter, were used by the aborigines as the palaces of their kings and the abodes of their rich and noble. The interior of some of them presents large square chambers, with stone benches running round them and niches cut in the walls, the latter having been intended to receive jars of milk and water.

 The aborigines were in the habit of embalming their dead, and caves and grottoes were also used as receptacles for the mummies. One famous grotto was found on the south side of Teneriffe. It was entered through a very small aperture, and the interior presented a large space, or hall, with several compartments, in which over a thousand mummies had been deposited. Very recently good specimens have been discovered in a perfect state of preservation in the island of Grand Canary. The hair was red-brown, and the teeth were of a beautiful whiteness. At the beginning of this century a cavern was discovered, whose catacombs are said to have furnished nearly all the cabinets of Europe with specimens. Caves are still used by the people as dwelling places.

 The rainy season is from November to February, and the dry from April to October. Water is very scarce. The camel is much used as a beast of burden in the Canaries. The chief productions are the cochineal insect, oil, grain, potatoes, sugar cane, and fruits of all kinds. The population numbers nearly three hundred thousand people, and, though many European nations are represented, the great majority are Spaniards, and the islands are under Spanish rule.

 We will suppose ourselves on a tour of inspection. Before we visit the one point of general interest, the Peak of Teneriffe, let us stop at this farm house, a good example of its class. It stands on the side of a ravine, and is built in rambling fashion. The owner lives in a distant town, and his farm is run by a fine, stalwart man, who dresses in the ancient costume of the country. After our camel has been relieved of its burden, and alms have been distributed among the beggars who have gathered round, we are shown into a large kitchen where supper is waiting.

Two tables are spread, one long and narrow, the other small. Our host takes his seat at the head of the former, and the farm laborers, to the number of twenty, range themselves along the sides, prepared to do ample justice to the meal, which, though coarse in quality, is abundant in quantity. We take our seat at the small table with the hostess.

An immense dish stands in the center of our table, and three others like it stand at intervals on the other. They are all filled with some kind of pottage. Each person is supplied with a wooden spoon, and, in company with five or six others, dips his spoon into the dish nearest him. This mode of partaking of food is certainly not the most agreeable, but it is best to accommodate one's self to the custom of the country, and thus avoid giving offense.

After the meal is finished, all stand up and join with the host in a thanksgiving. Then the servants leave the apartment, going out in an orderly manner, each one asking a blessing of the hostess and kissing her hand as he passes.

The kitchen is now lit up with pine torches stuck in the crevices of the walls. Dogs retire to the corners to gnaw the bones which have been given them, and various other little animals, tamed by the kindness of the family, come in to pick up whatever happens to fall in their way. Our hostess is not idle. As soon as the supper is over her distaff is in her hands, and she engages busily in spinning the flaxen thread.

The peasantry in many parts of the islands are extremely ignorant, the instances in which they are able to read and write being very rare. Neither are they musically inclined. A tambourine, rude pipes made of cane, and guitars are generally the only instruments used on festive occasions.

There are, however, many amusements peculiar to the islands. One of these consists of the marching of an illuminated procession by night through the principal streets of the town. All who take part in it are uniformly dressed in white trowsers and shirts. The greater number carry white paper lanterns with lighted candles on their heads, and, attaching themselves at equal distances to ropes, form two lines, which, marching down the street one on each side, preserve the center free from spectators. This center space is occupied by those who carry immense figures made of white paper over a framework of cane, representing grim giants as high as the housetops. Besides these, there are large figures of various other kinds of objects,—sun, moon, camels, donkeys, ducks, and geese, all marching at a wonderfully quick pace. A hole in the back of each figure admits of the entrance of the bearers.

But we must take our way toward the Peak of Teneriffe, or, more properly, Pico de Leyde, situated on the island of Teneriffe. Its height is 12,182 feet. On its summit is a crater half a league across, and sloping by an easy descent to the depth of one hundred and sixty feet. This enormous peak is seen piercing the clouds, and surrounded by a girdle, which gives it the appearance of a fortified city. Towns and villages, with their fields, gardens, and vineyards, stretch along its base and for some distance up its sides. These are succeeded by a woody region, composed chiefly of chestnuts and oaks, with an undergrowth of heaths and ferns. Still higher is a wide barren plain covered with pumice and blocks of lava, and inhabited only by a few rabbits and wild goats.

In ascending the mountain, the last five hundred feet have to be accomplished on foot, and the treacherous looseness of the soil makes the ascent extremely difficult. As we press forward, we notice several jets of steam and vapor issuing from among the stones and sand, and are told by our guide that these are "the Peak's nostrils." We also detect a slight smell of sulphur. After a few halts, we attain the summit. From this point we can see Grand Canary almost due south of us. Farther to the east is another of the group, looking like a dark streak on the ocean. As to the island of Teneriffe itself, we can see over its whole surface, and trace its boundaries by the fringe of white sea foam all around it.

This mountain has been seen from a ship's deck one hundred and fifteen miles distant, and Humboldt says it is visible from a cape one hundred and fifty-three miles away. But supposing we take the medium of one hundred and thirty-five miles as the distance at which the horizon can be made out from the summit of the Peak, then we can take in the astonishing circle of

A CARRINHO, MADEIRA.

nearly eight hundred miles of ocean,—an extent not equaled by the view from any other mountain on the face of the earth.

Madeira is the largest island of the Madeira group, which consists of two islands and three islets. Madeira lies in the Atlantic Ocean, about four hundred and forty miles off the west coast of Morocco, near the thirty-second degree of north latitude. It is thirty-five miles long and twelve broad. It consists of a mass of volcanic rocks, whose highest peak reaches an altitude of six thousand feet. Through the west half of the island runs a central ridge, about five thousand feet high, on which is an extensive plain called Paul de Serra. From the central mass, steep ridges extend to the coast, where they form perpendicular precipices from one thousand to two thousand feet high.

The road leading round the island is, in many places, exceedingly picturesque, passing between gigantic cliffs or along the front of precipices facing the sea. The mountain slopes of Madeira are clothed with unusually luxuriant verdure. Terraces are visible on all sides, and every available spot is turned to advantage.

Funchal Bay, on which Funchal, the capital, is situated, has been compared to the Bay of Naples, although smaller in size. There is the same crescent shape, and the same azure sea. The Loo Rock with its fort is much like the rock on which the Castel del Ovo is built, and there lies the hilly town with its background of mountain peaks.

But a closer inspection of the town is not as pleasing as the view from a distance. The streets are crooked, narrow, and poorly paved, and few of them have any sidewalks. The houses are, generally, mean and unpretentious, and irregular in construction, with stucco fronts, painted white, red, blue, orange, or green. It must be acknowledged, however, that these bright colors are quite in keeping with the sunny landscape.

There are few shops worthy of the name, the larger number being nothing but "poky little dens," with little or no window space. They are generally crowded to overflowing with a curious assortment of wares. Many of them, especially those belonging to cabinet-makers, shoemakers, and those of similar craft, have no front wall, and, consequently, as one passes along the street, there is nothing to obstruct a view of the interior, where artificers sit and chatter over their work as they busily ply the awl or chisel.

There are three good markets in Funchal, one for fish, another for meat, and a third for fruit. These markets are always crowded with animated buyers and sellers, forming a picturesque scene, and that is the great charm of the place.

The public garden is one of the prettiest places in Funchal. It is not large, but it contains a wealth of tropical vegetation which has been brought to absolute perfection. Just beyond, we come to an iron bridge which spans one of the three rivers that flow through the town. On crossing the bridge we enter upon the Rua Bella Vista, where the garden walls on each side of the street are covered with a countless variety of beautiful flowers. Some distance up on the left is the

AUSTRALIA AND THE ISLANDS OF THE SEA. 263

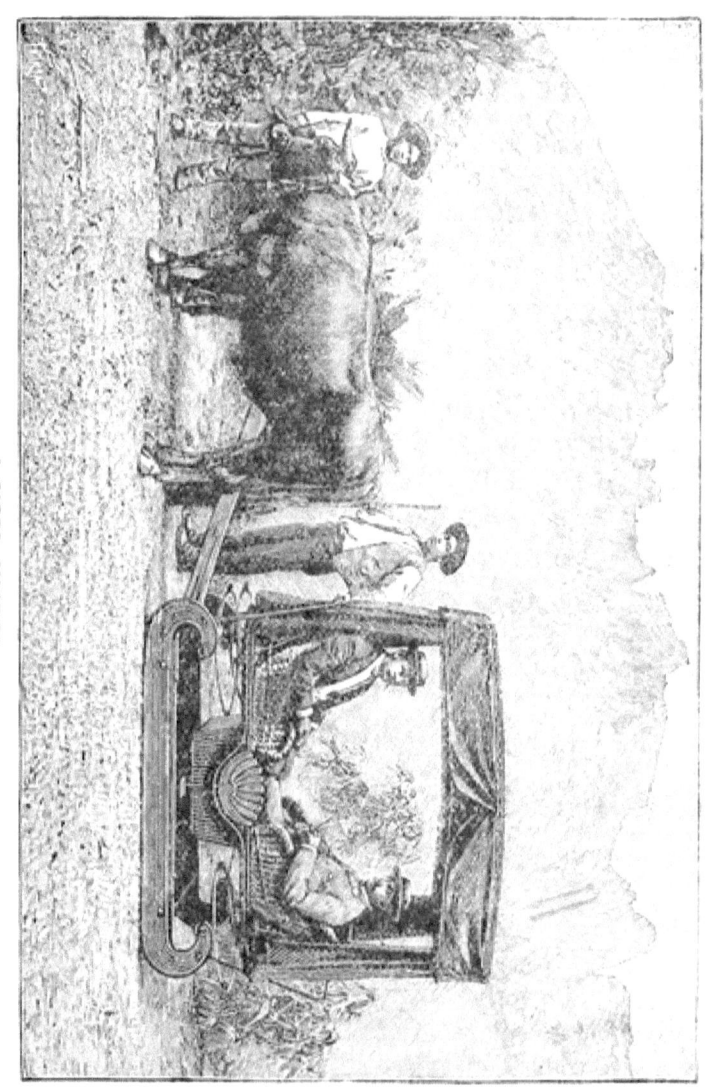

A CARRO, MADEIRA.

Portuguese Cemetery, a true "God's Acre." "Palms and tree ferns rear their feathery fronds above the tombs; trees of many kinds find a home, and are things of beauty in it; whilst all the place is full of the scents of myriads of flowers that are growing in such rich profusion everywhere, and the songs of birds that are fluttering about; and on every side are the signs of a loving care for the last resting places of the honored dead."

In traveling in Madeira, recourse must be had to the carro, the hammock, or the horse. The carro is the Funchal cab. It is an iron-shod sledge with awnings and curtains, and is drawn by a team of oxen. It seats four persons. A boy walks at the head of the oxen to direct them in the way, and this he accomplishes by tugging at a piece of stout cord fastened to their horns. The driver proper walks alongside armed with a goad, with which he prods the poor beasts whenever he wishes to accelerate their pace. Each prod is accompanied with a yell. The speed with which this peculiar vehicle moves is really astonishing, amounting to fully one and a half miles per hour. The sledge, or carro, is used in place of wheeled vehicles, as the latter would be utterly useless on account of the steepness of the roads. The only two-wheeled vehicles kept in the town are regarded as great curiosities, and are displayed only on notable occasions.

The *carrinho* is a modification of the carro, and is used for descending the steep mountain roads. No power of propulsion is needed for this vehicle, but, on the contrary, force is required to check its downward career. So ropes are attached to the four corners, and a stalwart Madeiran grasps hold of each rope, prepared to hold back instead of to pull. In this conveyance one or two travelers can safely and comfortably descend the steepest slopes. It is a sort of controlled toboggan.

The hammock, or rêde, is a combination of stout cord and canvas, covered with gayly colored cloths and fitted with a kind of hood to protect the traveler from the rays of the sun. It accommodates one person. A loop at the head of the hammock, and one at the foot, admits of its being suspended from a pole which is carried on the shoulders of bearers. These men are strong, wiry fellows, capable of traveling twenty or thirty miles a day over the worst sort of roads and under the intense heat of a tropical sun. A ride in a hammock must be indulged in to be properly appreciated. It is one of the most delightful ways of traveling.

The huts of the peasantry contain only one poor room, usually with no window, and no flooring except the bare ground. Oxen tread out the corn on the threshing floors just as they did in olden times. The implements of agriculture are few and rude. Parents and children are alike dirty, and the latter are innocent of all clothing except such articles as are absolutely necessary. In one thing alone they excel, and that is politeness. They run to the roadside to look at a stranger, but they invariably remove their hats and salute him as he passes. Should he speak to one of them, the villager remains with his head uncovered as long as the conversation lasts. If a villager desires to speak with a stranger, he remains hat in hand, and calmly awaits the request to make his business known.

The products of Madeira are those of both the tropic and temperate climes. In the lower portions of the island, groves of orange and lemon are mingled with the vineyards; higher up bananas, figs, pomegranates, and similar fruits thrive and grow. And still higher, apples, peaches, pears, currants, and other fruits of the temperate zone are found; some wheat, rye, barley, and Indian corn are raised, but not sufficient for home consumption. Coffee and arrowroot of excellent quality are also grown. The richest vine district, and the part where the famous Malmsey grape grows, is the valley of the Cama de Lobos on the south side of the island. In good years the quantity of wine produced is twenty-five thousand pipes. In recent years it has been reduced to fifteen thousand pipes, and, in 1852, a disease having destroyed the vines, the quantity was reduced to four hundred pipes. The island belongs to Portugal.

CHAPTER XXVI.

THE CHANNEL ISLANDS.

THE Channel Islands is the name employed to designate a group of islands in the English Channel, off the northwest coast of France. The principal ones are Jersey, Guernsey, Alderney, and Sark. They are officially comprised in the English county of Hants and the diocese of Winchester, and are the only portions of old Normandy now belonging to the English Crown, to which they have remained attached ever since the Conquest. They have cost the government a great deal, having been fortified at an immense expense. The population numbers about eighty-eight thousand. The language spoken is very peculiar; its basis being unquestionably the Norman-French, or Anglo-Norman. There are three well-marked dialects,—those of Jersey, Guernsey, and Sark.

The climate of the islands is peculiar, differing in many points from the climates of England and France. The days in summer are seldom hot, and the nights are pleasantly cool. The autumn is remarkably equable, night frosts being seldom felt before December.

Among vegetable productions, the ilex, or evergreen oak, is eminently characteristic, constantly retaining its bright green foliage. The elm is also common, and the beech grows well. The farmers, as a rule, do not approve of trees, as they think they harbor birds. Among shrubs the furze and bramble are the most prominent.

Both Jersey and Guernsey are rich in wild flowers. The great sea stock, the foxglove, several orchids, and numberless others brighten the landscape. Of flowerless kinds, the ferns are most interesting. Mosses are abundant, especially in Guernsey. In all the islands lichens grow freely on the rocks. The Guernsey lily, introduced from Japan, grows and flowers freely. The geranium remains green all winter. The magnolia grows to be a large tree. Myrtle, trained against the houses, is limited in height only by the house to which it clings. The fuchsia attains immense size, and is very common.

There are few native quadrupeds and reptiles. Wild geese, ducks, plovers, gulls, petrels, swans, cormorants, and bitterns abound. The variety of fish is great. The rockfish, the gar, the gigantic conger, and others never fail. Turbot, brill, dory, cod, mackerel, and mullet are almost constantly on the market. The swordfish, sunfish, angelfish, and even the sea horse, lamprey, and blue shark occasionally find their way into the bays. Shellfish are common, and in caves, bordering on the coast, are found the sea anemones and a multitude of species of zoöphytes.

Jersey is oblong in form and very compact, having a length of twelve miles and a breadth of five. It lies about sixteen miles west of Normandy and about forty-five miles south of Alderney. The north coast is characterized by bold and picturesque scenery, the others by large open bays terminated by rocky headlands. The interior is covered with trees, intersected by a network of roads running in every direction. The population of the island, according to the latest census (1891), was fifty-four thousand five hundred.

Jersey is celebrated for its breed of cows. They give, on an average, from four to five gallons of milk each day. Pears, grapes, and potatoes are exported in large quantities. Vegetables of all kinds grow to perfection. The cow cabbage is one of the curiosities of the island. It is raised for the sake of the leaves, which are used to carry butter to market. The stem grows to be eight or ten feet long and is used as a walking stick.

St. Heliers is the capital and chief town of Jersey. It has both an outer and an inner harbor, and a large floating dock of seventeen acres. The impression made on entering the town from the pier is not good, as several poor, narrow streets have to be traversed in order to reach the Royal Square. Here are situated the courthouse, the public library, and two of the principal hotels. Clean and well-paved streets lead from the square in all directions.

The churches of St. Heliers are numerous, the chief one being the parish church near the Royal Square. It is built in the early pointed Gothic style, and dates from the year 1341.

Victoria College, first opened for instruction in 1852, is a noble structure surrounded with terraces and public walks, and commands a fine view.

Fort Regent, a modern fortress begun in 1706, but completed only lately, stands on a lofty ridge of granite to the east of the harbor. Elizabeth Castle, an old and useless fortress, built on the rocks to the west, was constructed in Queen Elizabeth's time, and covered the ruins of an old abbey founded in the twelfth century. Close by, though on a detached rock, is a ruin called the Hermitage, of ancient date.

Prince's Tower is one of many points of interest in St. Heliers. The tower is neither ancient nor remarkable, but it is built on a tumulus, probably of great antiquity, and commands a fine view of the sea and part of the island.

Guernsey is second in size of the Channel Islands, and has an area of twenty-four square miles, two thirds of which are under cultivation. Its population, including that of the islands of Herm and Jethon, numbers thirty-five thousand. The coast line is deeply indented with bays and surrounded with sunken rocks. The surface slopes from the south, where the cliffs are lofty, to the north coast, which is low. The soil is not naturally rich, but with the aid of seaweed manure is rendered very fertile. The climate is moist, but healthy. The orchards furnish pasturage for a famous breed of cows, which compare favorably with the Jerseys. They are larger, of coarser structure, and greatly inferior in beauty of appearance; but they are rich and large milkers, and the color of the butter they produce is far deeper and richer than that of the rival race.

The process of making butter in Guernsey differs from the methods adopted elsewhere. The milk is poured into tall jars, set in a cool place, and left untouched until churning day. As the churning is done only once or twice a week, the cream on the older milkings is likely to be much wrinkled, and even moldy. The churns are immense in size, often holding sixty or seventy gallons. Cream, milk, and mold are all poured into the churn, and the churning never takes less than two and one half hours. The farmers claim that only by this method can they extract all the butter from the milk.

The town of St. Peter Port, the capital, is built on a steep slope, and boasts a superb harbor, being shut in from the sea by moles of massive granite. Its houses are comfortable, its streets are clean, and its markets commodious. The ancient town church has been restored without being spoiled, and is the finest church building in the Channel Islands.

The thatch-covered cottages in the interior of Guernsey are often picturesque, many of them having the characteristic round-arched doorway, which is as solid and substantial to-day as when it was built, centuries ago. This arch, so common here, is not often seen in Jersey.

Near the shore, north of the harbor of St. Sampson's, is Vale Castle, the restored ruins of which are now used as a barrack. In the same parish is the Vale Church, marked by its curious porch, while to the north of this, about one mile, is the most important Druid altar, or cromlech, of Guernsey. Of other important Druidical remains, the most curious is a tall monolith near Rocquaine Bay.

In the neighborhood of this church and harbor are the great granite quarries of Guernsey. Nearly one hundred and fifty thousand tons of kerbstone are exported, chiefly to London.

Alderney is about three miles long, and has a circumference of eight miles. Its population numbers two thousand. The coast is indented with small bays, only one of which affords even fairly good anchorage. Alderney was once rich in Celtic remains; but out of many, which modern barbarism has destroyed, one dilapidated cromlech alone remains. There is but one town in the island, St. Anne, situated on an elevated spot near the center.

And yet Alderney is an important place; for its possession, as a high authority affirms, "determines whether England or France shall command the British Channel." The original estimate of its fortifications was £600,000, but it has since been declared that the actual cost is more than twice that amount.

Though possessing such a warlike aspect, Alderney has long been associated with pastoral scenes. The Alderney cow has a world-wide reputation, and differs from the cattle in the sister islands chiefly in being much smaller.

Sark lies seven miles east of Guernsey and ten northwest of Jersey. It has an area of fourteen hundred acres, and consists of two high peninsulas, connected by a narrow isthmus. These are called Great and Little Sark, and the isthmus is one of the wonders of the island. The sea on the east and west sides has eaten into the land, leaving only a mere wall of earth and rock between the two parts of the island. This wall, which is broader at the base, narrows toward the top, which is just broad enough to admit a country cart. There is no protecting balustrade, and on each side there is a precipitous descent of rock for more than a hundred feet to the roaring sea below. This is about four hundred and fifty feet long. No small amount of nerve is required in crossing, especially if the wind is very strong.

One of the grand natural curiosities of Sark is "Le

Creux Terrible," situated in a field on the east side close to the shore. It is a huge natural chimney, circular in form, with sides formed of vertical, naked rock, and fully one hundred and fifty feet deep. At the bottom, two tunnels connect it with the shore, and through these the sea rushes when the tide flows. The spray is tossed almost to the surface, when the wind is high, and the seething water, boiling and roaring in the black crater, is a frightful sight.

Herm lies about two and one half miles east of Guernsey, or about halfway between it and Sark. The chief attraction to the tourist is Shell Beach, which extends for nearly three quarters of a mile along the shore, and is one mass of shells unmixed with sand or stones. Herm, too, has nearly forty varieties of sponges. It abounds in corals, and has some rare specimens of diminutive lobsters and other shellfish. There is a small harbor on the western shore, but dangerous currents flow along the coast. The population is very small. Quarries once in operation were long since abandoned.

CHAPTER XXVII.

THE ISLES OF WIGHT AND MAN, AND HELIGOLAND.

The Isle of Wight lies in the English Channel and is separated from England by straits named Solent and Spithead. Its length from east to west is twenty-two and a half miles, and its breadth at the center is thirteen and a half. It has an area of one hundred and forty-six square miles, and a population of seventy-nine thousand. It forms a part of Hampshire County, and is one of the most beautiful portions of the kingdom, presenting an endless variety of landscape in miniature. It rises in elevation toward the center, where a range of chalk hills traverses it from east to west. The highest point, St. Catherine's Hill, is eight hundred and thirty feet above the sea. The south, especially the southeast coast, termed the "Back of the Island," is characterized by precipitous cliffs, ravines, or "chines," and scenery of the most romantic kind. The Medina River partly separates the island into two nearly equal parts. More agricultural products are raised than can be consumed in the island, and this surplus, together with malt, wool, salt, and fine sand for the manufacture of glass, form the chief exports. In the western part are some wide downs, and about forty thousand fine-fleeced sheep are raised in the uplands.

"Chine" is the name given to any part of a cliff which is so broken as to admit of ascent. In some places these "chines" are very beautiful, their sides being covered with heather, fern, and numerous sorts of flowers, while a stream of clear water often runs along the bottom. But Black Gang Chine is more strange than beautiful, and forms a natural channel for the gradual ooze and subsidence of black clay and other substances diluted and set in motion by land springs and streamlets. From its eastern verge is seen the whole of the "Back of the Island" as far as Needle

Rocks, a coast line of twenty miles without a single break by any considerable river in the long forbidding line of cliffs. No settlement larger than a fishing hamlet breaks this desolate coast. And from this point the wide, flat, cultivated plain extends back for some miles to Newport.

Newport, near the center of the island, on the Medina River, is its capital. An old stone bridge crosses the river at this point. Newport has an ancient guildhall and market house, two assembly rooms, a neat theater, an excellent public library, two or three banks, and several other institutions. There is also an ancient church here in which Elizabeth, daughter of Charles I., was buried. She died a prisoner in Carisbrook Castle after her father's execution.

The site of this castle marks it as the natural citadel of the island. In remote times it was simply a Celtic earthwork. Later, William Fitz-Osborne, to whom the whole island was granted by the Conqueror, built its center and the castle keep, at the corner of the center rampart. Shortly afterward a high wall was run round the rest of the Celtic rampart, and, in 1086, the area of the castle grounds was twenty-six acres. No farther change was made until the time of Empress Matilda, when the famous well of Carisbrook was added. Then Anthony Woodville, brother of the Queen of Edward IV., built the great entrance gate. It is even now almost perfect, and is a complete example of purely military architecture as it was then understood. Its proportions are so ornamental and picturesque that its adaptation to its purpose is often lost sight of. Henry

VIII. made the first modification for the use of cannon, and Queen Elizabeth surrounded the whole by a complete parallelogram of bastioned defenses, still in perfect preservation.

Yarmouth and Cowes are two other of the principal towns of the Isle of Wight. Near the latter is Osborne House, a favorite resort of Queen Victoria. Yarmouth is a picturesque little place at the mouth of the Yar estuary. It has a miniature quay, a fortress, a palace, and a church. From the west the river is crossed by long narrow bridges and causeways leading to the castle and the quay. The poet Tennyson passed much time in the later years of his life at his pleasant country seat in Farringford, Isle of Wight.

The Isle of Man is in the Irish Sea, about thirty miles west of England, thirty-two east of Ireland, and less than twenty south of Scotland. Its extreme length is thirty miles and its greatest breadth is thirteen. It has an area of two hundred and twenty-seven square miles. A mountain chain extends throughout the length of the island. The highest point in the range is Snowfield (Snaefell), about two thousand feet above the sea level. Lead, zinc, iron, and copper are found in the mountains. The island has a good supply of water. Agricultural methods, usually quite backward, are constantly improving.

The legislative and judicial authority is vested principally in the House of Keys, a self-elected body of twenty-four members. The Crown appoints the Governor. The island was settled originally by a tribe of

Celts, called the Manx. Later it was held as a feudal sovereignty by the Earls of Derby, and more recently by the Dukes of Athole, from whom the rights were mostly purchased by Great Britain in 1765, the last right falling to the Crown as late as 1829. Although

TENNYSON'S HOUSE, ISLE OF WIGHT.

all the inhabitants speak English, the Manx language, derived from the ancient Celtic, is still in common use. The principal towns are Douglas, the capital, Peel, Castletown, and Ramsay. The population numbers nearly fifty-six thousand.

The climate of the island is extremely salubrious, with no extremes of heat and cold. Shrubs, which in some parts of England require great care and even artificial heat, in many sheltered parts of the island grow throughout the winter in the open air. Whole hedges of fuchsias of large size may be seen growing in magnificent perfection.

Before leaving the island, we will take a glimpse of a purely Manx village, situated upon the crest of one of the Mull Hills. It consists of about a dozen houses, and was noted, until the last few years, for its persistent retention of the old ideas and manners of the country. The community, small as it is, rarely married outside of its own limits. They kept up the old habits and dress of their fathers. Manx was the only language spoken among them. None of them had ever been outside of the island, except during their fishing voyages, and many of them had never been outside the limits of their own parish. Deeply impressed with religious feelings, and remarkably moral in their conduct, their prejudices were strong, their ideas were narrow, their ignorance of everything beyond the sphere of their daily lives was profound, and their belief in fairies and other spiritual beings was without limit.

Their houses were low, roughly built huts thatched with straw, while bundles of gorse, placed in the doorways, served instead of doors. Of course this is all rapidly passing away. The Manx dialect is fast being superseded by the English language. Owing to the advent of the "iron horse" and the regular arrival of mail steamers, their exclusiveness is fast passing away. The old national dress — the undyed wool jacket and the Sunday blanket — has almost disappeared. But their narrow ideas and their old-world superstitions are almost as strong and as operative as ever.

Heligoland is an island in the North Sea, belonging to Germany, about forty-six miles northwest of the mouth of the Elbe. It has an area of five and a fourth square miles, and a population of about two thousand. It consists of a rock rising to the height of two hundred feet, on which are a village and a lighthouse. A portion of the village is at the base of the cliffs, and the upper and lower settlements are connected by a flight of two hundred steps as well as by a passenger elevator. On account of the encroachments of the sea, the island is gradually decreasing in size. The inhabitants, of Friesian descent, are mostly occupied as pilots, or are engaged in lobster or haddock fisheries, which yield an annual revenue of £5000. Heligoland was held in high veneration in the Middle Ages. It is of some importance as a port in wartime, and was retained by England until 1890, when it was ceded to Germany, forming a part of the province of Schleswig-Holstein. Of late it has been much frequented as a watering place.

Heligoland, in common with all other places, has its Sunday character. Steamers arrive as usual, the theater is open, and all occupations are continued the same as on other days. But, nevertheless, the day has its peculiarities. Like the Jewish Sabbath, it begins at sundown. On Saturday evening there is no dancing on the island. On Sunday morning the band does not play, and the little church is filled with devout worshipers.

It is a curious little building of the seventeenth century; but its ruined tower has recently been rebuilt by the generosity of a native who had made a large fortune. A gallery runs round three sides, and on its front is a series of odd, and sometimes grotesque, illustrations of Scripture stories. The artist who painted these pictures was never famous, and their chief charm is his determination to make his meaning clear to the most casual observer. Everyone has heard of Satan's cloven hoofs, or of his lame foot. Our Heligolander has gone a little further, and has boldly represented him in the temptation of Christ, with a regular wooden leg having a round knob at the end.

The pews are painted all manner of bright colors, and are a part of a man's property, which he can bequeath at death to whom he will. At each side of the communion table is a private box with blue glass, the seats of the governor and magistrate. Behind the altar is a curious collection of ecclesiastical *bric-à-brac*, old hour glasses, old pictures, and a hundred odds and ends. The service as a rule is conducted in German, but once a week the minister preaches a sermon in English.

Heligoland claims to have a national dress. The men wear a white linen jumper, thick blue trowsers, and high boots, with smackman's hat for headgear. The women don a pretty little black silk cap, a striped green and red petticoat, with short dark skirt and white apron. But the real national costume is not worn in Heligoland every day. Men and women alike wear good warm clothing. The inhabitants are a happy, contented people, and their longevity is remarkable.

CHAPTER XXVIII.

THE BALEARIC ISLES.

This group consists of five principal islands and some smaller ones, in the Mediterranean Sea, the three most important being Majorca, Minorca, and Iviza. The united area is about two thousand square miles. They form a province under the control of Spain, and lie midway between her coast and that of Algeria.

Majorca is nearly square in form, the greatest distance from east to west being sixty miles and from north to south fifty. Its area is thirteen hundred square miles. The highest mountains of the group are those of Majorca, the loftiest peak attaining a height of forty-eight hundred feet. The climate is mild and agreeable, and the extremes of heat and cold are seldom of long duration. Fires are rarely required, except in the coldest weather.

The soil of these islands on the average is exceedingly fertile, and produces good crops of wheat, barley, olives, almonds, grapes, figs, oranges, beans, and hemp. Besides these, a great variety of other fruits and vegetables are grown for local consumption.

Pigs and sheep are largely raised in these islands, and form a great source of wealth; but goats and cattle are scarce, especially in Majorca, where cow's milk and butter are great luxuries. In the smaller islands pastures are provided, and the keeping of cows is fast becoming one of the chief sources of wealth.

The principal city, and the capital of the province,

is Palma, a fortified town on the southwest coast of Majorca. It is built in the form of an amphitheater, and is surrounded by a wall thirty-six feet thick, with

A MAN OF THE BALEARIC ISLANDS.

thirteen bastions and eight gates, three of which front the sea. The streets are straight, but narrow. Most of them are paved, and provided with footways laid with tiles. As you approach the city it appears to be a great mass of yellow and white buildings, with flat roofs or slanting tiled ones. On the flat roofs great cages for pigeons may be seen. The people are very fond of these birds and tend them with great care. In the morning the birds are allowed their freedom, but they all know their homes and return at night to their respective cages.

The most imposing object seen on approaching the harbor is the great cathedral, which stands close to the sea. It is lofty and of vast size; it is built of brick, with flying buttresses, manifold small pinnacles, and side buttresses so large and substantial that they have already outlived centuries. There is one solitary tower over the north doorway, which has narrow pointed windows and an open balustrade. The cathedral was commenced in the thirteenth century, and was finished at the end of the sixteenth. It is of a splendid amber color of an exquisite shade, which can only be produced by the lapse of time.

The interior is of the Gothic style of architecture, and on entering it you are awed not so much by its beauty as by its immensity. This impression is heightened by the fact that the whole interior is seen at once. The pillars which form the central nave are octagonal and very slender. They are architectural wonders, for in no other place are to be seen pillars of so great height resting on bases so small. Though the effect cannot be said to be pleasing, it is certainly wonderful. Other points of peculiar interest in this cathedral are the carved wooden reredos, dating from Mediæval times, and the tombs of Mallorcan bishops and kings.

Next to the cathedral, the Longa is the most remarkable building in Palma. It is a large, square, Gothic structure, dating from the first half of the fifteenth century. At each corner is an octagonal tower with indented battlements. From tower to tower runs an openwork, indented gallery of great beauty. The entrance is a Gothic doorway of remarkable size. The interior is a single square chamber. The arched roof is supported by fluted pillars, slender and graceful. From these start the moldings which gradually form the arches. This building was intended for an exchange and was used as such for many ages. Later it was employed for public meetings and as a ballroom. Recently it passed through the hands of restorers and workmen, by whom it was thoroughly repaired.

Nearly all traces of Moorish rule and reign have disappeared from Palma. An old palace with its beautiful courtyard is still to be seen, and also an old Moorish fountain. This fountain stands facing a street, and from it runs a thoroughfare on either side. A building of conical shape incloses the water, which is unseen. On each side of the fountain stands an orange tree, enlivening the structure with its glossy verdure and golden fruit.

Of the interior towns and villages of this island, there are few as interesting as Valdemosa. Long before the Spanish conquered the island this place was held in high estimation by the Moors. Later a king chose these hills for his summer residence, and built a palace here, which was converted into a convent in the last part of the fourteenth century. Little remains of this convent at present, its very chapel having been converted into a ballroom. The village is one of the poorest of its size in the island. While the convent flourished, provisions were to be had for the asking at

A WOMAN OF THE BALEARIC ISLANDS.

the convent gate. But this promiscuous charity had an evil effect on the men of the village. Many of them found a special protector in one or another of the rich monks, and preferred the convent's gifts to the scanty wages of mountain labor. But the wives and daughters were never allowed inside the cloister gates, and all the work fell upon them. This is largely the case still, and round-shouldered, high-backed women are to be seen everywhere, toiling down the rugged mountain paths with enormous loads of fagots on their shoulders.

Besides carrying wood, the women work with the hoe, and gather the olives and almonds. They are also employed in the orchards and gardens, for in no part of the islands is fruit grown in such variety and abundance as here. The men now busy themselves as charcoal burners or fishermen, or are employed on the adjoining farms and estates.

Minorca is situated about twenty-seven miles northeast of Majorca and has an area of about two hundred and ninety square miles. The coast is much indented with bays on all sides except the south, and the shore in most places is bold and steep. It has several excellent harbors, the best one of which is Port Mahon, the capital of the island. The climate of Minorca is mild, but not so equable as that of Majorca. The soil in general is not very fertile, that on the plains being scanty and chalky. The chief products are wheat, barley, wine, oil, potatoes, hemp, and flax. Fruits of all kinds abound, including melons, pomegranates, figs, and almonds. Cattle, sheep, and goats are raised. Stone is plentiful, and a soft kind is much used in building. The population numbers about thirty-nine thousand.

Iviza, though much smaller than the other islands, is the most varied in scenery and the most fruitful. Its coasts are much indented and rugged like those of Minorca, and its products about the same. It is occupied by about twenty-one thousand people.

CHAPTER XXIX.

SARDINIA, CORSICA, AND ELBA.

NEXT to Sicily, Sardinia is the largest of the islands in the Mediterranean Sea, having an area of nearly ninety-three hundred square miles. It lies directly south of Corsica, from which it is separated by the Strait of Bonifacio, a channel which in its narrowest part is only seven miles wide. The country is mostly mountainous, and some of the peaks of the central chain have an elevation of over six thousand feet. Many of these peaks are extinct volcanoes. The coasts are as a rule steep and rugged. There are many streams of water on the island, but only one of them is even partially navigable, and none of them has a long course.

The climate is mild, but in the low marshy lands, particularly in the neighborhood of some of the lakes, a deadly malaria prevails, especially in autumn. The inhabitants of these parts, who can afford to do so, migrate annually during the unhealthy months. Those who remain never leave their houses till an hour after sunrise, and return before sunset, carefully closing all doors and windows to prevent the entrance of the

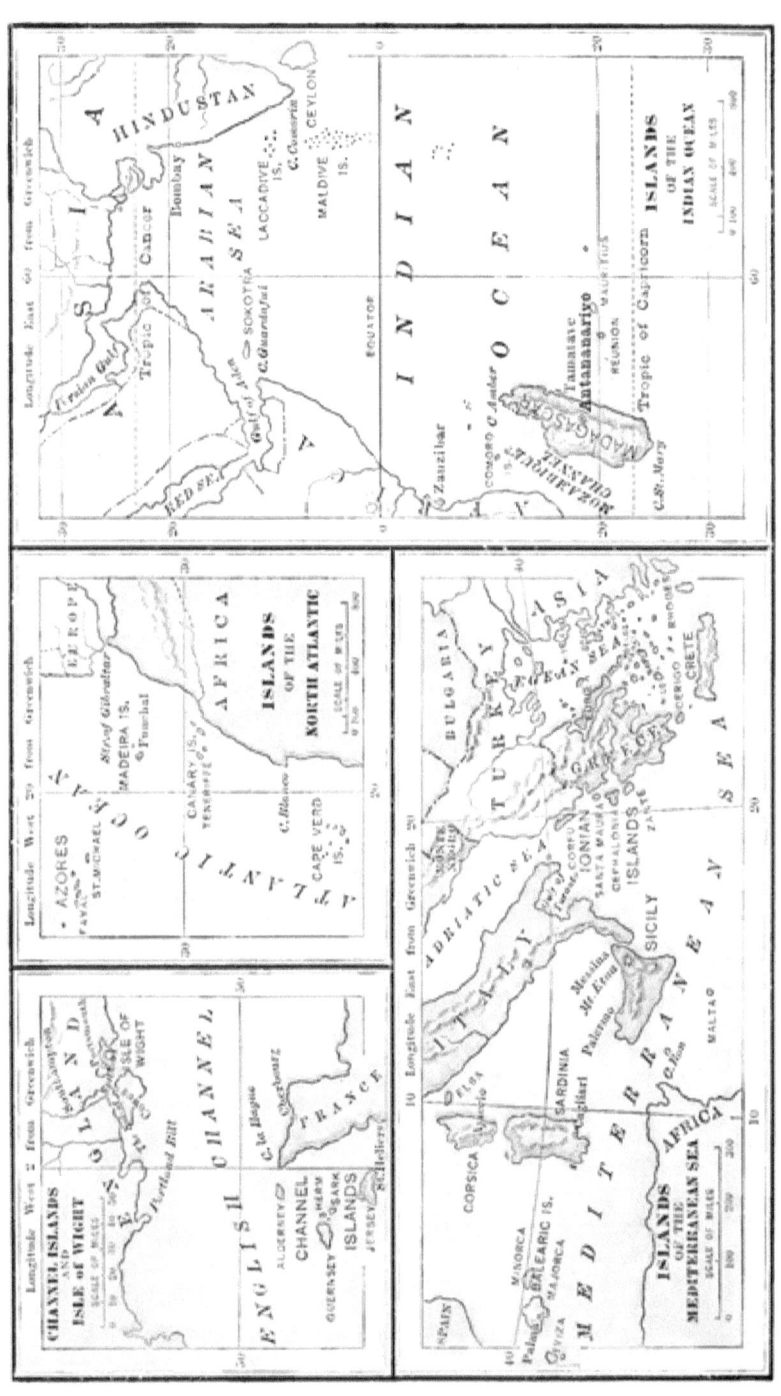

AUSTRALIA AND THE ISLANDS OF THE SEA. 289

TUNNY FISHING, SARDINIA.

poisonous gas. Between the mountain ranges are several wide valleys noted for their beauty and fertility.

The principal products are wheat, barley, maize, oranges and other fruits, all of which are esteemed for their excellent quality. Grapes are extensively raised; but from carelessness in the process of making the wine, it is of an inferior quality. Olive trees are numerous. Cotton, linseed, flax, and hemp are also produced. Among the trees which grow on the mountain sides are cork, chestnut, oak, and pine, which form a considerable item in the export trade. The manufactories of gunpowder, salt, and tobacco are also of importance. Sardinia is rich in minerals, but as yet its mines have been little developed.

The bullock is the favorite animal for draft, although horses are used to some extent. A small species of pony, much esteemed by the Roman matrons, is still found. Sheep, swine, and cattle are kept, and wild boars and deer are not uncommon. Foxes, rabbits, hares, and martens are so abundant that a large export trade in their skins is carried on.

The people bear a strong resemblance to the Greeks, and speak a dialect composed chiefly of Spanish, Arabic, and Italian. As a rule they are ignorant and bigoted, having been subjected to misgovernment and oppression from their emancipation from Roman rule until 1836, when feudal tenure was abolished and the enormous power of the clergy somewhat reduced. With few exceptions they are stupid and indolent, and often clothe themselves in sheepskins. Sardinia forms a part of the kingdom of Italy. The population of the island numbers over seven hundred thousand.

Cagliari is its capital city. It is situated on the northeast shore of a large bay on the south coast of the island, has a spacious and safe harbor defended by several forts, and is the emporium of all the trade of the island. Cagliari is very picturesque when viewed from the sea, as it covers the slope and summit of a promontory, the highest part of which is crowned by a noble castle.

A WOMAN OF SARDINIA.

The streets of the city are narrow, steep, and poorly paved. In the early morning they are swept by galley slaves, the dull clink of whose heavy fetters jars on the nerves. There is a loveliness in the fresh, gentle breeze of the early morning, which is peculiar to warm climates. But, as in other lands, the richer people do not value these fresh, calm hours, and it is only the poorer ones who are astir. The church bells are ringing for early mass, and the worshipers, chiefly of the peasant class, look very gay in their endless variety of dresses — for each class, and each trade, has its distinctive costume.

The little streets are a universal workshop, for every one plies his trade in the open air : the carpenter, the cobbler, the tinman, and the tailor — all hard at work. Everybody seems to be acquainted with everybody else, and what a chattering there is ! Pretty girls are picking grain to be ground in the family mill, and old women are busily spinning, while little children are eating figs and bread in the sunshine, and rolling round in the dirt, as childhood delights in doing the world over.

Down in the market place the noise increases and the scene defies description. Numerous dogs, lank, starved-looking creatures, roam about in all directions. Every morning, when the city gates are opened, crowds of them are waiting to enter. They go to the market and all round the town, devouring the refuse which they find.

As noon approaches, doors are shut and locked, shutters are closed, and quiet reigns everywhere. "Cagliari dines, and after dinner Cagliari sleeps." The Sardinian is fond of the good things of the table, and he is

also a firm believer in the siesta. Later in the day the city wakes up, and the people take a turn in the public walk that winds around the castle-crested hill on which the city stands. Lovely views are obtained of the surrounding country. There lies the great salt lake, where in the winter season may be seen large flocks of brilliant flamingoes. At sunset, the drums beat as a signal for the soldiers to retire to their quarters. There is no twilight here, for the sun goes down quickly.

May Day is the festal day of the patron saint of the city. From early dawn all is excitement. Bells are ringing, flags flying, and cannon firing, while the steep streets are full of life and brilliant with gay costumes. Peasants from the adjoining villages troop into the town, the women riding on pillions behind the men. All are gayly dressed; for the Sardinian is poor indeed who does not have a gay costume for festal occasions, no matter how humble his everyday attire may be.

First in the procession come the military, accompanied by all the drummers who can be mustered. Next come the gentlemen of Cagliari. These are descended chiefly from the old Spanish nobility, and have dark, olive-tinted complexions. They are mounted on richly caparisoned horses, which they manage with great skill. They are followed by peasants in their wild, native costumes, who play vehemently upon instruments of great antiquity.

Then comes the state coach, all gilding and plate glass. Within is an effigy of the saint, life-size, dressed in full canonicals, and surrounded by large lighted wax tapers. The vehicle is drawn by a yoke of cream-colored oxen, of a peculiar breed kept for this sacred purpose. An orange is stuck on the tip of each monstrous horn, while flowers and ribbons adorn the head and neck. And now comes the really wonderful part of the procession, — a great company of women. It would seem as if all the feminine population of Cagliari and the adjacent villages had made a vow to accompany the saint to Scaffa. Having reached Scaffa, the saint, or rather his effigy, will proceed, properly accompanied, to Pula, the place of his martyrdom, while the women will return to their homes. On the fourth day the saint will return, and the women will meet him at Scaffa, in the same manner as they have conducted him hither.

The island of Corsica has an area of nearly thirty-four hundred square miles. The central part is occupied by a range of mountains, branching off in all directions. There are three peaks over eight thousand feet high, and two over seven thousand. The island belongs to France. The most important resource is timber. Lead, antimony, and copper abound. Olives, almonds, figs, and grapes are raised extensively. Of the two hundred and ninety thousand inhabitants, only sixty per cent can read and write.

Ajaccio, the capital, is a delightful town, and far cleaner than any other in Corsica. The streets are gay and busy, and the inhabitants are pleasant and polite. One of the first sights to be visited in the town is the house belonging to the Bonaparte family, on the site of that in which Napoleon was born. The original homestead was burnt in the lifetime of the emperor. The present house is a large one, three stories in height, surmounted by a small turret. A black marble slab is placed above the door by which

BIRTHPLACE OF NAPOLEON, CORSICA.

you enter, giving the date of Napoleon's birth as the 15th of August, 1769. At present, this renowned dwelling place is let out in lodgings.

The men of Corsica dress very much like those who belong to the working classes in other countries. The only variety is caused by the wide-awake hat, the high boots, and the strap worn over the shoulder and supporting the large gourd which hangs at one side and contains the wine. As a rule, the men are lazy. They never carry anything except a gun, a stick, or an umbrella. It is not unusual to see them mounted on the backs of donkeys, with their pipes in their mouths, whilst their good wives trudge along behind, carrying babes and heavy burdens, the latter balanced on the head. The women dress in black or white, or some somber shade, the skirt and jacket usually being of different materials. A large white or black handkerchief is tied under the chin, and when pulled forward, forms a good protection against the rays of the sun.

The internal evil of this island has been the vendetta, or private revenge for the death of a kinsman. It has broken out again and again. It was the natural result of corrupt legislation among a people of violent passions and revengeful dispositions. In the thirty years previous to 1800, seven thousand murders were committed on its account. Then by strenuous measures the French government checked the evil. It was made penal for a man to carry a gun or any other weapon, and the law while in force worked well. During the last few years the law has been rescinded, and now every man carries his loaded gun.

Elba is the largest island of Tuscany, and lies in the Mediterranean Sea between Corsica and the coast of Italy, from which it is separated by a channel. It is triangular in form and rounded on the west coast. Its shores are elevated and steep, and deeply indented by seven gulfs, which form several good ports, the best of which is that of Porto Ferrajo, the capital. The area of

the island is ninety square miles, and the population numbers twenty-four thousand.

Elba is traversed by three mountain chains, which meet southeast of the capital. The highest point is 3134 feet in elevation. The climate, except in some low shore districts, is temperate and healthful. Iron abounds in many places, but is worked only at one point. By the treaty of Paris, in 1814, the island was erected into a sovereignty for Napoleon, and it was his residence from May 4, 1814, to February 26, 1815.

CHAPTER XXX.

SICILY AND MALTA.

SICILY is the largest island in the Mediterranean Sea, and forms an important part of the kingdom of Italy. It is nearly in the form of an equilateral triangle. The area is nearly ten thousand square miles; the population 3,365,000.

The coast, though presenting many small indentations, has few large bays, and there are no lakes worthy of the name. The streams are numerous, but small. The climate is excellent, and, with the exception of a few localities, very healthful. The average annual temperature is about sixty-two degrees. In the summer the sky is usually beautifully clear and serene, but in the autumn dews and fogs increase, and rain falls in frequent and heavy showers. The most annoying

CATANIA AND MOUNT ETNA.

wind is the sirocco, which blows from the deserts of Africa. Its stifling heat is intolerable, and during its continuance, which is generally three or four days, the natives confine themselves to their houses, closing all doors and windows carefully.

The interior of Sicily is finely diversified. A range of mountains commences in the northeast extremity of the island and stretches a little west of southwest, becoming gradually less elevated and throwing out numerous branches. This range resembles the Apennines of Italy, and strongly confirms the opinion that at one time Sicily formed part of the European continent. A tradition exists that the separation was accomplished by a tremendous convulsion of nature, at which time the narrow Strait of Messina was formed. The volcanic agencies, still active within historic times, especially in Mount Etna, support this theory. This mountain is the most remarkable natural feature of Sicily, and one of the greatest wonders of the world. It stands completely separated from the mountain range just mentioned, forming an immense cone, which, at its base, has a circuit of eighty-seven miles. It rises gradually from the plain until it reaches a height of over 10,800 feet.

The climate and soil of Sicily are both well adapted for raising vegetable products. The hilly country is clothed with fine timber, and the pastures support large flocks and herds. In the lower grounds cultivation is general, and the crops are often remarkably large, though the method of culture is careless and unskillful. The implements in vogue are such as were used centuries ago, and grain is still thrashed out by being trodden under foot by cattle. The most valuable crops are wheat, barley, and maize. Next to grain the most important products are those of the vine and olive. Many of the grapes are dried, but many more are converted into wine of various kinds and of an excellent flavor.

The olive trees of Sicily are remarkable for their size and strength. The olives begin to fall in August, but these are small and green and of little value. As the season advances, the olives change to a darker green, and, though still unripe, yield the dearest kind of oil, called virgin oil. In October they are fully ripe, and are almost black in color. Then they are gathered by men, women, and children. The men climb the trees, and shake them down on sheets spread below. The making of the oil lasts during the whole season. Men, dressed in the primitive costume of the country,—linen shirts, and trowsers reaching to the knees,—turn, with great labor and fatigue, a rude mill in which the olives are first crushed. As this process does not extract all the oil, the olives undergo another crushing in a mill as rude as the first. The people seem perfectly willing to expend a great deal of time and strength in order to make oil after the slow ancestral fashion, rather than submit to innovations in the way of modern improvements.

Silk is another source of income in Sicily. The raising of silkworms is a delicate task and is left to the women. In the month of May they take the "seed," or egg of the silkworm moth, roll it in a linen cloth,

SICILIAN TYPES.

and place it in their beds when they rise in the morning. This amount of heat is sufficient, but all doors and windows must be kept carefully closed, lest a chill breath of air should reach the dainty treasure, which, even in good seasons, costs over two dollars an ounce, and at other times is worth even four times that amount. When the seed is hatched, the young silkworms are placed in a flat basket which has previously been lined with the freshest and youngest of mulberry leaves. These must be renewed every day by placing fresh leaves above them. The worms devour an immense amount, and make a great noise while eating. When full grown they are fed no more. The women take them from the basket and place them on a dry twig, where they are left to weave the mysterious home in which their transformation takes place.

At first they wander restlessly from point to point of their twig, but at length they commence their work by throwing around them a fine white silk in which the chrysalis is enveloped. Then within that they weave their shroud of spotless white or shining yellow; this shroud, or envelope, is the cocoon. Their labor never ceases until their stock of silk is exhausted, when they fall asleep to wait the day of their resurrection. For many of them it never comes. In their helpless state, as chrysalids, they are taken and baked in an oven or roasted in the hot noonday sun. In the month of August, when both crops of silk are in, men take the cocoons and put them in large caldrons filled with boiling water. The silk is loosened, and with great dexterity men catch up the flying threads and throw them on a large reel stand-

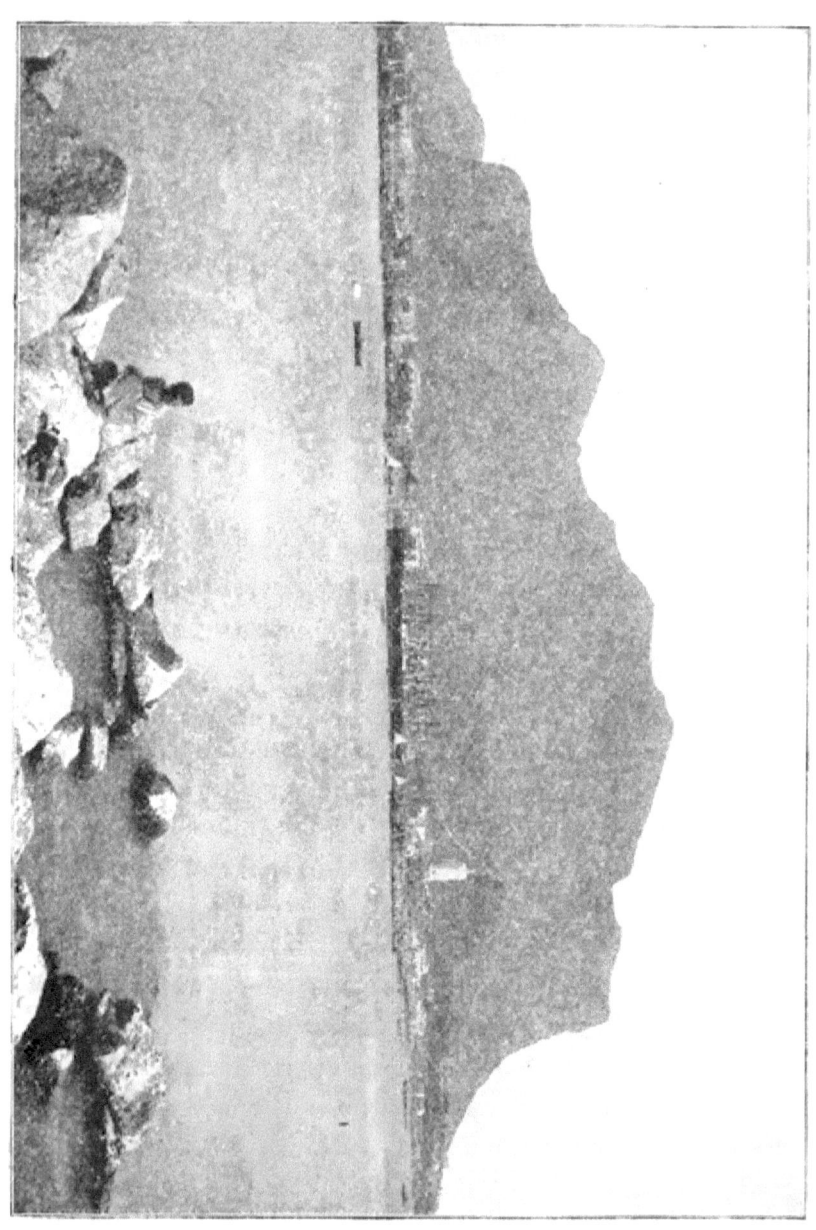

PALERMO, SICILY.

ing near. It turns swiftly and unwinds the beautiful silk fiber.

Palermo, a fortified town, is the capital of Sicily. It stands on the north side of the island in a rich valley, at the base of Monte Pellegrino. It is built in the form of an amphitheater, facing the sea, and is surrounded by an old wall. The valley has been called the golden plain, because of its great fertility. It tapers to a fine point where the mountains meet, and spreads out toward the sea like a cornucopia. The whole of this area is covered with olive, orange, palm, almond, fig, and locust trees, whilst the Judas bush and flowering plants innumerable adorn every open space.

Palermo was probably founded by the Phœnicians, and was a stronghold of Carthage nearly three hundred years before Christ. An antique cathedral and the grounds in which it stands form the most picturesque spot in modern Palermo. A host of statues of holy or distinguished natives surrounds the inclosure in front of the cathedral, which, though lacking somewhat in the dignity of its outline, is splendid in the golden color of its stone and in the magnificence of its decoration.

The older portions of the cathedral were built in the tenth century by an English archbishop, called Walter of the Mill. All that remains of his work, however, are the crypt and portions of the south and east walls, the rest having been rebuilt at different times. The noble, isolated clock tower, which adjoins the archbishop's palace, is united to the cathedral by two arches across the street. The cupola, which has been said to spoil the effect of the whole, was added in modern times. The interior is of excellent proportions, and contains two beautiful holy water basins, the silver shrine of St. Rosalia, the statues of the Apostles, and the Tombs of the Kings, which are most deserving of mention, as

THE CATHEDRAL, PALERMO.

they form one of the most interesting groups of royal sepulchers in the world. At the back of the second chapel is the monument of King Roger, "mighty duke, and first King of Sicily." In the first chapel is the tomb of Frederick II., and beside it that of his daughter, Queen Constantia, "in whom the glorious dynasty of the Norman kings came to an end." Besides the cathedral, there are nearly three hundred other churches in Palermo.

The palace is now the residence of the prefect of Palermo. Part of it, built in the early part of the eighteenth century, was decorated with red Sicilian marble. In the Parliament Hall and the neighboring chambers are paintings by Sicilian artists. On the second floor, in the Norman tower, the angles are decorated by small Norman pillars; and the ceiling and walls are brilliant with mosaics, representing on the ceiling various kinds of animals, and on the walls Norman hunters, crossbows, and stags.

Palermo is the residence of the military commandant of the island, and has an arsenal and shipyards. Its university, founded in the fourteenth century, has over seven hundred students and a library of forty thousand volumes. The town has a botanical garden and many learned societies. Its manufactures consist chiefly of silks, cottons, oilcloth, leather, glass, and gloves. The population, in 1894, was two hundred and seventy-six thousand.

Sicily is divided into seven provinces, each one of which is presided over by a prefect. Each province is subdivided into three or four districts, and these again into numerous townships. Over each district is placed a sub-prefect, and over each township a mayor. Of course this insular self-government does not supersede the necessity of sending Sicilian deputies to the national parliament at Rome; for, having been liberated from the tyranny of the Bourbons by the victories of Garibaldi, in 1861, Sicily was annexed to the kingdom of Italy.

AUSTRALIA AND THE ISLANDS OF THE SEA.

About sixty miles south of Sicily in the Mediterranean Sea lies a group of three islands and two islets known as the Maltese Islands. The largest of these, Malta, is seventeen miles long, and contains an area of ninety-five square miles. It is of an oval form, and is deeply indented on all sides except the south, where the coast forms an almost unbroken line. There are several large bays on the coast, but by far the most important is the double bay formed by the opposite sides of the peninsula on which the capital, Valetta, stands. In its early history Malta was held successively by the Phœnicians, Carthaginians, and Romans. According to some writers Malta is thought to be the mythical island of Ogygia, where the nymph Calypso entertained the wandering Ulysses; her grotto is still pointed out to tourists. The Apostle Paul was shipwrecked on Malta in the year 62 A.D.

Fruits, particularly figs and oranges, are abundant and are of an excellent quality. The blood orange, which is the boast of the island, is most delicious. It is produced by grafting the slips of the common orange on a pomegranate stock. The pulp inclines to the color of red, but not so much in mass as intermixed in streaks; and hence its name. The blood oranges sell, in Valetta, for twice as much as the best of the common varieties.

Malta is a British fortress; the harbor is defended by two forts, St. Angelo and St. Elmo, and, though very different from Gibraltar, it is perhaps as impregnable. In the case of the latter, nature has done her utmost, while in Malta art has exhausted her resources for defense. A bird's-eye view of the island comprehends a mighty array of fortifications, the very names of which it would be tiresome to enumerate.

Vaietta appears to be a very ancient city, and yet its age is little more than three hundred years. This appearance is owing partly to the style of architecture,

MALTA.

and partly to the nature of the building material, which is a soft, crumbling freestone, that, when first quarried, seems totally unfit for permanent structures. On exposure to the air it hardens, especially on the surface.

The houses of the island are, in general, lofty and majestic in appearance. The roofs form a flat terrace, and are used as places of promenade and observation.

The windows are few and narrow, and resemble the loopholes of a castle. Those on the lower floor are heavily barred on the outside, which gives a prisonlike look to the edifices. These bars are not to protect the glass, but to keep out burglars, a fact which does not speak very well for the character of the people.

The balconies form a curious feature of the Maltese houses. Some of them are very uncouth, but their oddness does not make them seem out of place. The supporting stonework is fantastically carved, and the frame above is painted with various colors, as green, red, and blue. Some of them are the size of small parlors. They are neatly finished within, ornamented with pictures and flowers, and furnished with chairs and table. Members of the family spend whole hours in them, and receive their visitors there.

The people are a hardy, capable race, but very poor and ignorant, and many of them are without regular employment. Not Valetta only, but all Malta, swarms like a beehive, and a large number of the people are without money or habitations. Hundreds of them have no other bed than the cold, hard pavement. The men, as a rule, are sparely built and a little under the medium height, but very active and muscular. Their complexions, naturally swarthy, are made still darker from their wearing caps without visors. Their color is similar to that of the people in the Barbary States, and their short crisp hair and rather flat noses would indicate a similar origin.

When abroad, the women draw over their dress a sort of black robe, and, in place of a bonnet, cover their heads with a black silk mantle, which hangs down over the shoulders; the part which covers the head is provided with a piece of whalebone, inserted in the hem, which holds it in position and keeps it from dropping over the eyes. On Sunday, when hundreds of women are out, the streets wear a funereal look.

A STREET IN MALTA.

The religion of the island is Roman Catholic, and fully one third of the property of all Malta is held by the priests. The English, by whom the island is governed, have never interfered with the religious faith, forms, or usages of the people.

Six miles west of Valetta, near the center of Malta, stands the old capital of the country, Città Vecchia. It has a venerable appearance, its gray walls and towers crowning a commanding eminence. We ascend to it by a rugged path, not unlike the channel of a dried mountain torrent, and enter the city through a barrier of considerable strength.

We have come, as all others do, to visit the famous catacombs. They are very extensive, and their origin is lost in antiquity. It is probable that the object at first was simply to quarry stone for the city, but later they were used as receptacles for the dead, and as retreats, and even abodes, by the living. The early Christians fled to them for refuge. Afterward, the members of sects called heretical sought asylums in them from persecution; and, in later times, the inhabitants of Malta were glad to fly to them for safety from the attacks of the Goths, Vandals, Moors, and Turks.

Provided with tapers, we descend into the labyrinth by a narrow flight of stairs, and take especial care to follow our guide closely. We enter first a gallery, narrow and gloomy, pierced on either side with openings into ancient sepulchers resembling the mouths of ovens. They are of different sizes, made to accommodate every age from the infant to the adult. We next traverse a long passage, which opens occasionally into small chambers, the sepulchers of which are superior to those which we have just examined.

Some of them are cut in such a way as to raise the head of the body three or four inches, the rocky pillow being carved so as to fit the form of both the head and the neck. Proceed as far as we may, we see in advance of us long, dismal passages stretching beyond into the darkness. The air in these mansions of the dead is so close and stifling that we hasten from their melancholy solitudes, glad to come forth once more into the sunshine of a summer day.

CHAPTER XXXI.

THE IONIAN ISLANDS.

The Ionian Islands are found in the Mediterranean Sea off the west coast of Greece and Turkey. They consist of seven large islands with several smaller islets. The united area is nearly eleven hundred square miles. The population numbers two hundred and thirty thousand, and is composed of one third Jews, one third a mixed race, and one third Greeks.

The surface of the islands is mountainous and is mostly covered with heath, but in some of the larger islands there are fertile plains. About half the land is cultivated, and yields barley, wheat, and other grains. Wine is made chiefly in the four largest islands. Olive oil is prepared mostly in Corfu and Zante. Currants, cotton, and flax are also produced. Shipbuilding is an important industry.

As a group the islands are rich in natural advantages. Although the soil of all may be characterized as barren, still the vine will grow when planted, even in loose stones, and the labor expended is repaid a hundred fold. With corn, wine, and oil in abundance, having coasts indented with innumerable small bays and creeks, and situated in the highway of the European nations, the islands exert considerable influence on Greece, with which they combined in 1863, and formed the United Kingdom.

It is said that Corfu is the most beautiful, Cephalonia the largest, Santa Maura the wildest, Zante the

THE GATE OF CORFU.

prettiest, and Ithaca the most romantic of the Ionian Islands. This last island is believed to be the one described by Homer, and selected by him as the home of the wise Ulysses.

The views of Corfu, obtained on approaching it from the sea, are extremely grand. But, after visiting Zante, and seeing its excellent drainage, and taking note of the industry which has caused the Cephalonians to cultivate every nook of their Black Mountain, one will not be surprised that the neighboring island, so much more richly endowed by nature, should be so inferior through the shiftlessness of men.

The landing at Corfu, which is the principal town on the island of the same name, has a low, narrow, and dirty entrance, and is crowded with men and animals.

Its architecture presents a most conglomerate appearance. On leaving the citadel, one sees the palace. Facing this is the esplanade, skirted on one side by a shady walk and on the other by a rather handsome row of houses. The town on the north side ends in the market place under Fort Neuf, where all merchandise is landed. The encircling street is called the "Line of Wall."

The Jews still live separate in separate quarters, which in former times were closed with ponderous gates and guarded with detachments of soldiers, — so hostile was the feeling of the other inhabitants toward this much-persecuted race.

The average Corfu peasant loves to lounge away his time in the market place, eager to hear every trifling piece of news. He is utterly devoid of ambition and is extremely lazy, being satisfied to subsist upon what nature provides for him. Bread, salt fish, and the olive form his daily food. The oil of the olive gives him light, and its wood supplies him with fuel. His wife weaves cloth from coarse cotton or brown goat's hair, and thus supplies him with sufficient clothing. The greatest exertion he ever makes is when he goes to town once a week. This journey he accomplishes on the back of his faithful mule, while his patient wife trudges along behind on foot, carrying the household bundle.

Besides Sunday, the Greek Church enjoins the keeping of numerous holidays, which are usually the saints' days of some favorite church. On such days, the people assemble and make presents to their priests. The chief festival occurs on Ascension Day. Many booths are then erected throughout the olive groves. Jars of wine are kept in constant circulation, and lambs roasted whole are quickly divided among the hungry people. After the feasting, the dancing begins, and it is then that the ancient native costumes of the women are worn and are seen to the greatest advantage.

In one village the women wear blue satin jackets, having open bosoms covered with white embroidered cambric. The dress skirt, also of white cambric, is cut short and embroidered, and shows to excellent advantage the velvet slippers which are adorned with large silver buckles.

The women of another village wear black and red jackets, with red stockings and black velvet slippers with gold buckles. In each village the women wear the style of dress adopted by their society; and, no matter what it may be, it always shows off well in contrast with that of the men, which is made of brown goat's wool. These festivals are the only occasions on which the women are allowed to mix freely in public.

Funerals are conducted in a manner quite different from our own. On the way to the grave, the priest, dressed in his gayest robes, walks on ahead, chanting the service. He is followed by several young boys carrying lights, banners, and images. Then comes the open bier, the deceased being dressed in his best clothes. The mourners and friends follow. The Greek cemetery is clean and well kept, the abode of the dead forming, in this respect, a striking contrast to that of the living.

The peasant's home usually consists of two dark rooms on the ground floor. A large part of one of these is taken up by an oven, while the corners serve as receptacles for all sorts of things. The other room, which has but one small opening for the admission of light and air, is used as a sleeping room by the women and children. Over this room is a sort of loft, with a floor of loose reeds, which is reached by means of a ladder, and is used as a sleeping room by the men, who, wrapped up in their cloaks, sleep in any corner they find convenient.

But all of the people are not as poor as this. The house of the farmer, though not differing much externally from that of the peasant, is really much more commodious and much better furnished. The entry serves as both cellar and general storeroom, and a score of large casks for wine and oil are ranged along each side.

A proper stairway leads into the upper story, which is divided into two rooms. That devoted to the women is of large size. Besides the large bed, which is about seven feet square, it contains several old Venetian chests, in which are the household linen and the costumes worn only on feast days. These chests are ornamented with rich carving. Two mirrors, several pictures of Greek saints, and the wedding wreath of the housewife adorn the walls. There are tables, benches, and chairs, and the room appears both comfortable and substantial.

CHAPTER XXXII.

CRETE AND THE GRECIAN ARCHIPELAGO.

CRETE lies in the Mediterranean Sea south of the Grecian Archipelago, from which it is separated by the Cretan Sea. It has a length of one hundred and sixty miles, a varying width of from six to forty miles, an area of 3300 square miles, and a population of 294,000. It is the chief island between the southern extremities of Greece and Asia Minor.

A chain of mountains extends throughout the length of the island, and Mount Ida, near its center, is nearly eight thousand feet in height. Cultivated trees are to be seen everywhere, especially the olive and the orange. The fruit of the latter is so fine that it is famous throughout the Archipelago. But of vegetables there is a great scarcity, and the upper parts of the mountains are mostly bare. Other products are lemons, tobacco, raisins, cotton, honey, oil, wine, and silk.

Besides the classical interest which attaches to Crete, from its heroic and mythological associations, and from its having been a chosen seat of the arts and sciences, there is the higher interest which arises on account of its having been one of the first places in the world to receive the Gospel. The Christian faith was introduced into the island by St. Paul, and his disciple Titus was the first bishop of Crete.

But a visit to the island at the present day leaves a melancholy impression on the mind. Poverty exists everywhere, and many of the people do not have enough to eat. During the three years' insurrection, which began in 1865, many villages were plundered and burned. A few of the people are Mohammedans, but the great majority are Christians. They make few complaints, and are not accustomed to begging. No doubt misrule and oppression have had much to do with reducing them to their present condition.

For ten centuries Crete repelled all foreign aggression, but was at length subdued by the Romans, who subsequently ceded it to the Marquis of Montferrat, by whom it was sold to the Venetians in 1204, when it obtained the name of Candia. It was afterward taken by the Turks, in whose possession it remained till 1830, when it was ceded to Mehemet Ali, viceroy of Egypt, who in turn was obliged, in 1841, to restore it to Turkey. The tithe is the only regular impost, but the manner in which it is collected greatly increases its oppressiveness. Much injury has also been done lately by the introduction of a debased coinage, first by the government, and next by the merchants. Added to these, are the barbarities perpetrated by the Pasha's troops, which, if not thoroughly attested, would be quite incredible.

In 1868 the Cretans rebelled against Turkish rule, and as a result Turkey agreed to give Crete practical autonomy. Her promises were not fulfilled, and in the spring of 1897 trouble broke out again. Greece came to the defense of Crete, and, for a while, made a noble and heroic stand, of which ancient Greece herself might have been proud. But the Greek army soon met with disastrous reverses, and, in a short but active campaign in Thessaly, was totally defeated by the Turks, and compelled to pay the whole expenses of the war. The affairs of Crete were then submitted to the ruling powers of Europe for arbitration.

The majority of the Cretans are a little above the medium height. Their hair and eyes are dark, and their faces oval, with pointed chins, aquiline noses, and full cheeks. The dress of the men consists of long boots, baggy blue trowsers gathered at the knee, a red sash, a blue waistcoat corresponding to the trowsers, and a jacket. Over this is worn a short capote, usually white, with a hood to cover the head. Sometimes a skullcap is used instead.

The Ægean Sea, or Grecian Archipelago, is the name given to that part of the Mediterranean Sea lying between Asia Minor on the east and Greece and part of Turkey on the west. Its length from north to south is about four hundred miles, and its breadth two hundred. The sea in general is very deep. In many places less than a mile from land, no bottom has been found with a two-hundred fathom line.

Some of the islands are of volcanic origin, while others are composed of white marble. Most of them are high, having an altitude of fifteen hundred to eighteen hundred feet. They are divided into two groups, in one of which they lie in the form of a circle, while in the other they are scattered somewhat in a line. The former lie off the eastern coast of Greece, while the latter skirt the west coast of Asia Minor. The first group, containing seven principal islands and many more of inferior size, belongs to Greece. Of the second group, there are twelve islands of considerable size and many small ones; these all belong to Turkey.

Delos, Rheneia, and Tenos are three of the islands in the first group and occupy a position in the northeastern part. In Greek legends, Delos is noted as the birthplace of Apollo. The ruins of the Temple of Apollo are still visible, forming a vast heap of marble fragments, columns, bases, and entablatures.

Both Delos and Rheneia are destitute of trees, and on the latter we find an ancient necropolis containing the graves of those whose bodies were removed from Delos at the time of the Peloponnesian War. It is over half a mile long, and is a scene of wild desolation. Broken stones lay strewn about in all directions, interspersed with sides and lids of sarcophagi.

The island of Tenos lies north of Delos, and a town of the same name occupies its southern extremity. It is one of the most attractive and fertile of the group; is well watered by springs, and has an excellent climate. Tenos produces much barley, silk, wine, figs, oranges, and honey. Its mountains furnish fine marble of various colors. Silk stockings and gloves are extensively manufactured.

For purposes of cultivation, the mountains of Tenos are carved into terraces, giving evidence of vast labor employed in their construction. The people are very industrious, and their villages have a flourishing appearance, the whitewashed houses being surrounded by olive, orange, and fig trees. The flat roofs and trim gardens are like those of northern Italy; and this is not surprising, since the island was held by the Italians for nearly five hundred years. The people are extremely superstitious, and have both a Greek archbishop and a Roman Catholic bishop. Population, 22,000.

The rugged island of Scio, near the coast of Asia Minor, belongs to Turkey. Before the Christian era it was famous as a center of literature and art. It is one of the several spots claimed as the birthplace of Homer. The present population is about 36,000.

Patmos and Rhodes, the former one of the smallest, and the latter one of the largest, are two of the best known islands of the second group. Patmos is famed as being the place of the banishment of St. John. At the present day it is one of the least accessible of the islands of the Archipelago, since, on account of its remote position and the unproductiveness of its soil, steamers never touch there. It is a bare, irregularly shaped mass of rock, twenty-eight miles in circumference, having on its east side a deep indentation which forms a secure harbor. It is almost divided in two near the center; for in this part, within a distance of little more than half a mile of each other, are two isthmuses only a few hundred yards wide, and rising but slightly above the level of the sea. The southern half of the island belongs to the monks, and the other to the civil community.

The population numbers about four thousand, and is composed of Greeks. They are mostly a seafaring people, engaged in the sponge fisheries. The principal town takes the name of Patmos and is sometimes called St. John. It consists of about two hundred houses, and stands on the edge of a mountain, being reached by a steep and rugged ascent. On a height above the town stands a large convent surmounted by several irregular towers. A neighboring grotto is the supposed abode where the apostle John saw the vision which he has recorded in the book of Revelation.

Rhodes has a length of forty-six miles, and an area of five hundred and seventy square miles. Its inhabitants, nearly thirty thousand in number, are principally Turks, Greeks, and Jews. It is traversed by a mountain chain covered with forests, which have long supplied good timber for shipbuilding. Its valleys are well watered and are very fertile. Its principal exports are wax, honey, wine, figs, oranges, lemons, pomegranates, and manufactured silk.

AUSTRALIA AND THE ISLANDS OF THE SEA.

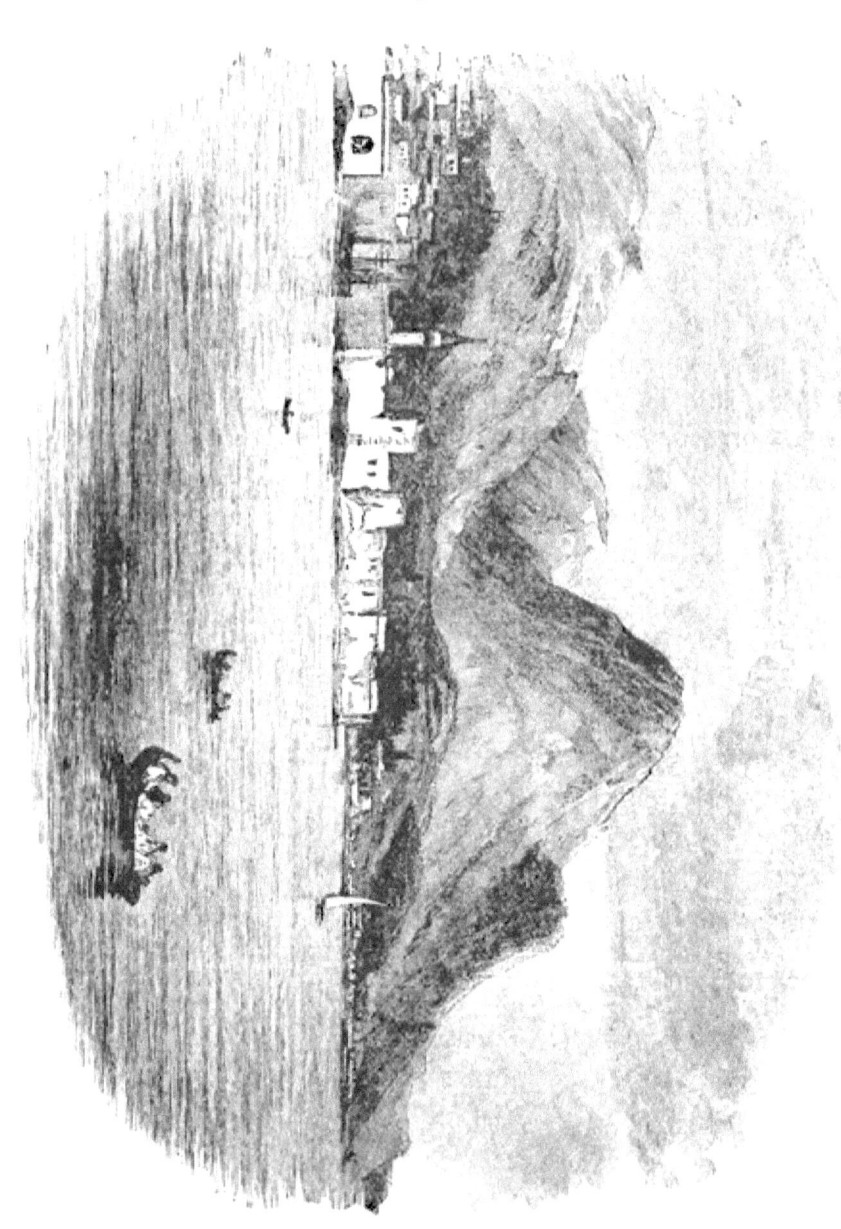

Rhodes is governed by a Pasha, whose jurisdiction extends over the whole group. Its chief city has the same name, and is built at the northeast extremity of the island, thirteen miles from the nearest promontory of Asia Minor. It is inclosed by walls built by the Knights of St. John.

As a commercial station, Rhodes occupies an admirable position, on account of its nearness to the mainland, and of its being a natural point of departure for Egypt and the East. It is said that "in ancient times it was surpassed in grandeur by no other city, and hardly equaled by any." Its commerce, its political institutions, its school of oratory, and its school of sculpture enjoyed a world-wide renown. It was the residence of many great men. Tiberius chose Rhodes as his place of voluntary exile, and it was here that Cicero studied. But little remains of the magnificence of those times except the Hellenic foundations of the moles, and the many sepulchral monuments of gray marble which are to be seen in the city and suburbs.

The military history of Rhodes is full of interest; it has withstood some remarkable sieges. That of 1522 was, perhaps, the most notable, when four thousand five hundred soldiers and six hundred knights withstood for five months the Ottoman fleet of three hundred ships and one hundred thousand soldiers, commanded by Suleïman I. "This resistance is one of the most glorious exploits of martial Christianity." The knights were granted an honorable capitulation, and with four hundred inhabitants they abandoned the island, which since that time has belonged to the Turks.

Starting from the suburb on the northern side of the city, we have on our left the first harbor, that of the galleys, which was outside the walls, but was defended by a strong round tower at the extremity of the mole, called the tower of St. Nicholas. Some believe that this fort occupies the site of the famous Colossus of Rhodes, one of the seven wonders of the world; but other authorities claim that the statue stood on the low ground at the southwest corner of this harbor. This statue was one hundred and five feet high, and represented the Rhodian sun god, Helios. It commemorated the successful defense of Rhodes in 303 B.C., was twelve years in completing, and stood 66 years, being at last thrown down by an earthquake.

We next pass through the gate of St. Paul. A figure of the saint stands above the gate, holding in one hand a volume of the gospel, and in the other a sword. This gate does not lead into the city itself, but into the circuit of walls which incloses the great harbor. Through the wall which borders this harbor, the city is entered by the finest of all the gates, that of St. Catharine. It is surmounted by a figure of the saint standing between St. Peter and John the Baptist. Immediately within this, on the right hand as we enter, is the cross wall separating that part of the town in which dwelt the ancient order of Knights, and which occupied about one third of the area of the town, from the part occupied by the citizens. Taking our way through this latter section, and following a line of streets which cross it transversely, we have the Jewish quarter on our left. Many of the handsomest of the old dwellings are to be found here. They are solidly built and elaborately decorated.

In the other portion of the city, by far the most interesting part, is the Street of the Knights. It descends in a straight line by a gradual slope toward the port. The buildings on either side are of rough brownstone, with projecting latticed frames of wood, thrown out by the Turkish families that dwell there. This street contains the Priories, which were the headquarters and places of meeting of the different nationalities of Knights. Their escutcheons and those of the most distinguished men may, in many cases, be seen on the façades.

Throughout the island the courtyards, in which the houses are built, are often covered with tessellated pavements of pebbles. In some of the dwellings the rooms are floored with them, and the patterns are often elaborate and beautiful. The walls are frequently hung with the plates of the Rhodian ware, which collectors prize so highly. These plates are regarded by the people as heirlooms in their families.

In some parts of the island the villages are built with curious uniformity. Every doorway is surmounted by a pointed arch, and the window and chimney of each house occupy the same relative position.

Cyprus is the easternmost island in the Mediterranean and the third in size. It has a length of one hundred and forty-eight miles, and a breadth of forty, with an area of three thousand seven hundred miles, and a population of two hundred and nine thousand.

The whole island is occupied by a range of mountains known in heathen mythology as the third range of Olympus, whose two culminating points, Santa Croce (Olympus) and Thrados, are seven thousand feet high. On the northeast side of the island the slopes are steep and rugged, and one of the elevated valleys contains Nicosia, the modern capital of Cyprus. The slopes are even bolder on the south side, and present a deeply serrated outline with thickly wooded sides, furrowed by deep valleys. In the southwest the mountains yield excellent asbestos; also talc, red jasper, copper, silver, gold, and emeralds. The name of the island is supposed to have been derived from the Greek word (*kupros*) meaning copper.

Cyprus is deficient in water, having but one river of any importance. The climate is in general healthful. Temporary blindness is sometimes caused by the sun's reflection from the white chalky soil; and to avoid sunstroke the natives wrap their heads in thick shawls.

About one third of the cultivable surface of Cyprus is under tillage. Of vegetable products, cotton and corn are the most important. Excellent wheat, barley, tobacco, and madder are raised. Silk is produced abundantly in several vicinities, and sponge fishing is a prominent industry. Wine is the most noted production of the island, and is of excellent quality.

The women of some of the towns and villages do beautiful embroidery, and make silk net which will bear comparison with the finest European lace. They also weave some cotton, woolen, and linen fabrics. Good morocco leather is made in Nicosia; and calicoes, imported from England, are here dyed in brilliant colors and exported to Syria, Smyrna, and Constantinople. On the west side of the island the peasantry distil rose, orange, and lavender water, and myrtle and laudanum oil. The island of Cyprus is under British rule, being governed by a resident High Commissioner, assisted by an Executive Council. For many years Cyprus has been explored and excavated for relics of antiquity, and some remarkable specimens have been found here. In 1845, a bas-relief on which was sculptured the figure of Sargon, king of Assyria 722–705 B.C., was found in a good state of preservation. This monument is at present in the Royal Museum of Berlin.

CHAPTER XXXIII.

ISLANDS ON THE EAST AFRICAN COAST.

MORE than two hundred miles from the east coast of southern Africa, in the Indian Ocean, lies a large island called Madagascar. It was discovered in the latter part of the thirteenth century by a Venetian traveler, and was valued by European nations chiefly as a vast hunting ground for slaves until 1816, when the trade was suppressed. From three thousand to four thousand were shipped annually from its ports.

The greatest length of the island is one thousand miles and its greatest breadth three hundred and fifty. Its area is estimated at two hundred and thirty thousand square miles. At the time of its discovery, the natives called their island by a name which means "in the center of the sea."

Through the country from north to south extends an elevated tract of land, rising by successive terraces to the center. The highest points reach an elevation of ten thousand feet. This plateau is surrounded on all sides, except the southeast, by a strip of low land from twenty to fifty miles wide, some parts of which are actually below the level of the sea, from which it is protected only by the beach thrown up by the surf. It is also surrounded by a forest which extends to the low plains, and, in some cases, to the sea.

No country in the world is better watered than Madagascar. But few of its rivers are navigable; for during the first part of their course they fall rapidly, and, when they come to the lowlands, they spread out into lakes, and reach the sea only with sluggish streams.

On the low coasts, often running parallel with the sea, are chains of lakes formed in some cases by the overflowing of the barred rivers, and in others by the sea. In the interior of the island several large lakes are reported to exist.

The heat on the coasts is often excessive, and rains are frequent there, but on the highlands of Ankova the thermometer seldom rises above eighty-five degrees.

Madagascar is rich in vegetable productions. Among the most important trees is one whose leaves are made into a kind of cloth, and from whose bark is extracted a drink resembling spruce beer. There are many kinds of gum trees, one of which yields a gum greatly valued as a powerful cement. Another tree produces a highly fragrant allspice. Dyewoods, fig, ebony, orange, peach, and mulberry trees also grow here. Coffee, which has been introduced, thrives well.

There are few formidable wild animals in Madagascar. Its beasts of prey are confined to a small leopard, a wild dog, a wild cat, and a species of fox. Crocodiles are numerous in the rivers. There are many kinds of snakes, some of which grow to a great size. Apes are found in the woods. But the wealth of the country consists in its cattle, which are mostly humped like those of India.

A HOVA WOMAN AND CHILD.

Coal, rock salt, sulphur, and copper are all found in the island. Excellent iron abounds in several parts of the country. The natives take the ore and put it in pits or kilns covered over with clay. Near the edges of these they place hollow tree trunks, and, by means of pistons placed in these and worked by hand, they provide the necessary blast for the smelting of the ore.

The government, until recently, has been a sort of monarchical despotism, modified by changes in the religion and habits of the court under the teaching of Christianity. A body of judges used to sit constantly in public to hear complaints and to administer rude justice, not according to any written law, but rather by traditional usage. There are twenty-five tribes, each having its own chief, subject, in old days, to the monarch. Recently the French, having claimed rights under a treaty made in 1885, have taken Antananarivo, the capital, and have established a protectorate, which gives them virtual possession of the island.

The name of the capital, Antananarivo, signifies "the city of a thousand." It is located upon the summit and slopes of a hill which rises from a plain to the height of five hundred feet. The houses are built upon terraces. There are but three or four streets in the city; from these streets, branch innumerable pathways leading between the houses. They are so narrow that in many places it is impossible for two people to meet and pass each other.

The hill has three elevated points. The highest of these is called by a name which means "hill for observing." Near to this one is "the crown," or "the top of the town," on which the palaces stand. The third, the "whitehill," is the site of a memorial church.

The royal palaces are the most conspicuous buildings in the town. They are grouped together in a large courtyard, and are about a dozen in number. The principal entrance is on the north side, and consists of a picturesque gateway, forming a triumphal archway, which is approached by a massive flight of stone steps. On each side of the archway are Romano-Doric columns. In the center above the arch is a peculiar square

TATTOOING A CHIEF, MADAGASCAR.

panel with a large mirror set in it, and directly above this is a figure of the national falcon made of copper.

Near to the great palace is the palace church. Its tower rises to the height of 112 feet, and, at the time of its completion, it was the only building in the country whose roof was covered with slates.

The population of Madagascar has sprung from different races. The fairest race, the Hovas, is the ruling one, and has established its sway over nearly the whole of the island. The Hovas are distinguished from the other people by their light olive complexion, the absence of thick lips, and by their activity. They are well made; but rather below the medium height. The next race in importance is the blackest, and lives on the western coast.

There are no roads in Madagascar, but merely tracks which may be traveled by men or cattle. The people are accustomed to make long journeys on foot. Men employed by the government to carry letters or dispatches acquire wonderful powers of speed and endurance. Many of them are able to travel two hundred miles in four days, over rough and rocky hills often slippery with mud, across unbridged streams, and through dense forests and deep sloughs.

The national carriage consists of two poles of tough, light wood, held together by iron rods with nuts and screws. On the hindmost of these rods, and to each of the poles, is fastened a framework of iron, which is covered with leather and stuffed, and has a back against which one may lean. In front is a footrest made of wood, and at each side are pockets for holding small articles. There is no cover overhead, but a large sunshade is fastened to one pole, and a piece of canvas, which serves as a protection against rain, is secured to the other.

Four runners carry this on their shoulders. When well trained, they keep step so well that the motion is not unpleasant. If the distance is short, two extra men run alongside to relieve two of the bearers, who in turn relieve the other two. When the distance is great, eight men are required, the two sets changing off with each other at regular intervals and without stopping. From six to seven hours is an ordinary day's work, but the bearers frequently travel eight or nine without inconvenience.

Mauritius, an island in the Indian Ocean east of Madagascar, has an area of seven hundred square miles and a population of three hundred and seventy thousand.

Port Louis, the capital and the only town, lies in an extensive valley; and as our ship approaches the outermost anchorage a view of unsurpassed beauty presents itself. Far away in the distance is the well-known Peter Botte Mountain; just behind the city rises the majestic Pouce, wooded to its summit; to the east lie the gentle slopes of Citadel Hill, bastion crowned; and to the west, abrupt and rugged, Long Mountain Bluff rears its signal-topped head. The city covers an area of ten square miles, and has a population of sixty-two thousand. It has a fine natural harbor, capable of affording anchorage to vessels of heavy burden, which, even during hurricane weather, can ride safely.

The entrance to the channel is through coral reefs, well marked out by buoys, and has an average depth of thirty-five feet, and within the harbor of fourteen feet. It is well defended by forts George and William, and the citadel, which stands back of the city, also overlooks and commands it.

The streets of Port Louis are many of them macadamized, and are kept fairly clean. Several rivulets flow through the town. In wet weather they become rushing torrents, bringing down masses of mud and débris. In dry weather they become almost stagnant, and add largely to the malarious condition of the city.

In the interior the houses are very plain, and consist of drawing-rooms and dining-rooms and a few sleeping apartments, all of which have the strong Z-shaped bar on the outside of the hurricane shutters. Nearly all of the houses have small pavilions, which contain two or three bedrooms for guests.

Chaussée is the principal street for shops, and is in the oldest part of the town. The buildings are wooden, and are old-fashioned-looking on the outside, contrasting strongly with the interiors, where all indicates the latest Parisian fashion. You may buy any article of a lady's toilette, from a Lyons silk dress to a plain English calico. Jewelers' shops shine resplendent with gold and gems, especially diamonds, and you wonder how so small a place can find purchasers for such costly articles.

A curious feature of this and other streets is the juxtaposition of one of these elegant magazines with a Chinese store retailing such articles as charcoal, salt fish, cocoanut oil, rice, wood, and lard. The continuation of Chaussée is called Royal Street, and it extends nearly to the northern limit of the city. Most of the shops here are built of stone.

The division between the two parts of this street is made by the Place d'Arms, which stands in front of the quays, and is shaded by three kinds of trees, one of which is the flamboyant of Madagascar. This tree is covered with magnificent scarlet, yellow, and white flowers, which, lying against the soft delicate green of the foliage, form a bouquet of transcendent beauty. Seats are placed under the trees, and there planters, merchants, and women discuss the affairs of the island.

Large cages of native birds are displayed in the markets, conspicuous among which are the pretty scarlet cardinals with their mates, and greenish yellow canaries that sing so sweetly. These are all offered for sixpence a pair. Beautiful foreign birds are also for sale, brought from India, Australia, New Guinea, and Brazil. These command large prices.

Perhaps few places in the world can boast such a variety of fish, many of which are of gorgeous colors. The most esteemed are the mullets, Dame Berry, cordonnier, pike, and eels. Fine crabs and crayfish are abundant. Shellfish are sold in large quantities. Large sharks, rays, and other monsters are sliced and sold to the natives.

At a distance of seven miles from Port Louis are the celebrated Botanical Gardens, founded in 1768. In them are growing the nutmeg, clove, and other spice trees, beside a large variety of useful and ornamental trees, obtained with great trouble and at large expense from both hemispheres. On Sundays and holidays, this place is a favorite resort of the city people, who enjoy its shady avenues and thatched pavilions.

St. Pierre's well-known romance, "Paul and Virginia," has spread a sort of halo round Mauritius for nearly a century. The two tombs shown as theirs are two commonplace brick and mortar structures. They are situated in what was once a fine garden. A little rivulet flows between them, and they are shaded by stately palms and feathery bamboos.

Réunion, also called Bourbon, one of the Mascarene Group, lies in the Indian Ocean, four hundred miles east of Madagascar. It has an area of nine hundred and sixty-five square miles, and a population of one hundred and seventy thousand. It forms a French colony. The capital is St. Denis. The island is of volcanic origin and is elliptical in form.

It is traversed from north to south by a chain of mountains which divides it into two portions, differing in climate and productions. The highest summit is that of an extinct volcano, 10,100 feet high. Three other peaks are respectively 9500, 7300, and 7218 feet, the last being an active volcano. There are many narrow valleys, but no extensive plains.

Réunion was counted at one time one of the healthiest spots in the world. But the climate has recently undergone a great change, and serious diseases attack every foreigner after a residence of four or five years.

The prevailing winds drive the rain clouds to the east side of the island, and often originate the most terrific hurricanes. On such occasions the waves, usually three to four feet high, rise to fifty feet in height, and rage with inestimable fury. The sky changes to a copper color, the temperature rises to its maximum intensity, the barometer sinks to its lowest point, rain falls in torrents, and the wind blows with resistless might. Réunion has no good port, and its anchorage is very insecure. In one year, eleven large vessels were wrecked near its shores.

The chief products of the island are sugar, coffee, cloves, maize, rice, tobacco, dyewoods, and saltpeter.

Zanzibar is an island on the east coast of Africa, near the sixth degree of south latitude; it formerly belonged to the Sultan of Muscat, but is now a British protectorate. It is separated from the mainland by a strait twenty-five miles wide, thinly beset with coral reefs and islets. This island, like all others near the coast, is of coral formation. It has been raised above its original level and in some places attains a height of two hundred and fifty feet. The soil is extremely rich, and the greater part of the island is still in its natural state. The mango, banana, papaw, plantain, and various Indian fruits grow wild, with several species of palm and the stately cotton tree. The natives cultivate rice and millet (which grows to a height of ten feet), but the cultivated fields are few in number.

The plantations of the Sultan, or Seyyid, contain not less than five hundred thousand clove trees, the produce of which is excellent. He has planted also nutmeg and cinnamon trees, obtaining his workmen from Mauritius and Réunion.

There are few wild animals in Zanzibar. The interior thickets are occupied by wild hogs, and a few civet cats lurk about the villages. With the exception of the guinea fowl, wild birds are few. The ass is here the universal beast of burden.

The principal towns are Zanzibar and Uzi. In traveling through the country between these towns, the stranger is agreeably surprised to find that the narrow roads

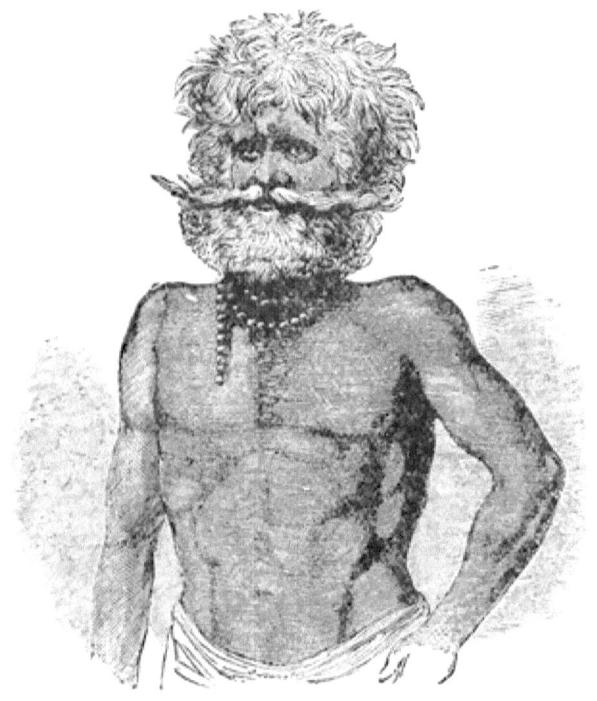

A FAKIR OF ZANZIBAR.

are everywhere neatly fenced, like garden walks, with hedges of palma Christi or some other suitable plant.

The city of Zanzibar is the principal commercial port on the eastern African seaboard; it has a population of thirty thousand, mostly blacks. The Central, or Fort, Quarter is the seat of government and of commerce.

The material of which the houses are built is "coral-rag," a substance at once easily worked and durable. The best houses are on the Arab plan. A dark narrow entrance leads from the street, and the center of the tenements is a quadrangle. There are no shady trees, bright flowers, or green verdure as in similar houses in the southern part of Europe. Here the "Dár" is simply a dirty yard, paved or unpaved, generally encumbered with piles of wood or hides, and tenanted by dogs, poultry, donkeys, and lounging slaves. A steep, narrow staircase of rough stone connects it with the first floor, the "noble quarter." There are galleries for the several stories, and doors opening upon the court admit light into the rooms.

"Koranic sentences on slips of paper, fastened to the entrances, and an inscription cut in the wooden lintel, secure the house against witchcraft." Arabs here, as elsewhere, prefer long narrow rooms. The reception hall is usually on the ground floor. The protracted lines of walls and rows of arched and shallow niches are unbroken save by a few weapons. Pictures are almost unknown; chandeliers and mirrors are confined to the wealthy. What in our houses would be bald and barnlike, here suggests coolness and simplicity. A bright tinted carpet, a tasteful Persian rug for the dais, matting on the lower floor, a divan in the older houses, and a half dozen stiff-backed chairs of East Indian blackwood in the later ones, compose the upholstery of the Zanzibar "palazzo."

Sokotra lies off the eastern extremity of Africa in the

AUSTRALIA AND THE ISLANDS OF THE SEA.

A ZANZIBAR VILLAGE.

Indian Ocean. It has an area of about fourteen hundred square miles and a population of ten thousand, mostly Bedouins, with some settled Arabs, negroes, and descendants of Portuguese.

Its center is a chain of mountains, rising to the height of five thousand feet. Round this a low belt of land, two to four miles wide, skirts the sea. The climate is more temperate than on the adjacent continent. Among the products are aloes, various gums, tamarinds, tobacco, dates, millet, and ghee. Sokotra was formerly occupied by the Portuguese, but was annexed by Great Britain in 1886.

CHAPTER XXXIV.

THE LACCADIVE AND MALDIVE ISLANDS.

BETWEEN ten and twelve degrees north latitude, in the Indian Ocean, is a group of small islands of coral formation known as the Laccadive Islands. They are so low that, were it not for the cocoa palms with which they are so thickly studded, they would scarcely be discernible. The soil of all of them consists of a light, white, coral sand, and beneath this, a few feet down, is a stratum of coral.

Of the eight inhabited islands, four belong to Great Britain, and the other four to the estate of a native ruler. The people are of mixed Hindu and Arab descent, and are Mohammedans.

Kiltan Island, which belongs to the British, is typical

of the other Laccadive atolls. It is a long, oval reef inclosing the usual lagoon, with one entrance at the northwest corner. The reef is surrounded by a shelving bank, varying in breadth from one eighth of a mile to a mile. Beyond the edge of this bank the line drops at once into very deep water. The lagoon is very shallow and nearly dry at low water, and the island is covered with cocoa palms from one end to the other. This tree yields its ripe fruit week after week throughout the whole year, and is highly prized by the natives. They deem trees which ripen their fruit only once a year as rather unsatisfactory freaks of nature, and therefore set no great value upon the trees which bear breadfruit, limes, horse-radish, and plantains, all of which have been introduced into the islands.

In the central portion of the palm grove which covers the island, about two hundred houses are scattered, containing nearly eight hundred people. The walls of most of these houses are solidly built of blocks of coral rock, and the roofs are composed of palm leaves laid on rafters made of wreck wood or split trunks of palm trees.

Grain, pulse, bananas, and vegetables are cultivated; but the natives depend upon the mainland for rice. One of the commonest shrubs is a coarse heliotrope.

In some of the islands the people are very much troubled with rats, which live up in the crowns of the palm trees, and often drop the nuts on the heads of people passing by. They also seriously damage the crops, and make themselves disagreeable generally. The government, anxious to succor the people, sug-

346 THE WORLD AND ITS PEOPLE.

PALM GROVE AND NATIVES, LACCADIVE ISLANDS.

gested sending cats to the islands. But these the people had already; and, as there was a plentiful supply of fish below, the cats could not be persuaded to run up ninety feet of the bare trunks in search of rats, of whose existence they were ignorant.

Then the government sent over a lot of snakes and mongooses. The former the people quickly exterminated, not seeming to think them a desirable accession to the community; and the latter did little good, as they could not climb the trees. Then the government tried owls. But the people called them by an evil name, and declared they kept them awake at night and "made the children scream and the old women foretell death and ruin."

At last the government gave it up, and the native men are still assembled at regular seasons, according to their custom, for a "koot," or rat hunt. The younger men climb the trees and drive the vermin down, to be dispatched by those below. The rats scurry from tree to tree, only to find a fresh foe in each. Of course many escape, but the numbers are thus reduced.

The people are a peaceable, order-loving population. They have been accused of plundering wrecks; but about the worst that can be said of them is, that when they find abandoned wrecks on the reefs, and useful articles scattered about handy, they very naturally help themselves. Until lately, no inducement was ever held out to them to act otherwise. They have always treated shipwrecked mariners with kindness; and now that salvage has been offered them, this petty pilfering will probably become less common.

The Maldive Islands are situated in the Indian Ocean, about three hundred miles from Hindustan. They are coral atolls and are arranged in seventeen round or oval groups, each one being about ninety miles in circumference.

Standing in the center of one of these atolls, you see all around you a great reef of coral, which protects the inclosed islands from the impetuosity of the sea. These reefs each have four openings, varying in width from thirty to two hundred yards.

To those who sail near the islands they appear of exceeding whiteness. This is due to the fact that all the shoals and reefs are covered with a fine white sand. Some of the islands have fresh water; but others do not, and in that case the inhabitants go to a neighboring island to get it. They also employ simple contrivances for catching rain water. They stretch a cloth horizontally, with a stone in the center of it, and underneath they place a vessel which catches the water as it filters through. They also tie cocoa leaves tightly around the tree trunks near the bottom, and the rain, as it runs down, is conducted into vessels.

The sea yields all kinds of fish, and this is the principal food of the natives. They use besides a great deal of poultry, which runs wild and costs them nothing but the catching. The islands abound in pigeons, ducks, rails, and other birds that may be used as food. The people are much troubled with rats, mice, and ants, which destroy their grain, provisions, and fruit. To escape these pests, they often build their storehouses and granaries two or three hundred yards from the shore.

The principal island of the group is called Mali. It is about six miles in circumference, and is the most fertile of all. It is the residence of the Sultan and his court, and for this reason the most thickly inhabited of any. The Sultan pays a yearly tribute to the Governor of Ceylon on behalf of the British Government.

There are no walled towns, but the houses in the villages are generally separated by streets into quarters and neatly arranged. Those of the better class are built of wood, or occasionally of stone; those of the poorer people being constructed of cocoa thatch, twigs, and mud, with thatched roofs.

The outer garment worn by the men consists of a large robe of cotton or silk reaching to the ankles. For a belt they use a large handkerchief embroidered with silk and gold, folded in three plaits, and tied in a knot in front. Over this they wear a piece of silk of bright color, reaching to the middle of the thigh; and last of all gird themselves with a long silken sash, letting the ends hang down in front. On their heads they wear bright-colored turbans of silk or cotton.

The women also wear a long robe of finest cotton, bordered with blue and white and reaching to the feet. It is fastened at the neck with two gilt buttons. On their arms they wear heavy bracelets of silver, sometimes reaching to the elbow, and weighing three or four pounds. They also wear silver chains around their waists, which are not seen except when the robe is very transparent. They braid their hair, of which they take the best of care, and fasten it in a knot at the back of the head, drawing over it a gold netting, which the richer women stud with precious stones. In each ear, beginning with the lobe and running around the cartilage, they wear twelve golden ornaments, the holes being bored in early life. They color their finger nails and their feet red with the sap of a certain tree, this being their notion of beauty. The people are of a dark olive complexion with black hair.

As to their religion, they are Mohammedans. They say prayers before meals. They use no table, but sit crosslegged on a mat on the floor. Instead of linen, they use large banana leaves, — the food being placed on these in covered dishes. They deem it bad manners to eat otherwise than in the greatest haste; and they never converse while taking food, even when company is present. After the meal is over, betel is served as dessert. They have no regular time for meals, but eat whenever they feel inclined to do so.

CHAPTER XXXV.

THE MALAY ARCHIPELAGO — SINGAPORE AND BORNEO.

THE Malay Archipelago is the largest and most important group of islands on the globe. It lies between Asia and Australia, and is washed by the Indian Ocean on the west and the Pacific on the east. It is more than four thousand miles in length from east to west and about thirteen hundred in breadth. This includes New Guinea on the east and the Philippine Islands on the north, all of which are excluded by some geographers.

The archipelago is usually divided into three groups. The first group contains the Andaman and Nicobar islands, with an area of over three thousand square miles. The former are in the Bay of Bengal. The native population is very scanty and in the lowest state of barbarism. The Nicobar Islands lie in the Indian Ocean south of the Bay of Bengal. They are covered with trees and are in a fertile condition. They are subject to frequent hurricanes and are very unhealthy. The second group includes the Sunda and Molucca islands, with an area of nearly six hundred and sixty thousand square miles. This group contains eight divisions, the chief of which are the Borneo group, the Sumatra, the Java, the Moluccas, and Celebes. The third division takes in the Philippine Islands, with an area of one hundred and fourteen thousand square miles.

Borneo is more than four times as large as New England. New Guinea contains twenty-five thousand more square miles than Borneo; being, next to Australia and Greenland, the largest island in the world. Sumatra is nearly half as large as Borneo. Java and Celebes are each larger than the state of New York. Eighteen others are as large as Jamaica, while there are many smaller islands and islets.

One of the principal volcanic belts on the globe passes through this archipelago. A curved line, which may be traced by numerous active volcanoes and many more inactive ones, extends through Sumatra and Java and thence through thirteen other islands or groups of islands to Morty Island. Here there is a break of two

A SULTAN OF BORNEO.

hundred miles, and the belt commences again in the North Celebes, passes through two other islands, and thence to the Philippine Islands, along the eastern side of which it continues to the northern extremity.

In this whole region earthquakes are of frequent occurrence. Slight shocks are felt every few weeks or months, while more severe ones, shaking down whole villages and doing more or less damage, are sure to occur in some one of the islands almost every year. In Java, in 1772, forty villages were destroyed, when a whole mountain was blown up by repeated explosions, a large lake being left in its place. This island alone contains more volcanoes than any other known district of the same extent. They are about forty-five in number, with an average height of ten thousand feet.

There are two aboriginal races in the Malay Archipelago. One is of Malay extraction and has a brown complexion; the other is the Papuan, or negro, race, and is black. The brown race is about four inches below the average European in stature. They are robust and rather clumsy. The face is square, with hollow cheeks and projecting jaws. The mouth is large, the nose small, the eyes small and black, and the hair lank. The Javanese are the most civilized of this race and the darkest. The negro race rarely attain the height of five feet and have feeble frames. The skin is of a sooty black, not polished like that of the African. The lips are prominent, the chin small, and they have a wild, malign look. They increase in numbers toward the east and are in sole possession of New Guinea.

Politically, the archipelago is subject to a sixfold

division: the independent native states and tribal territories, the Spanish possessions, the Portuguese, the Dutch, the English, and the Sarawak. The Dutch power is by far the most influential. The Spanish possessions are confined to the Philippine and Sulu Islands. The English possess Singapore and several others. The Dutch claim nearly all the rest, including an area of more than seven hundred and thirty-six thousand square miles, and a population of thirty-three million.

Singapore, the chief British possession in the Malay Archipelago, furnishes a great variety of Eastern races, as well as many different religions and ways of life. The government, the garrisons, and the principal merchants are all English. Besides these there are the Chinese, who form the great mass of the people. Many of them are merchants, farmers, and mechanics. The boatmen, fishermen, and most of the police are Malays.

The town of Singapore contains some handsome public buildings and churches. Hindoo temples, Mohammedan mosques, Chinese joss houses, and quaint Chinese bazaars occupy conspicuous places. The long suburbs show many Chinese and Malay cottages, besides good European houses. The Chinese are the most noticeable people in the place. The merchants are usually fat-faced, pleasant men. They dress in the loose white smock, and wear brown or blue trowsers, which differ from the clothes of the poorest coolie only in being of finer quality. The hair is braided, and hangs in many cases nearly to the heels.

Singapore tailors sit *at* a table and not *on* one.

Barbers clean ears as well as shave heads, and for this purpose keep many curious little picks, tweezers, and brushes. Blacksmiths and carpenters live in the outskirts of the town; and while the former seem to be

ELEPHANT AT WORK, SINGAPORE.

engaged mostly in making guns, the latter busy themselves in the construction of coffins.

Men crying their wares walk up and down the streets, while some carry a portable cooking apparatus on a pole balanced by a table at the other end, and serve up a meal of shellfish and rice for the modest sum of four or six cents. In the interior the Chinese are engaged in cutting down trees, in agriculture, and in the raising of pepper, which is an important export.

The island is covered with hills about three hundred feet high, many of which are still occupied by the original forests. Here and there among them tiger pits are concealed. They are about twenty feet deep and built with slanting sides, being larger at the bottom than at the top. Tigers are still so numerous that on an average a Chinaman a day is devoured by them. Elephants are largely used for heavy hauling.

Borneo lies directly east of Singapore and may be said to form the great central mass of the archipelago. The seas surrounding it are called by various names. On the west and north, it is washed by the China Sea. On the east it is separated from Celebes by the Strait of Macassar, and from Java on the south by the Java Sea.

The general character of the shores is that of mangrove wastes or low level plains, covered with dense forests and subject to inundation. Little is known of the central part of the island, but it is believed to contain immense plains of great fertility. The highest mountain in the interior attains an elevation of fourteen thousand feet; from a lake at the foot of this mountain issue several rivers. The river mouths are nearly all choked with sand bars, making them quite inaccessible from without for vessels of even moderate size.

The wet season begins in September, and ends in April. During this time great quantities of rain fall, attended with much thunder and lightning. In the so-called dry season showers fall nearly every day.

There are countless forms of vegetable life in this prolific island. The cocoanut, the betel, and the sago are much prized by the natives, and of all the fruits the durian is the greatest favorite. It grows on a lofty tree somewhat resembling the elm. The fruit is about as large as a cocoanut, though slightly oval in shape. It is green in color, and is covered on the outside with short, stout spines, very strong and sharp. The rind is so tough that it never breaks with a fall. From the base to the apex fine faint lines may be traced, and here, with a sharp knife, the fruit may be divided. The five cells are of a satiny white color, are oval in shape, and are filled with a mass of creamy pulp, in which are embedded two or three seeds about the size of chestnuts. This pulp is the edible part, and its consistence and flavor are simply indescribable. "It is neither acid, nor sweet, nor juicy; yet one feels the want of none of these qualities, for it is perfect as it is. In fact, to eat durians is a new sensation worth a voyage to the East to experience."

Borneo and Sumatra are both inhabited by the orang-outang, and this immense ape is believed to be confined to these two large islands. It is a very strong and powerful creature, and its arms or front legs are so long, that when it is standing nearly erect they rest upon the ground. Its height is about four feet, and its outstretched arms measure from seven feet two inches to seven feet eight inches. It lives in the forests, and travels in the tops of the trees, seldom descending to the ground. It walks deliberately along a large limb, selecting one whose branches intermingle with those of an adjoining tree. When it reaches these, it grasps them with both hands and seems to try their strength, after which it swings itself lightly across to the large limb and proceeds as before. It never seems to hurry; yet a man in the forest below has to run to keep up with it. When night comes, the animal selects a place to sleep, not more than fifty feet from the ground, breaks large branches from the trees, lays them crisscross, and thus forms a bed. It seldom sleeps in the same place more than two nights in succession.

The orang is not an early riser, never leaving its bed until the sun has dried the dew on the leaves. It feeds through the middle of the day, and lives almost altogether upon fruit, only occasionally eating buds, leaves, and young shoots. Its preference is for unripe fruits, some of which are very sour and others intensely bitter. It always wastes much more than it eats.

The population of Borneo is composed of Chinese, Europeans, Malays, and Dyaks, who are the aborigines. The title rajah is sometimes conferred by the government and often assumed by a landowner. The natives are closely allied to the Malays, and more remotely to the Siamese, the Chinese, and other Mongolian races. They have a reddish brown or yellowish brown skin, straight black hair, a small nose, and high cheek bones.

Their houses are all raised on posts, and are from two to three hundred feet long by forty or fifty wide. The floors are made of strips split from large bamboos, so that each may be nearly flat and about three inches wide. These make an excellent floor.

The bamboo is put to innumerable uses. The Dyak

A DYAK OF BORNEO.

makes baskets, hen coops, fish nets, and bird cages of it, and uses it to assist him in climbing trees. Thin, long bamboos are used as vessels for carrying water into the houses. Cooking utensils are made of it, and rice and vegetables may be boiled in them to perfection. Many other uses might be mentioned, but a sufficient number has been enumerated to show how valuable the bamboo is, especially to a race who have not the means of utilizing the wood and iron common to more civilized races.

CHAPTER XXXVI.

SUMATRA AND JAVA.

SUMATRA lies directly under the equator. It is separated from the Malayan peninsula on the east by the Strait of Malacca, and on the southeast from Java by the Strait of Sunda. The east side of the island is an immense plain, nearly as level as the sea. On the west coast are three or four separate chains of mountains running parallel with the shore. There are about twenty peaks that rise to a height of eight thousand feet.

The streams on the west coast are numerous, but are little more than mountain torrents. On the east side are several large rivers, forming extensive deltas at their mouths.

The animals of Sumatra resemble those of Borneo. The only antelope known in the archipelago is the wild buck of Sumatra.

The chief city is Palembang, built on a fine curve in a river of the same name. It is said that the natives are true Malays, never building a house on dry land if they can find water to set it in, and never going anywhere on foot if they can reach a place in a boat. Consequently the stream is much narrowed by the houses

A YOUNG ANTELOPE, SUMATRA.

built on piles on both of its banks, and by a row of houses even beyond these, built on bamboo rafts and moored to the shore by rattan cables.

About three miles out of town is a hill which is held sacred by the natives. Its summit is shaded by fine fruit trees inhabited by a colony of squirrels, which have become quite tame. They have somewhat the movements of mice, advancing a few feet, then suddenly pausing and gazing intently with their large black eyes before advancing again. The Dyaks, by their kindness, often obtain the confidence of wild animals.

A GIRL OF SUMATRA.

Where the Malay villages are not built near a stream they are somewhat peculiar and very picturesque. A space of a few acres is surrounded by a fence, and the houses are built within it with no reference to regularity. They are raised upon posts about six feet from the ground, some being built of planks and others of bamboo. They are totally unfurnished inside, the floor being covered with mats upon which the inmates sit or lie. The appearance of a village is very neat, the ground being swept before the principal houses.

During the wet season the people live exclusively

upon rice, which is cooked dry and eaten with salt and red peppers.

Java is the chief seat of Dutch power in the East. It is an extremely mountainous country, being traversed throughout its whole length by two chains, forming ramifications sloping gently down to the sea. Both chains are thickly set with volcanoes, active and extinct, rising to a height of from six thousand to twelve thousand feet.

The animals are not like those of Borneo and Sumatra. Neither the elephant nor tapir are found here, but in the west part the one-horned rhinoceros is not uncommon. In some districts the royal tiger, the panther, and the tiger cat keep the people in constant terror.

Java possesses exceeding fertility, and an unrivaled vegetation covers the ground. Laurels, chestnuts, oaks, magnolias, and myrtles are common. The coasts are fringed with cocoanut trees, and vast rice fields are found farther inland. Coffee is extensively cultivated and yields a large harvest.

The mode of government is unique and interesting. The series of native rulers is still retained, from the princes called regents down to the village chiefs. With each regent is placed a Dutch president, who is looked upon as an elder brother, and whose orders take the form of recommendations, which are, however, implicitly obeyed. Along with each president is placed an inspector, who, at stated times, visits every district, hears complaints against the native chiefs, and looks after the government plantations.

The religion of the Javanese is Mohammedanism. Until recent years, the Colonial Government discouraged all efforts directed toward the conversion of the people to Christianity. The Mohammedan creed was regarded as better adapted for supplying their religious

DRYING COFFEE, JAVA.

needs. Of late years, however, a more liberal policy has prevailed.

Batavia is the capital of Java, and, when the prosperity of the Dutch East India Company was at its height, it was appropriately styled the " Queen of the East." It was the center and headquarters of the company, and it was also the emporium through which the whole commerce of the East passed to and from Europe. The Dutch possessions of Ceylon, the Cape of Good Hope, and the Moluccas depended for their supplies upon Java. But since the foundation of the town, the seashore has silted up to such an extent that the original harbor of Batavia has been abandoned and a new port constructed at a point six miles to the east. The harbor works at Tanjon Priok, as the present port of Batavia is called, and the railway which connects the town of Batavia and port, are among the many improvements begun since 1875. Ocean steamers of four thousand and five thousand tons' burden can now be moored at these wharfs, and there is a convenient and constant service of trains between the port and the town.

Batavia may be divided into three parts. First, there is the business quarter, the oldest, where the houses are tall and are built with balconies and verandas, and where the streets are narrow; second, the Chinese quarter in the center of the town, containing the bulk of the population, closely packed in their green dwellings; and third, the Dutch town, where the officials, the military, and the merchants reside. The town is divided by a stream and intersected by numerous canals. A railway runs from one end of the place to the other and the tramway runs from the town gate on the north to the statue of Meester Cornelis on the south. Batavia has a population of 112,000, Surakarta 102,000, and Surabaya nearly 150,000.

The Javanese are natural artists, and nowhere is this inborn perception more clearly manifested than in the color and form of their dress. They wear light cotton and silken cloths admirably adapted to the climate. Both men and women alike wear the "sarong," a long decorated cloth, wound around the lower limbs and fastened at the waist. Over this the men wear a short open jacket, and the women a long cloak, fastened at the waist by a silver pin. A long scarf is flung gracefully over the right shoulder. It is used by the mothers to carry their babes, and as a belt by the men when engaged in active work. On their heads the men wear a square cloth which resembles a turban, over which is worn a large straw hat for protection against the sun. The women wear nothing, but occasionally carry a bamboo umbrella for a similar protection.

A JAVANESE FRUIT GIRL.

The better class of natives use European furniture, but the poorer class have none except a bed and a chest for clothes, both made of bamboo. The staple diet is rice and dried fish, with vegetables and fruit. The cooking arrangements are very simple, nearly everything being cooked in a frying pan.

Rice culture is a prominent pursuit of the Javanese. The land of Java is naturally divided into two classes: that capable of being inundated by streams, called

"sawah," and the remainder, called "gaga." On the latter the mountain rice and Indian corn are grown. On the former rice is grown in terraces, a perfectly natural and perpetual supply of water being gained from the high mountains. The small fields are worked with a hoe, and the large ones with a plow, and then inundated. After ten or fifteen days they are hoed or harrowed again, and finally small trenches are cut for the water to flow from one terrace to another. When the earth is a mass of liquid mud, the young plants, sown in beds a month before, are transplanted carefully into this soft mud. Inundation is necessary until the rice is nearly ripe. It is reaped with a short knife, by means of which the reaper cuts off each separate head with a few inches of stem. The ears are threshed in the hollow trunk of a tree, being stamped with a heavy piece of wood having a broad end. The men do the plowing, harrowing, and weeding, the women, the planting, reaping, and threshing.

The Javanese are particularly skillful in the making of mats, of which there are many kinds. A light sort of covering for the floor is made from the leaves of the wild pineapple. A stronger kind is made from the bark of a species of palm, and is used to cover walls and ceilings. Mattings are also made from canes imported from Sumatra.

The carpenters are very clever, and easily imitate European designs handed to them. In spite of this aptitude for higher industries, however, the present commercial system compels the mass of the people to remain mere peasants.

CHAPTER XXXVII.

TIMOR AND NEW GUINEA.

The island of Timor is about three hundred miles long by forty broad. It possesses no active volcanoes with the exception of Timor Peak near the center of the island.

Besides the natives, it is inhabited by Malays, Chinese, and Dutch. The natives are tall, of a dusky brown color, with large features, aquiline noses, and frizzly hair. Their villages consist of curious little houses not to be seen elsewhere. They are oval in form, the walls being made of sticks about four feet long driven into the ground close together. From these rises a high conical roof thatched with grass. The door, three feet high, is the only opening.

One of the chief products of Timor is sandalwood, which grows on the mountains. It is of a fine yellow color and possesses a fragrance which is delightful and wonderfully permanent. It is shipped chiefly to China, where it is burnt in the temples and the houses of the rich. Beeswax, a still more important and valuable product, is formed by the wild bees, which build huge honeycombs, suspended in the open air, from the large branches of trees, seventy or more feet from the ground. They are of a semicircular form and often three or four feet in diameter.

New Guinea, or Papua, lies north of Australia, between the Asiatic seas on the west and the Pacific Ocean

A NEW GUINEA COUNCIL HOUSE.

on the east. Its greatest length is fifteen hundred miles, and the equator passes just a little north of its most northern point, called Cape of Good Hope. This vast island is known chiefly from the reports of navigators. Its interior has never been thoroughly explored by intelligent travelers. The western half of the island belongs to the Dutch, the southeastern portion to the English, and the northeastern portion to the Germans.

The chief town is Dori, about one hundred miles south of the Cape of Good Hope. It has a good harbor, at one extremity of which is an elevated point jutting out into the water and forming, in connection with several small islands, a sheltered anchorage. The houses all stand in the water and present an odd appearance. They are very low, and the roofs look like inverted boats. They are reached by means of rude bridges. The houses, bridges, and platforms are all supported by small sticks placed with no reference to regularity and looking as if they would fall down. The floors are also formed of sticks equally irregular, and with such large spaces between, that one unaccustomed to the performance walks across the floor with difficulty. The walls are made of bits of boards, pieces of old mats, palm leaves, or anything else the people can pick up that will answer the purpose. Under the eaves of many of the houses hang human skulls, the triumphant relics of their battles with the fierce tribes of the interior, who often sally forth to fight with them. Near the center of the village stands a large boat-shaped council house, supported by larger sticks than the ordinary houses.

PORT MORESBY, NEW GUINEA.

The natives are of a deep brown color, and many of them are tall and well proportioned. Their lips are extremely thick and their noses very wide, often being curved downward by the weight of the ornaments attached to them. But their distinguishing characteristic is a great mass of frizzly hair, which stands out from their heads in every direction. They call it a mop, and are very proud of it. They keep a six-pronged bamboo comb stuck in it, with which, when they have nothing else to do, they assiduously comb the hair to keep it from getting matted.

The people of Dori are great carvers and painters. They cover the outsides of their houses with rude yet characteristic figures. The prows of their boats, which are cut out of solid blocks of wood, are ornamented with masses of open filigree work. The wooden beaters, used in tempering the clay for their pottery, their tobacco boxes, and other household articles, are tastefully and often elegantly carved. This love of art, in a people who have no idea of order, comfort, or even decency, seems strange indeed.

Their clothing consists of filthy bark, rags, or sacking. They never cut roads through the brush, but scramble over fallen trees and wade through pools of mud and water whenever they go to or from their provision grounds. They live almost wholly upon roots and vegetables, and have fish and game only as an occasional luxury.

New Guinea and the adjoining islands are the home of many varieties of birds of paradise, one of which, called the red bird of paradise, is especially beautiful. There are in all more than sixty known species of birds on the island. The most numerous is that of the parrots; and New Guinea may well be called the land of cockatoos. The mammals are few in number, and are mostly marsupials. Like Australia, New Guinea is the home of the kangaroo, of which there are two kinds, one having the peculiar habit of living in the trees.

CHAPTER XXXVIII.

THE MOLUCCAS AND CELEBES.

The Moluccas, or Spice Islands, about eight in number, lie between New Guinea and Celebes. They are very fertile, producing nutmegs, cloves, and other spices, and also sago, fine woods, and fruits. They belong to the Dutch. The natives are a mixed race, characterized by pronounced features, dark skins, and frizzly hair.

The only indigenous mammal is the bat. The opossum, deer, and pig found here were probably introduced. Of birds, the most handsome is the fruit pigeon. It feeds upon mace, and its loud booming note is heard continually. The calao is a large bird of the hornbill species. Snakes are numerous, the largest being the python, which grows to the length of thirty feet. When twelve feet long, it is capable of swallowing a dog or a child. It has been known to climb up the posts on which the houses stand, and take a comfortable position on the roof. When in such a place, a practiced hand is required to dislodge it, and the ensuing scuffle is likely to be a lively one.

AUSTRALIA AND THE ISLANDS OF THE SEA. 375

Celebes lies east of Borneo, and is crossed by the equator. It has an area of over seventy-six thousand square miles. Celebes is properly the name of the east part of the island only, the west being called Macassar. The island consists of four large peninsulas stretching to the east and south and separated by deep gulfs. The

THE CALAO, MOLUCCAS.

loftiest mountain is not more than seven thousand feet high. The largest lake is said to be in the central part of the island, but has never been visited by Europeans. The largest river is supposed to have its source in this lake, and is navigable for some distance from its mouth for vessels of considerable size.

Though very hot, the climate is tempered by the sea

breezes and is remarkably healthful. The east monsoons last from May to November and the west ones the rest of the year. The soil generally consists of a vegetable mold from ten to twenty feet thick.

The island is destitute of large carnivorous animals. Deer, antelopes, and wild hogs abound; also monkeys, moles, rats, mice, and scorpions. Pouched animals are found here, also the chameleon and flying dragon. These are kept from overrunning the country by numerous snakes, from the tiger python down to the small cobra, whose bite is deadly poison.

Dense forests clothe the mountain sides, among which are found the oak, teak, cedar, nutmeg, palm, and countless other trees. The coffee tree, sugar cane, indigo, and tobacco are cultivated, and maize and mountain rice, of which there are three varieties, are also produced.

The town of Macassar, on the southwest peninsula, is a Dutch settlement and the capital of all the Dutch possessions in the island. It is defended by Fort Rotterdam. It has admirable local regulations. All European houses must be kept whitewashed, and at four in the afternoon each person must water the road in front of his house. No refuse is thrown into the streets, but covered drains carry away all impurities into large open sewers, into which the tide is admitted at high water and then allowed to flow out, carrying all sewage into the sea.

One continuous street along the seashore constitutes the principal part of the town, and is occupied chiefly by Dutch and Chinese merchants. This street extends

AUSTRALIA AND THE ISLANDS OF THE SEA. 377

VEGETATION AND MALAY TYPES IN CELEBES.

for more than a mile and gradually merges into one containing native houses of miserable character, but built exactly in a straight line and backed by fruit trees. This part of the street is generally thronged with a native population, whose dress consists of cotton trowsers about twelve inches long and a checked scarf of gay colors worn round the waist or over the shoulders in a variety of ways.

Parallel with this street run two short ones, which form the old Dutch town and are inclosed by gates. After passing the private houses, we come, at the southern extremity, to the fort, a church, and a road at right angles to the beach, on which are built the houses of the governor and chief officials.

The people of Celebes have attained a considerable degree of civilization, and are both industrious and peaceable. They dress well, live in fairly good houses, and are making considerable progress in education. All this is largely due to the admirable form of government adopted by the Dutch, which has been styled a "paternal despotism."

CHAPTER XXXIX.

THE PHILIPPINE ISLANDS.

The Philippine Islands form an important group in the northern part of the Malay Archipelago. They belong to Spain, and, next to Cuba, form its most important colonial possession. There are over four hundred islands in the group, the two largest being Luzon and Mindanao.

The coasts of the larger islands are extremely rugged. Their grand mountain ranges are clothed to their summits with a gigantic, ever-teeming vegetation, and the plains between are exceedingly rich in their tropical fertility.

Among plants cultivated for use are the palms, hemp, coffee tree, indigo, tobacco, cloves, nutmeg, and red and black pepper vines. Rice, maize, wheat, yams, sweet potatoes, and many kinds of fruits are also raised.

The buffalo is used in tilling the fields and as a beast of burden. The woods are full of pelicans, pigeons, herons, eagles, wild ducks, and quails. The jungles swarm with humming birds and parrots. The lakes and rivers are alive with fish, crocodiles, and alligators. The most dreaded of the snakes is the boa constrictor.

The total population numbers about seven millions, of whom one million belong to the Papuan negro race and independent Indian tribes; more than three and a half millions are Malay Indians; fifty-five thousand are Chinese, and the rest are Europeans and mixed races.

Manila, the capital of the group, is situated on Luzon Island, near the mouth of a river and on a bay of the same name. The city proper forms the segment of a circle between the river and the sea, and its suburbs extend over numerous islets formed by the river and its branches, and are easily reached in all parts by boats.

The population of the city, which numbers about one hundred and fifty-four thousand, consists of Spaniards, Creoles, Malay Indians, Mestizos, and Chinese.

MESTIZO GIRLS, MANILA.

The city is divided into two sections, the military and the mercantile, the latter being the suburb. The military part is surrounded by high walls and is bounded on one side by the sea and on the other by an extensive plain, where the troops are drilled, and where, in the evening, the Creoles go in their carriages to exhibit their elegant costumes and to inhale the sea air. This public promenade has been styled the "Champs-Elysées" of the Malay Archipelago.

A bridge connecting the two parts of the city spans the river. The military town is inhabited principally by Spaniards, and its aspect is rather dull and monotonous. All the streets are perfectly straight, and are bordered by wide granite footpaths.

The houses, large and spacious, are built in a particular manner, so as to withstand the shock of earthquakes. They have but one story above the ground floor. The upper part is occupied by the family and is surrounded by a gallery, opened or shut by wide sliding panels, the panes of which are mother-of-pearl. This permits the light to enter and excludes the heat.

Numerous canals intersect the suburb where live the rich merchants,— Spanish, English, Indian, and Chinese. The newest and most elegant houses are to be found along the banks of the river. They are simple in their exterior, but contain the most costly inventions of English and Indian luxury. Precious ware from China and Japan, gold, silver, and rich silks greet the eye of the guest on entering one of these habitations. Each house has a landing-place from the river, and small bamboo palaces serve as bathhouses, to which the residents resort several times in the course of the day to relieve the fatigue caused by the intense heat.

The people of the interior seem to be a mixed race, resulting from the union of the aborigines with Chinese, Japanese, and Malays. They are tall, with long hair

VOLCANO OF MAYON, PHILIPPINE ISLANDS.

and thin beard. They have a brasslike color, inclining to European whiteness, with vivacious eyes, large nose, and high, prominent cheek bones.

They are passionately fond of music and dancing. They are of frugal habits, requiring nothing for their sustenance except water, rice, and salt fish. They venerate the aged and are very hospitably inclined. A stranger appearing at mealtime before an Indian hut is invited, even urged, to take a place at the humble board and partake of the family cheer.

In the year 1896 trouble broke out in the Philippine Islands, and Spanish troops were immediately sent to quell the disturbance and reduce the people to subjection. As they were fighting for what they deemed were their rights, they were not easily conquered, and in the spring of 1897 large numbers of soldiers were withdrawn from Cuba and sent to coöperate with the Spanish troops in the Philippines. The war has continued, with varying successes, and with the usual Spanish barbarities.

CHAPTER XL.

ISLAND GROUPS OF OCEANICA.

THE Caroline Islands form one of the great archipelagoes of Oceanica, and lie between the Philippines, the Marshall Islands, and New Guinea, extending from three to twelve degrees north latitude. Including the Pelew Islands, which, from the character of their in-

HOGOLEN ISLANDERS IN CANOE.

habitants and the history of their discovery, form part of the archipelago, they extend over a distance of two thousand miles from west to east. They are divided into numerous groups. All of the Carolines except three are atolls. The climate is mild and agreeable in spite of the hurricanes which now and then sweep over the islands.

The greater part of the inhabitants of the Carolines belong to the Malay race. They are excellent seamen, and live almost wholly upon the produce of their fishing. The natives of the Hogolen Islands, one of the groups, are a cruel and treacherous race, often attacking vessels which approach their shores. They arm themselves with knives, brass-hilted cutlasses, spears, and slings, using the latter weapon with great dexterity and murderous effect.

On the Bornabi group are the ruins of a fortified town, not built by the aborigines, but by some civilized people. The stones in the walls are eight or ten feet in length and must have been carried hither from some other land, as no rock of this kind exists in the neighboring islands. It is believed they were erected by Spanish pirates several centuries ago, this group being a stronghold of these lawless rovers.

In some of the islands the houses erected are of a superior order, when compared with the dwellings of savages in general. The erection of a house is looked upon as an honorable employment, and the future occupant is assisted by all his friends and their dependents. The roof has a very steep pitch, and in its center is supported by tall posts. It is thatched with palm leaves, which overhang the walls about a foot at the eaves. The space between the uprights is filled up with small canes and bamboos fastened together with twine. The twine is of different colors, and is so woven as to present figures on the outside walls. The floor is laid of bamboo, a space four or five feet square being left in the center for a fire, the smoke from which finds its way out through crevices in the roof and walls.

The largest houses seldom exceed forty feet by twenty, and the lower classes of people are contented with those ten feet by six, or even smaller. But the war-canoe houses, which serve the purpose of council rooms and halls for feasting, are often a hundred feet in length by forty wide. The canoes are suspended at the sides of the house when not in use.

The principal mechanical tool is the hatchet, made of a hard white stone, broken to a shape resembling our hatchets, and sharpened to a fairly good edge on rough rocks. For lighter work sea shells are used. Dogfish skin is used for polishing. It is surprising how dexterous the natives become, and what excellent work they often perform, with these simple tools.

Vines are often used for cordage. The fibers of the plantain and banana tree are very fine and soft, and are used in the manufacture of sashes. They are drawn from the pith of the tree, and are woven into a texture which much resembles silk. The mats for sails, clothing, and beds are braided by the women. The sails are woven of split rushes. The mat worn about the body is made of the tuft of leaves growing at the top of the cocoa palm. After the leaves are bleached, they are strung together. The mats upon which they sleep are made of rushes. The natives have a great love of music and a fairly accurate ear.

There are only two musical instruments in use,— a drum and a pipe, or sort of fife. The drum is made by stretching a piece of fishskin over a hollow log. The fife has three finger holes, and is blown by the nostrils instead of the mouth of the player. For war trumpets they use shells or conchs.

Next to singing, the favorite amusement of the natives is dancing. Night dances are held in the canoe houses,

NATIVE SWORD AND DRUMS.

with no light other than the moon and stars shining in at the great open door. They stand up in rows, and their dancing is merely stamping in time to the singing, and the precision with which they do this is quite astonishing.

The religion of the people is extremely singular, since it seems to be a worship of mind or life independent of the body. They have no temples, altars, offerings, or sacrifices, but worship a world of spirits. Aside from the general and universal worship of the ancestors of the chiefs, each family worships its own ancestors. The profession of the priests is hereditary. Their support is drawn chiefly from presents; for, though they own land, their possessions are small. They are held in great respect by the people, and are the confidants and advisors of the chiefs.

Spain claims several of the groups of the Caroline Islands as dependencies of the Philippines, but she has no settlements on them and no representative of her authority. Among these are the Ladrones, or Marianne Islands, fifteen in number; but five only are inhabited. They are of volcanic origin, very fertile, and densely wooded. The government is a sort of oligarchy, where the power is so subdivided that some chief can take note of every man's actions; and all offenses, whether great or small, are promptly punished as soon as committed.

The Marshall Islands are included in the Mulgrave Archipelago in the Pacific Ocean. They are low and of coral formation. It is in the Marshall Group that the natives have made the greatest progress in civilization. This is due to the fact that they are directly in the track of vessels. They have a population of fifteen thousand, and are under German protection.

Next to the Marshall Group the Gilbert Islands are of most importance. There are fifteen of them, and the highest land in any one does not exceed twenty feet.

The soil, composed of coral sand and vegetable mold, is only a few inches deep. The natives cultivate the cocoanut and the pandanus, which are the chief articles of food. They give especial care to a species of the taro. The breadfruit tree grows on the north islands. The inhabitants resemble the Malays, and the population of the entire group is about thirty-six thousand.

The Solomon Islands are in the Pacific Ocean, between latitude five degrees and twelve degrees south, and about five hundred miles east of New Guinea. They are of volcanic origin, and there is one active volcano. The surface is elevated, well wooded, and fertile. The shores are steep, with fringing reefs. They were first discovered by a Spaniard, who gave them the name of the Islands of Solomon in order that his countrymen, supposing them to be the islands from which King Solomon procured his gold, might be induced to colonize them.

The natives of the Solomon Islands are divided into two distinct classes: those who live on the coast, and those who inhabit the interior. Hostilities nearly always exist between them, and it not unfrequently happens that the language of the one is unintelligible to the other, showing that feuds are of many years standing.

The houses of the chiefs and principal men are elaborate, and often have a staging in front on a level with the lower edge of the aperture that serves as an entrance. This staging is protected by an overhanging roof, and on it the inmates are wont to sit and lie about

NATIVE OF THE SOLOMON ISLANDS.

during the afternoon and evening. In the best houses spaces are partitioned off for sleeping rooms and there are raised stages for mats.

The tambu houses are sacred buildings, and have many and varied uses. Women are not allowed to

A TAMBU HOUSE, SOLOMON ISLANDS.

enter them. But the front of them is a common place of resort for the men, especially during the afternoon, and they are at liberty to sleep in the building itself at night.

Wild fruits and nuts occur throughout all the islands in large quantities, and are much used as food by the natives. The flesh of the large monitor lizard is much prized, and even the crocodile is not rejected. The natives are also addicted to cannibalism.

All the people — men, women, and children — are inordinately fond of smoking tobacco. The weed has in fact established itself between trader and native as the principal currency. The practice of chewing the betel nut is also prevalent throughout the group, and is practiced by both sexes.

The Solomon Island songs, though often monotonous, are in keeping with the wild character of the islanders. The Pandean pipe is the musical instrument in common use among them, and the Jew's harp of foreign manufacture is also much in demand.

The Fiji Islands form a group in the South Pacific between 15° and 19° south latitude, and 177° east and 178° west longitude. They comprise nearly two hundred islands, of which about eighty-one are inhabited. Two of the islands only are of large size.

These islands are of volcanic origin; all are mountainous, and some of the peaks rise to the height of several thousand feet. They are covered with a luxuriant vegetation to their very summits.

The fruits include breadfruit, of which there are nine varieties, cocoa, shaddocks, and the papaw apple. The yam, of which there are six sorts, is the chief food of the natives. Sugar and tobacco are cultivated.

The savages number over one hundred thousand. They have been decreasing in the last fifty years. Formerly cannibalism was frightfully common.

The native Fijians are above the average height of

Europeans, the men often measuring six feet. They are not corpulent, but large, muscular, and powerful. Nearly all of them are broad-chested and have sinewy arms, stout limbs, and short necks. The head is often covered with a large amount of long, black, frizzly hair, sometimes growing low on the forehead. They wear a thick round or pointed beard, and sometimes a mustache also. The face is oval; the nose is well shaped, with full nostrils; the eyes are black and marked by a restless but penetrating gaze; and the large mouth is made conspicuous by white, handsome teeth. They vary in complexion, but the pure Fijian stands between the black and copper-colored races. He is neither dull nor stupid, and is capable both of love and hate. His loyalty is both strong and lasting, and at the same time he is noted for his undying revenge. In a social way, he is cautious and clever.

The native houses vary very much in different localities. In one district a village looks like a collection of large wicker baskets, in another like a cluster of rustic arbors, and in another like a number of large hayricks of either oblong or conical form. Some tribes introduce just enough framework to receive the covering for the walls, the inside of the house being a single room. Other tribes introduce center posts and other supports on the inside, and along one side build a gallery on which to store their property. The walls of a house are from four to ten feet high, and the roof steep and lofty. The thatch covering the roof frequently reaches to the ground, concealing the walls from sight.

The furniture of Fijian houses is very scant and

SUGAR LOAF MOUNTAIN, FIJI ISLANDS.

simple. Where the house is high, an elevated place along one end serves as a divan by day and a bed by night. It is covered with a thick layer of dried grass and elastic ferns, upon which are from two to ten mats. It is also furnished with two or three wooden or bamboo pillows. Ornamental baskets, gourds, and bottles for scented oil hang on the walls. Besides these there are fans, sunshades made from the leaves of the cabbage palm, a dish made of dark wood for holding oil, and a few wooden or wicker dishes for food. Along the foot of the walls rest oblong wooden bowls with four feet, or round earthen ones with none.

The people usually have two meals a day, the principal one being in the afternoon or evening. They like their meat very fresh, and some of the smaller fishes are eaten alive as a relish. Their manner of drinking is peculiar. They throw the head backward, open the mouth wide, elevate the vessel several inches above the lips, and then pour a stream of water down the throat. To drink in this manner from a bamboo which is from two to ten feet long is no easy task. The longest bamboo holds about two gallons, and to slake one's thirst from the open end, while a native gradually raises the other, often results, for a novice at least, in a cold bath.

"Sleep and tobacco are among the leading comforts of the Fijians." Although tobacco has been known for but comparatively few years, it is universally used by men, women, and children.

Missionaries to the Fiji Islands first landed in 1835. Their numbers have never been large, but the work accomplished by them has been marvelously great. Cruel practices and degrading superstitions have been lessened, and thousands have been converted to Christianity. Marriage is sacred, the Sabbath is regarded, and hundreds of schools have been established. The language has been reduced to written form, and a grammar and dictionary have been printed.

NATIVE CANOE, FIJI ISLANDS.

In 1874 the islands were annexed to the English government. Within the last fifty years a great many white people have settled there and established themselves as planters, shopkeepers, and traders. A few of them are Americans, some are Germans, but the majority are English.

The New Hebrides are an island group in the Pacific Ocean between latitude fourteen degrees and twenty degrees south. There are five principal islands. The natives are of the Papuan race. A few of the islands are of coral formation, and nearly all of them are surrounded by coral reefs.

The four most important trees in the islands are the cocoanut, the breadfruit, the orange, and the sandalwood. There are also several varieties of palms, among them the beautiful and useful fan palm. The breadfruit tree is not unlike an ash in form, but its leaves are very large, every one spreading out like the open hand of a mighty giant. The wood of the tree is soft, easily worked, and very durable. Canoes are usually hollowed out of the trunk of this tree. The breadfruit is either round or oval, and about six inches in diameter. In appearance and consistency it bears a considerable resemblance to fine wheaten bread. It is easily cooked, and may be either boiled or roasted. The bread, when cooked, is nearly pure white, soft, delicious to the taste, and very wholesome and nourishing.

There are two crops each year. The winter one is the smaller, and is ready in July and August. The summer crop comes on in December and January. The fruit cannot be kept fresh more than a day or two after it is picked. But the natives have a way of preserving it, when the crop is very plentiful or is blown down by a hurricane. They dig pits three or four feet deep and about three in diameter, line them with cocoanut leaves, cut the fruit into three or four pieces, throw it into the pits, and cover it with leaves and earth. It then under-

FAN PALM, NEW HEBRIDES.

goes a sort of fermentation. After a while they take it out, work it, and replace it. When thus prepared, it will keep for several months.

When first discovered, these islands were governed by numerous chiefs and under chiefs. In heathen times there was no union, and no concerted action. In some of the eastern islands the missionaries, assisted by an English lawyer, prepared a civil constitution for the natives. But the result was disappointing. These good men very soon concluded that the best policy was to let the framework of society remain as it was.

The Loyalty Islands are five in number, two large and three small ones. Lifu is the most northern and the largest. Mari, discovered in 1841, is densely settled by a wild race of small stature. This island has been visited by whalers and traders for many years, and the natives understand enough of the English language to make themselves understood in bartering transactions. The Mari natives have taken to civilization better than most of the races of the western isles in the south Pacific. They wear European clothing, if they can afford it, and the chiefs occasionally build good houses, and even manage to buy an occasional whale boat of fair size.

Although traders had for many years carried on their business of bartering with the aborigines of New Caledonia, this island was but little known until the French took possession of it in 1854. It is more than seven hundred miles from Queensland, and six hundred from

HOUSE IN NEW CALEDONIA.

the Fiji Islands. It is an elongated tract of mountainous land, rising in many places to the height of three thousand feet. It has a length of about two hundred miles, and an average breadth of thirty. The hills of New Caledonia are not covered with profuse vegetation, but they are rich in minerals,— how rich remains yet to be ascertained. The range skirting the eastern shore supplies nickel ore. The nickel region extends for about sixty miles, and nearly all the white inhabitants have been, or are, in some way interested in this metal. Noumea is the capital. The French army and navy is well represented, for this is a French penal station. The number of prisoners is about three thousand.

The marked feature of a native village is the conically shaped house of the chief. It is from thirty to fifty feet high and has an addition of ten or twelve feet of ornamentation, which usually consists of a vertical pole to which large sea shells are fastened at regular intervals. The middle post or axis which supports this structure is the straight stem of a pine tree. The roof is covered with a thatch of fine grass, and is perfectly water tight. The dwelling part of the house is cylindrical in form, with a height of about nine feet.

The men, in common with other savages, are exceedingly lazy. They loiter about in the bush or on the shore, and their slings and spears afford them some amusement. The women are busy enough. They collect the shellfish, fetch wood and water, and attend to the plantation. The only recognized meal of the day is prepared toward sunset. The meal is cooked in an open space, inclosed by a wall of dried cocoanut-palm leaves, arranged so as to form a sheltering screen. There are two or three large ovens inside this inclosure, and by this method of coöperation the one meal of the whole community can be cooked and distributed at the same time.

The natives of New Caledonia belong to the Papuan race. The men are remarkably muscular and, so far as the term applies to dark-colored races, handsome. The

A NEW CALEDONIA FISHERMAN.

women, who perform the drudgery, age rapidly, and their wrinkled foreheads and oftentimes closely shaven heads render them the reverse of beautiful.

CHAPTER XLI.

SAMOAN, FRIENDLY, AND SOCIETY ISLANDS.

In the Pacific Ocean, fourteen degrees south latitude, is a group of thirteen islands of volcanic origin, called the Samoan, or Navigator Islands. Only four of these are of any importance. The most easterly is called Manua, and rises to the height of twenty-five hundred feet. The largest island is named Savaii, and its highest point is four thousand feet above the sea.

The climate is variable, though warm. In the winter heavy rains and strong winds prevail. The soil is very fertile, yielding twenty kinds of breadfruit, bananas, sugar cane, coffee, sweet potatoes, pineapples, yams, and tobacco. Banyan trees, tree ferns, several varieties of palms, and orange trees grow in abundance. Rattans, ninety feet in length, bamboos, and wild nutmeg trees are common.

In 1875, the United States secured a naval coaling station at Apia, on the Island of Upolu, and four years later England, Germany, and the United States agreed to respect each other's rights in Samoa. Malietoa, a man of excellent character, was proclaimed king, and two others, vice-kings. Malietoa, resisting false claims, was deposed and one of the vice-kings declared his successor. The other fought against him, and in the fray several Germans were killed, which gave Germany a pretext of declaring war. Finally, a conference of the Powers at Berlin reinstated Malietoa as king, and

HOUSE OF THE KING, SAMOA.

a strict neutrality of the foreign powers was guaranteed.

Upolu is a very beautiful island. Its chief city, Apia, has a fine harbor, formed by a coral reef running nearly the entire distance across the bay. The entrance is narrow, and another reef divides the harbor into two parts. From the sea, the appearance of Apia is tropical and fascinating in the extreme. The cocoa palms, the picturesque mountains, and the charming bay form a scene which an artist may well admire. The village is almost hidden by dense groves of cocoa palms and breadfruit trees. On the extreme left the palm groves are dotted with foreign residences. The middle ground is occupied by small white cottages and native houses, savage and civilized life being strangely blended together. The French missionary church occupies a central position among these.

The beach road is the chief thoroughfare in Apia. Not far from the center of the town a small stream of water crosses the road, and is spanned by a bridge. Here most of the natives of Apia do their washing. Every day men, women, and children may be seen standing or sitting in the water, laughing and washing away with great energy. The women usually sit in the water, with a flat stone before them, and on this they beat the clothes until they think them clean. Then they rinse them, after which the clothes are wrung out and spread in the sun to dry.

The native house of Apia has a roof resembling a ship's hull, keel uppermost. Its shape is usually oval, and it is thatched with grass and leaves. There are plenty of mats on the floor, a hole in the ground for lighting a fire, a kava bowl hanging on the wall, several bamboo pillows, an old chest or two, and perhaps a musket.

Kava is the popular beverage of the Samoans. It is prepared from the root of a shrub, a species of pepper, which grows to the height of five or six feet. In order to prepare the drink, the root is cleansed and cut into small pieces. These are then distributed among young men and women who have perfect teeth, and who chew the pieces until they are reduced to minute particles. The pulpy masses, mouthful after mouthful, are then thrown into a large wooden bowl. Water is poured on, and the mass is worked about with the hand until the strength and flavor of the kava is thoroughly extracted. Kava has medicinal properties, and when drunk in excess produces an effect similar to that brought about by the use of opium.

The Samoans are true Polynesians, of the lightest color of the race. They are of fine physique, and, both in appearance and manner, are prepossessing. In mental and social disposition they hold the highest position in the Pacific. Though they have had a great deal of war among themselves, they do not love fighting for its own sake. In all their wars they respect the lives of non-combatants, such as infirm persons, children, and women. They have never been given to infanticide or human sacrifice. They are never treacherous. They always treat their women with respect, and their children with extravagant affection.

In spite of missionary teaching, the men still tattoo

SAMOAN PRINCESSES.

their bodies from the hips down to the knees. A tattooer's profession is very lucrative. His instruments resemble combs, and are made of human bone of different sizes. The operation takes from two to three months, during which time the patient remains in some retired place. All this time the relatives of the young person bring mats, money, and food, and if the quantity does not suit the tattooer, he "goes on a strike," refusing to proceed until sufficient liberality is displayed. Of course the requisite gifts are sure to be brought, for no Samoan could endure going half tattooed.

The Samoans, both in person and domestic life, are scrupulously clean, bathing two or three times a day, and preferring the water of the rivers to that of the sea. The young women are fine in form, if not in feature, although some of them would be considered beautiful in any country. A young woman is often selected as Queen of the Village, and while she holds that position everybody must obey her commands. The Samoan language is soft and liquid in pronunciation, and has rightly been styled the "Italian of the Pacific." It is difficult to learn, as one of its accents misplaced changes the whole meaning of the word.

These Pacific islands are subject to violent hurricanes. On March 15, 1889, there were warships of the United States, Germany, and England riding at anchor in the harbor of Apia, when suddenly a terrific storm burst upon them, causing them to drag their anchors, hurling some of them upon each other, and dashing others upon the beach. Courageous natives rescued many of the struggling sailors, but many were drowned.

AUSTRALIA AND THE ISLANDS OF THE SEA.   409

HARBOR OF PANGO-PANGO, SAMOA.

The English man-of-war, *Calliope*, succeeded in escaping to sea, in the midst of the fearful commotion, and, as she passed the United States warship *Trenton*, our manly tars, forgetful of their own imminent peril, gave lusty cheers, to which the Englishmen responded. It was a grand thing to do; facing death and yet cheering the sailors of another nation who were escaping from it. The *Trenton* finally settled in shoal water, and all but one of the four hundred and five souls on board escaped death as by a miracle.

Robert Louis Stevenson, the noted English writer, went to Samoa on account of his health, and lived there for several years, becoming greatly endeared to the natives. He died near Apia in 1894, and was buried high upon the side of one of the mountains which in life he had loved so well.

The Friendly Islands, sometimes styled the Tonga Group, comprise about thirty-two larger islands and a hundred and fifty smaller ones. The great majority are of coral formation, but some of them are volcanic in their origin. The principal island of the group is Sacred Tonga, which contains about seventy-five hundred inhabitants out of a population of twenty-five thousand in the entire group. These islands were discovered by Tasman in the seventeenth century, but the name Friendly was given to them by Captain Cook.

The climate is very mild, but humid. Earthquakes and hurricanes are common, though the former are not destructive. Yams, sweet potatoes, bananas, cocoanuts, breadfruit, sugar cane, and the hog-plum are the

A LANE IN SAMOA.

principal products. The various islands were formerly governed by independent chiefs, but nearly all of them are now under the rule of one chief or king.

On the island of Tofua is an active volcano, situated near the middle of a large inland basin. For a great distance around this point the surface of the earth is torn to pieces by the eruptions which have taken place. But few people live upon this island. They are always warned of an approaching eruption by a great rumbling noise and by the trembling of the earth.

In some of the other islands occasional volcanic force is displayed. Three quarters of a mile northeast of Tofua is a lofty conical island with a volcano sometimes in action. In October, 1886, an eruption occurred on another island of the group, which had a population of nearly five hundred people at the time. The inhabitants all escaped to an island thirty-five miles distant. Their own island was covered twenty feet deep with volcanic dust, and in one place a new hill two hundred feet high was formed.

The natives of the Friendly Islands greatly resemble those of the Samoan Group. They are equally light in color, and the young children are almost white. Their countenances are generally of the Asiatic cast. They are tall and well proportioned, and their muscles are finely developed. The women are remarkable for their personal beauty, and have considerable respect shown them, which varies, however, according to their rank.

Their ranks of society are king, chiefs, attendants of chiefs, the common people, and slaves. Originally, there were persons connected with the heathen priesthood who were considered superior even to the king, and to whom he was expected to do homage. The manner of investing the monarch with kingly dignity is peculiar. The chiefs of the various islands assemble, and the ceremony takes place at a kava meeting. The kava here drunk is like that of the same name prepared

NATIVE HOUSE, FRIENDLY ISLANDS.

by the Samoans. Two of the principal chiefs, called fathers, sit, the one at the king's right hand, and the other at his left. Their office is to relieve the king and to act on his account. The other chiefs sit on either side, forming a large circle, and the mass of the people occupy a place in front. Before the kava is served, the chief at the king's right hand makes a speech, in which the object of the meeting is set forth. Other chiefs, and the king also, speak in turn. When the kava is poured out for the king, the right-hand chief salutes him with the title expressive of his office.

The first attempt to introduce Christianity was made in the latter part of the eighteenth century. Now nearly all the islanders are Christians. The majority of them can speak English, and many of these have learned writing, arithmetic, and geography. The women have nearly all been taught to sew.

The Cook Islands lie between the Friendly and Society islands. They have an area of three hundred square miles and a population of eight thousand. The people are of Malay race, and many of them have become civilized through the efforts of English missionaries.

The Society Islands form an important group in the South Pacific between latitude 16° 11' and 17° 53' south. The group consists of the island of Tahiti and a great number of comparatively small islands. All the islands are mountainous. In Tahiti the loftiest summit is 7300 feet above the sea, and there are two other peaks near it, measuring nearly 7000 feet. A coral reef encircles the island at the distance of two or three miles, presenting an effectual barrier against the violence of the waves, and, on account of frequent openings in it, forming several harbors, where the sea is always tranquil and the largest vessels may ride in safety. The best of these harbors, and the only one much used, is Matavai Bay on the north. The scenery

A WOMAN OF THE FRIENDLY ISLANDS.

of all the islands is beautiful, and almost every one of the group has been described by navigators in rapturous terms, as realizing their ideas of an earthly paradise.

Papeete is the capital of Tahiti. It is a small town, consisting of several streets shaded by fine trees, the branches of which almost meet overhead. The French Government House is at Papeete, and quite outrivals the palace of the native sovereign. It is two stories in height, and entirely surrounded by a covered veranda inclosed with Venetian blinds. The French obtained possession of the island in 1845, and the defeated natives were obliged to accept the French protectorate. They are a good-humored, gay, and cheerful people, and are honest, well behaved, and obliging. Some of them have been converted to Christianity and can both read and write. They are passionately fond of music, and many of their compositions are extremely melodious.

The people have some strange customs, the strangest of which consists in giving away one of their own children occasionally and adopting that of a friend in its place. Another peculiarity is the source from which they derive their names and also change them. That of Pomare, the present native queen, arose from a former king, who was seized with a violent fit of coughing after dark: *po* signifies night, *mare*, cough, and the name has descended from generation to generation of crowned heads. When the eyes of the dying rest on any particular article of furniture or clothing, members of the family adopt it for a name and drop the one formerly held.

AUSTRALIA AND THE ISLANDS OF THE SEA.

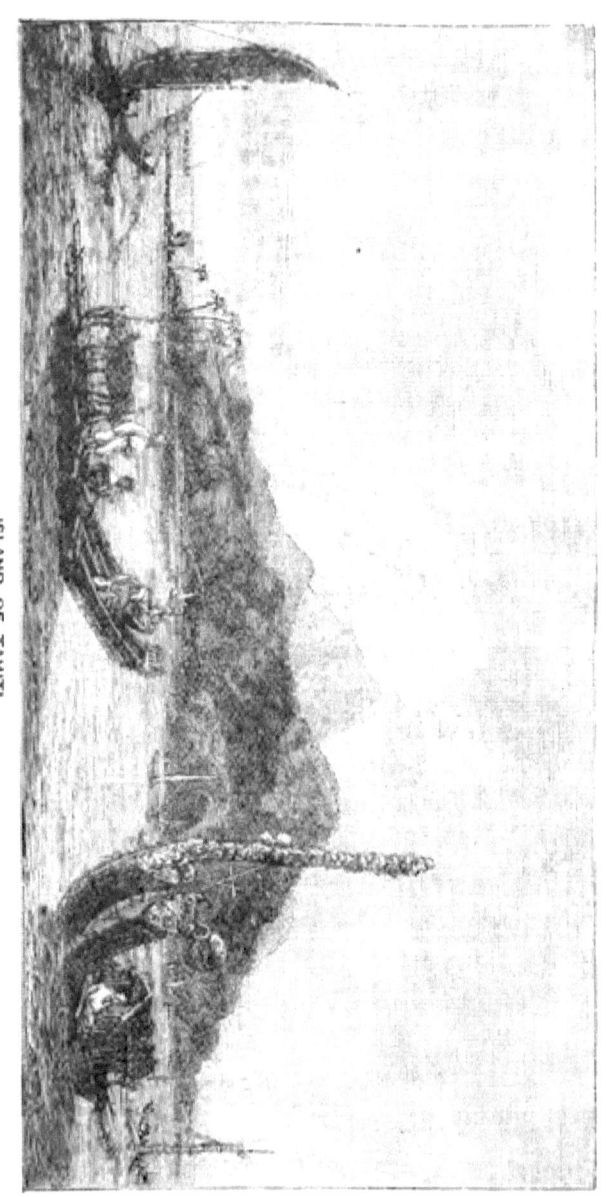

ISLAND OF TAHITI.

CHAPTER XLII.

THE HAWAIIAN ISLANDS.

When these islands in the Pacific Ocean, twenty-one hundred miles southeast from San Francisco, were discovered, in July, 1778, by Captain James Cook, he named them the Sandwich Islands, in honor of Lord Sandwich. They had been previously visited by Gaetano, an Italian navigator, in 1542. Their original name, Hawaii, is now retained. When Captain Cook first landed, he was regarded as a god. The natives had expected an old deity to return, and supposed the distinguished navigator was he. They gave him homage, and offered sacrifices to him; but in about thirteen months an altercation ensued, in consequence of the theft of a boat by the natives, and Captain Cook was killed. A monument, erected in 1877 on the island of Hawaii, the largest of the group, marks the spot where he fell. His death is regarded to this day by the natives as a stain upon their history.

The Hawaiian Group consists of eight mountainous islands with seven insignificant islets, some of which are mere rocks jutting out of the sea. Their origin is volcanic, and coral reefs abound on their shores. They lie in the North Pacific Ocean, between the parallels of latitude eighteen and twenty-two. Their area is about sixty-six hundred square miles, and the population about one hundred thousand.

The people who first came to these islands voyaged

all the way from Tahiti, more than twenty-three hundred miles to the north. The ancient canoe, which still is somewhat in use, was made from a log hollowed out, with an outrigger to keep it steady. Sometimes double canoes, carrying sixty men, were built, which sailed very swiftly, rigged with a triangular sail and

NATIVE CANOES, HAWAIIAN ISLANDS.

also propelled by paddles. The people fought with clubs and spears in their numerous battles among themselves, and used bows only to kill rats. They made various tools from the shell of a large clam, which cut like an ax. Their clothing, which was very scanty, was made by beating out the inner bark of trees.

Cocoanut trees, some of which are a hundred years old

and a hundred feet high, are still quite numerous and give a very tropical appearance to the landscape. The natives ascribed the origin of the cocoanut to divine power. A legend says that a young woman, daughter of one of their gods, lived in a cave. She had a lover who was god of the eels. When he was compelled to leave her, he told her to cut off his head and plant it. She did so, and from it sprouted a tree, the parent of all the cocoanut trees in the world; on each nut are invariably found the two eyes and the mouth of the young man.

The taro root was and is the principal food of the natives. It was imported from the South Pacific, and from it, when prepared by pounding and fermentation, *poi* is made and many nutritious dishes. The natives eat *poi* with their fingers. The common habitation of the natives was a grass house, made of a very stout, fibrous plant, and having no opening except a low door. They kept their food in calabashes and, with a few mats to sit and sleep upon, enjoyed life without much necessity for work. A few of these grass houses may be seen at this day.

The first king of all the islands, named Kamehameha I., died in 1819. He had conquered all the native chiefs and reigned supreme. Kamehameha III., under the influence of the missionaries, gave the people a constitution and laws, and also divided the lands between himself, the chiefs, and the people. The language was reduced to writing, and young and old learned to read, write, and sew. Some industrial schools were also established, and a time of prosperity followed, dis-

AUSTRALIA AND THE ISLANDS OF THE SEA. 421

A COCOANUT GROVE, HAWAIIAN ISLANDS.

turbed mainly by the interference in affairs of the islands by foreign officers, whose acts were afterwards disallowed by their governments.

The monarchy continued until 1893, when the queen, Liliuokalani, was deposed by the Provisional Government, which afterwards, in 1894, was merged in the Hawaiian Republic, proclaimed July 4 of that year by President Sanford B. Dole, its first chief magistrate. There have been some attempts to restore the ex-queen since that time, but these insurrections have been overcome without much bloodshed. The president, his council, and other officials are mostly Americans, with some natives of prominence. The government has been administered with a firm hand and with success. There is a prevailing sentiment among the people that annexation to the United States will give Hawaii future peace and prosperity. On the 16th of June, 1897, a treaty annexing Hawaii to the United States was signed by Secretary of State, John Sherman. If ratified by the Senate, this country will for the first time have extended its boundaries beyond the sea. It is expected that an oceanic cable will soon be laid, which will connect Hawaii, not only with the United States, but also with Australia and other countries.

Honolulu, on Oahu, is the chief city and capital of the islands. Oahu is not the largest island, although its harbor has made it the most important. Hawaii, the most southern island, is the largest, being about the size of the state of Connecticut. Its population, however, is scattered, and it has no good harbors where ships may approach the wharves. People who land on

A GRASS HUT, HAWAIIAN ISLANDS.

any island except at Honolulu must go ashore in boats, sometimes through openings in the coral reefs; and in some places they are hoisted, in a sort of cage, to the top of a cliff by a crane, which swings them from the boat beneath to a platform on the shore.

Of the present population on these islands, about twenty-five thousand are Japanese, most of whom have come to work on the sugar plantations; fifteen thousand Chinese, who carry on industrial and agricultural pursuits; eight thousand Portuguese, many of them emigrants from the Azores; a mixed population of some thousands of foreigners; between two and three thousand Americans, many of whom were born on the islands, and about thirty-four thousand natives and half-whites, being all that are left of the two hundred thousand natives who inhabited the Sandwich Islands when discovered by Captain Cook.

The native race is contented, docile, good-natured, and easy going; the men are excellent sailors, and in general appearance both men and women are large and rather fine-looking. They love music and deck themselves with flowers, which grow profusely.

They are easily influenced for good or evil. They are able to read and write, live in frame houses, imitate the foreigners in their dress, and their children are well cared for in schools. A fund of many hundred thousands of dollars was bequeathed for native education by Mrs. Bernice Panahi Bishop, the last of the kingly race, whose memory is perpetuated by the fine school buildings, and by a magnificent museum containing curios and relics of ancient Hawaii.

Let us now take a sort of tourist's view of the city of Honolulu with its twenty-three thousand inhabitants, a picturesque town of many contrasts, both in its population and its scenery. The whites live in spacious houses, generally of one or two stories, without much

NATIVE MUSICIANS, HAWAII.

architectural pretension, but surrounded by a most luxuriant vegetation. Areas are filled with tropical plants, imported and given away by the government to rich and poor alike. The mango, the breadfruit, the magnolia, the India palm, and the cocoanut tree abound. Rare flowers of rich variety bloom on every hand.

Everywhere one sees the Chinese or Japanese servant

in native costume, the native with flowers woven into wreaths for the hat or the neck, and native women galloping, always astride, on their rough horses, with a lasso tied to the pommels of the saddles. Foreign sailors from the men-of-war riding at anchor in the safe harbor appear in neat white uniforms. Tramway cars, with horses or mules attached, run in the principal streets. There are electric lights all over the city, telephones to the number of thirteen hundred in use, and elegant stores, with rich treasures in the windows direct from China and Japan. There is a Chinese quarter, where the original customs of the Flowery Kingdom may be seen. All the bustle and stir of an enterprising seaport appear in the lower streets and on the wharves, which mark a commerce greater than any other Pacific port except San Francisco.

One may see a fine public library; two native churches, which will seat from fifteen hundred to two thousand people; a Roman Catholic school, with five hundred native boys in attendance; an elegant Protestant church, of stone, which cost $130,000; and schoolhouses, one of which, the High School, was the most elegant private house in the city, built by a princess, but is now occupied by pupils of the higher grades; the Lulani palace, and the government building. There is every indication of American and European thrift and enterprise. It is a rare type of New England civilization in a variegated setting of tropical scenery and dark-skinned races. As the steamers come in from the American coast, brown native boys dive for nickels; and as the steamers go out, the passengers are loaded with gar-

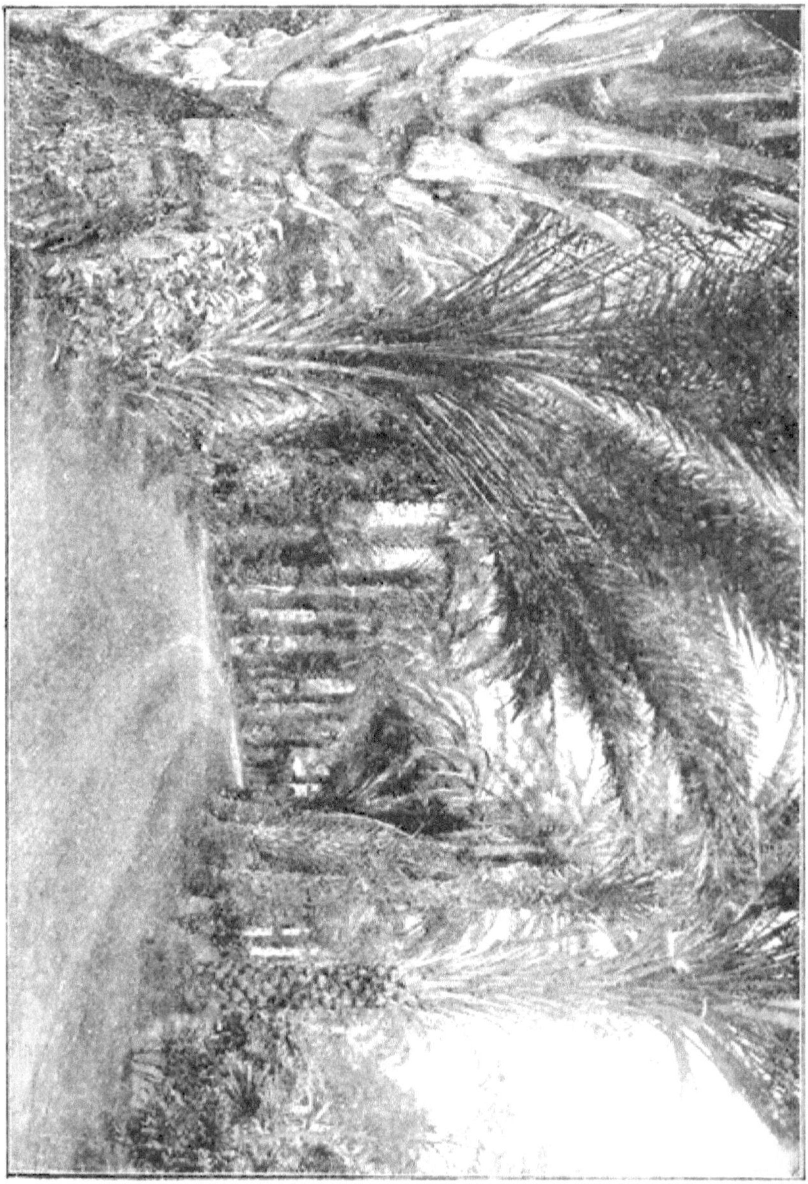

AVENUE OF ROYAL DATE PALMS.

lands, and the magic word "Aloha" (Love to you) is heard on every side.

One of the most wonderful and characteristic natural features of these beautiful islands, "The Paradise of the Pacific," is their volcanoes, active and extinct. On the island of Hawaii are two volcanic mountains, Mauna Kea and Mauna Loa. From a distance both look depressed, scarcely more in appearance than a curved line, like the back of a whale; and yet they are twelve thousand and fourteen thousand feet in height, respectively. On the slope of Mauna Loa, four thousand feet from its base, is the active crater of Kilauea, nine miles in circumference and three miles in diameter.

Looking down from the cliffs which inclose the black surface of lava, seven hundred feet below, one sees steam jets bursting from the seams and crevices. And descending, a trail leads, after a walk of two and a half miles, to the lake of fire, which lies elevated like a low dome amid the heaps of lava, and is the active portion of the crater. This lake is about eight hundred feet across and one thousand feet in length. It is a deep cavity filled nearly to the brim with red-hot lava. Burning jets fly twenty or thirty feet into the air and fall in fiery spray upon the seething surface. It does not throw up cinders or hot stones; its eruptive action is not explosive; but as one stands near its edge, great lava cakes roll on each other, while the boiling, surging lake spouts fountains of fiery substances into the air, twenty or more jets at once. A lurid glare crimsons the clouds at night, and the rush of steam from blow holes near by fills the air with stupendous noises.

On the 8th of July, 1894, this fiery lake overflowed its banks, and on the 12th the lava surface fell two hundred and seventy feet in twelve hours, causing the banks to fall in on all sides, and engulfing about eight acres of the floor of the larger crater. Huge walls, or cliffs, stood out boldly about the sunken lake, and billows of fire dashed against the sides of the crater.

The sugar cane, grown on the fertile plateaus of these islands, has given millions of wealth to the enterprising white men who have brought thrift and enterprise to bear upon these sunny lands, so that Hawaii bids fair to become one of the wealthiest, as well as most lovely and salubrious, of all the islands of the sea.

Were it not for the fact that the scourge of leprosy makes it necessary to separate many lepers from the people, and to place them on the island of Molokai, about fifty miles from Honolulu, this group of islands would be almost an ideal habitation. Twelve hundred of these poor people, mainly of the native race, are kept by the government in comparative comfort, on a peninsula inclosed by lofty cliffs on one side and a billowy sea on the other, where everything which is possible is done for the amelioration of their condition. Father Damien, who went to Molokai in 1873, did much for them, but fell a victim to the dread disease sixteen years later.

Putting this one plague spot out of mind as well as we can, we may believe, with a recent writer, that an inexpressible charm is exercised by lovely Hawaii over all who breathe her balmy air. "No alien land in all the world," writes Mr. Clemens, "could so longingly

A HAWAIIAN BELLE.

and beseechingly haunt me, sleeping and waking, through half a lifetime, as that has done. Other things leave me, but that abides. Other things change, but that remains the same. For me, its balmy airs are always blowing; its summer seas flashing in the sun; the pulsing of its surf beat is in my ear; I can see its garlanded crags, its leaping cascades, its plumy palms drowsing by the shore, its remote summits floating like islands above the cloud rack; I can feel the spirit of its woodland solitude; I can hear the plash of its brooks; in my nostrils still lives the breath of flowers that perished twenty years ago."

CHAPTER XLIII.

TIERRA DEL FUEGO AND OTHER ISLANDS OF SOUTH AMERICA.

TIERRA DEL FUEGO, the "land of fire," comprises a group of islands at the southern extremity of South America between latitude 52° 40′ and 56° south. It is separated from the mainland by the long and intricate Strait of Magellan, while the other sides are washed by the three oceans, — the Atlantic, Pacific, and Antarctic. The largest island is East Tierra del Fuego, or King Charles South Land; the four islands next in size are Navarin, Hoste, Clarence, and Desolation. There are numberless smaller islands, of which the one at the extreme southern point, terminating in Cape Horn, is the most remarkable.

Many mountain peaks on these islands exceed five thousand feet in height, and the culminating point is estimated at sixty-eight hundred feet. They are either covered with perpetual snow and ice, or clothed with stunted forests.

The climate is intensely disagreeable. Mist, snow, and rain, accompanied either with constant storms or violent and sudden gusts of wind, follow one another in rapid succession. But this climate is far from being unfavorable to the native vegetation; and hence in some places large woody-stemmed trees of fuchsia and veronica, which in our country are treated as tender plants, have been seen in flower not far from the base of a mountain with two thirds of its height covered with snow, and with the temperature at thirty-six degrees. Another peculiar vegetable product is a bright yellow edible fungus, about the size of a small apple. Sea fowl are numerous on the shelving cliffs.

YAHGANS.

Tierra del Fuego contained, when discovered, and still maintains, three distinct tribes of Indians. One tribe resemble the Patagonians in color, stature, and clothing. Their bodies were bulky, their heads and features large, but the hands and feet were comparatively small. Their color was a rich reddish brown. Their heads were covered with coarse, thick, black hair. They were a land tribe and seldom built canoes. They subsisted entirely upon what the land produced.

Another race occupied the islands lying west of Cockburn Channel. They were natural sailors. They built canoes and spent a great deal of time upon the water, either for pleasure or to obtain food.

The third tribe inhabit the islands south of East Tierra del Fuego and the very narrow south beach of that island itself. They live farther south than any other known people, and are called Yahgans. They are described by early navigators as low in stature, badly proportioned, and evil-looking. Their color is between dark copper and bronze. Their coarse, dirty, black hair heightens a villainous expression of the worst description of savage features.

The Esquimaux clothe themselves in fur and live in huts, which at least give shelter from storm and cold. The Yahgans, on the contrary, go nearly if not quite naked, and often sleep unsheltered from the frost and snow.

The Falkland Islands belong to Great Britain and are about two hundred in number. They are in the South Atlantic, two hundred and fifty miles northeast of Tierra del Fuego. Only two of these islands are of any considerable size, East and West Falkland. The former has an area of three thousand square miles and the latter two thousand.

The climate is salubrious and equable, there being no extremes of heat or cold. Thunder and lightning are rare, but rain and high winds are frequent. There are no trees, but in November and December a great variety of sweet-scented flowers covers the ground.

The tussac grass is the most singular and useful plant here. All the small islands of the group are covered by it as with miniature palms.

The Falkland Islands were discovered by Davis in 1592, and were afterward visited in 1690 by Strong, who gave them the name they now bear. They belong to Great Britain.

Juan Fernandez is a rocky island in the Pacific Ocean about four hundred miles off the coast of Chili, of which it is a dependency. It is eighteen miles long and six miles broad and rises to the height of three thousand feet above the sea. Its shores are steep, and, viewed from the ocean, it presents a desolate appearance. But the northern half of the island, in which is Cumberland Bay, contains some fertile valleys, producing figs, grapes, sandalwood, cork, and other timber trees.

This is the island of Robinson Crusoe. There are two instances of men, one of a Mosquito Indian and the other of Alexander Selkirk, who lived alone upon this island for several years. Selkirk's manner of life during his solitude was in most particulars very remarkable; but there is one circumstance which he relates which was verified by Mr. Walter, who visited the island thirty-two years afterward. Selkirk tells, among other things, that he often caught more goats than he wanted; he sometimes marked their ears and let them go. The first goat killed by Mr. Walter's men at their landing had its ears split, whence they concluded that it had formerly been under the power of Selkirk. It was an

AUSTRALIA AND THE ISLANDS OF THE SEA. 435

NATIVES OF THE FALKLAND ISLANDS.

animal of most venerable aspect, and dignified with an exceedingly majestic beard. During their stay they met with many others marked in the same way.

The Galapagos Islands form a group in the Pacific Ocean on and near the equator, seven hundred and thirty miles west of the coast of Ecuador, South America. There are six principal and seven small islands. Albemarle, sixty miles long by fifteen broad, is the largest and reaches an elevation of four thousand feet. They are of volcanic origin, and much of the surface is covered with lava. They derive their name from the turtles of enormous size (in Spanish *Galapagos*) which frequent their shores. Iguanas and other reptiles are also common. A small colony of Spaniards has been planted on Charles Island, forming a penal settlement. The other islands are mostly uninhabited.

CAPE HORN.

CHAPTER XLIV.

KURILE, ALEUTIAN, AND PRIBILOF ISLANDS.

The Kurile Islands, numbering about twenty-five, stretch from Yesso to the most southerly point of Kamchatka. The archipelago forms part of the Japanese Empire, having been exchanged by Russia, only a few years ago, for part of an island then belonging to Japan. The population is small.

The nearest island to Yesso is separated from it by a channel ten or twelve miles wide. It is mountainous, the highest peak being over seven thousand feet high. The largest island of the group, northeast of this one, is of volcanic formation, and has bold and rugged scenery. There is one active volcano, beside a beautiful volcanic cone rising about four thousand feet above the sea.

Salmon are extremely plentiful, and large numbers are caught during July and August, especially at the mouths of the rivers. Bears and foxes are numerous in all of the larger islands, and in the northern ones many seals are captured.

The inhabitants of the Kuriles belong to a race called Ainos. The story of this tribe is an unhappy one. In their far northern home they were accustomed to cross from one small island to another in their poor little canoes, carrying with them all their possessions, consisting of skin garments and implements for fishing and hunting. Their only aim in life was hunting, sealing, and fishing. At the command of the Japanese

A KURILE MOTHER AND CHILD.

government, their huts were destroyed, they were taken on board a ship and carried to this rocky island, where there is scarcely any vegetation.

All over the Kurile Islands are to be seen the remains of an extinct race of pit dwellers. The present inhabitants are wholly ignorant of their ancestors, and do not know whether they built structures over pits or not. Their own houses or huts are built entirely above the ground.

Until quite lately, the Kurile islanders destroyed their huts when they left one island for another. They also burnt the huts of persons who died. In connection with all the Aino huts is the "skull trophy." It is always placed at the east end of the hut on a line parallel with its wall and only a few yards away from it. It is constructed of biforked poles. Upon these are placed the skulls of the bears, wolves, and foxes killed by the owner of the hut.

In shape, the garments of the men resemble short tunics. They are made of sea birds' skins, with the feathers on the inside. The garment worn by the women is much longer, reaching nearly to the feet. The sleeves are very long. In bad weather this garment is fastened with a girdle and pulled up to the knees, showing the long yellow boots. A gayly colored handkerchief of Russian make is fastened round the back of the head, and another is tied round the neck, and thus the women resemble Italian peasants. Moccasins or long boots of salmon skin or seal skin are worn by both men and women.

The Ainos are a small race of people. The average

height of the men is a little more than five feet and two inches; that of the women, four feet ten inches. They are dirty and uncivilized, and have neither schools, churches, hospitals, nor public buildings of any kind. They are simple, gentle, and courageous. Crime among them is rare, and prisons are unknown.

The Aleutian Islands extend from the Peninsula of Kamchatka in Asiatic Russia to the promontory of Alaska in North America. They are divided into three groups, the one nearest to America being called the Fox Islands. All these islands are bare and mountainous. The coasts are rocky and surrounded by breakers.

The climate is severe, and only for a short time is the monotonous rigor of winter interrupted by a cloudy spring and a hot summer, both of which are subject to sudden changes in temperature. Few trees grow, but there are plenty of low scrubby bushes of birch, willow, and alder, beside grasses, moss, and lichens. Timber for building purposes is obtained from driftwood brought by the Japan Current. The people employ themselves in hunting and fishing or in making implements for the prosecution of these industries. Fur traders have settlements here for the capture of seals and sea otters, which abound on the coasts, and of the Arctic fox, which roams over the islands. Dogs and reindeer are common.

The population numbers about two thousand people. The natives are a race kindred to the Kamchatkans. They are low in stature, but plump and well built,

AUSTRALIA AND THE ISLANDS OF THE SEA. 441

ALEUTIAN ISLANDERS.

with short necks, swarthy faces, black eyes, and long, straight black hair. Nominally they are Christians, having been converted by the missionaries of the Greek Church. The islands form a part of Alaska Territory, and belong to the United States.

A great many kinds of birds frequent the islands in the summer time, while some remain throughout the entire year. Among them are various kinds of gulls, ducks, and owls. The Pacific eider duck, the rock ptarmigan, and the tufted puffin are the most valuable.

The Pribilof Islands, in the Bering Sea, consist of the islands of St. Paul and St. George with several islets. They were discovered in 1786 by the Russian navigator Pribilof. They are far enough south to be beyond the reach of permanent ice floes, and far enough from the mainland and the Aleutian Islands to have remained unknown to savage men. Hence they afforded the seal the happiest shelter and isolation, for their position is such as to surround and envelop them with fog banks that fairly shut out the light of the sun nine days out of ten during the summer, which is the breeding season. Ocean currents from the Pacific, warmer than the normal temperature of that latitude, coming up from the south, ebb and flow around the islands. About the end of October cold, strong winds from the Siberian steppes carry off the moisture and clear up the air. By the end of January they usually bring great fields of broken ice from the north, and until May or June the islands are completely ice bound.

Nearly half of the shore of St. Paul is a sandy beach,

while on St. George there is less than a mile of it all put together. Just above the Garden Cove Beach, under the overhanging bluffs, several thousand sea lions hold exclusive possession. On the north side of St. George Island, a grand bluff wall rises abruptly from the sea. Upon its numberless shelf margins, and in its countless chinks and crannies, millions upon millions of water fowl breed during the summer months.

Six miles southwest of St. Paul is a bluffy islet called the Russians' Otter Island, because in olden times the Russians are said to have captured thousands of sea otters on its stony coast. Six miles east of this is a small rock called Walrus Island, which is frequented every summer by hundreds of male walrus, to the exclusion of the other sex. This rocky islet is also the home of tens of thousands of screaming water fowl. The inhabitants of St. Paul resort for eggs to this island, where, in a few hours, tons of them may be obtained. Were it not for this, they would be obliged to go to the westward, and suspend themselves over lofty cliffs by means of ropes, as their neighbors at St. George are only too glad and willing to do.

Since the United States have controlled these islands, the condition of the inhabitants has been greatly improved. The houses in which the natives live were built by the Alaska Commercial Company. The agents of the company instruct the people about beautifying their homes and keeping them clean.

A schoolhouse was built on each of the two large islands by the company. At first the older people looked upon the enterprise with suspicion; they feared that if the children forgot the Russian language, they would also forget their religion. The government officer had told them that it was absolutely necessary to have an English school kept; that the company paid the money, and the children would be obliged to attend. The matter was talked over, and it was finally agreed that the children should go to the English school from nine o'clock to twelve, and that from one o'clock until nine the next morning, if they wished it, they should have the use of the building and fuel in order to teach them Russian. The two languages used on the islands are the Aleut and the Russian. The Aleut is the common language, and the Russian is the language of trade. In time, English will take the place of Russian.

Each island has its church, which is the Greek Church. The bishop resides in San Francisco, and visits the islands occasionally.

In 1896 British and American commissioners were appointed to investigate the seal-fishery question. In 1897 the government of the United States attempted to make a temporary arrangement with Great Britain, providing that joint measures be employed for the better protection of the herds against indiscriminate slaughter. The attempt did not succeed, partly because the British commission does not believe the extinction of the herds to be so imminent as the American commission believes it to be. The same commissioners were reappointed in 1897, and the United States assigned three revenue cutters to do patrol duty. In addition, a special high commissioner was dispatched to England for official conference on the subject.

INDEX.

Abaco, 179.
Adelaide, 40.
Ægean Sea, 321.
Ainos, 439.
Ajaccio, 295.
Alderney, 266, 271.
Aleutian Is., 440.
Althing, 117, 126, 128.
Andaman, 351.
Andros, 179.
Angra, 248.
Ankova, 331.
Antananarivo, 333.
Anticosti, 171.
Antigua, 238.
Antilles, Lesser and Greater, 187.
Apia, 405.
Arafura Sea, 14.
Arctic Archipelago, 159.
Atolls, 65.
Auckland, 88.
Australia, 13.
Azores, 248.

Bahamas, 177.
Balearic Isles, 282.
Barbados, 233.
Batavia, 364.
Bêche-de-mer (bäsh′de mâr), 70, 72.
Bermudas, 172.
Bischoff, Mount, 76.
Bonifacio Strait, 288.
Bornabi Group, 385.
Borneo, 351, 357.
Bourbon, 339.
Bridgetown, 233.
Brisbane, 36.

Cagliari, 291.
Calao, 375.
Canary Is., 255.

Cape Breton I., 165.
Cape Verd Is., 242.
Cap Haitien, 211.
Caribs, 241.
Caroline Is., 383.
Carpentaria, Gulf of, 14. 15.
Carrinho, 260, 264.
Carro, 263, 264.
Ceiba, 191, 228.
Celebes, 351, 375.
Cephalonia, 314.
Ceylon, 364.
Channel Is., 266.
Charlottetown, 169, 171.
Christophe, 211.
Città Vecchia (věk′kê ä), 312.
Cockatoo, 48, 374.
Cod fisheries, 161.
Colossus of Rhodes, 327.
Columbus, 200, 209, 220, 226. 239.
Cook Is., 414; Captain, 60, 84, 416
Coolies, 192, 201.   [418
Coral polyp, 64; Reefs, 65.
Corfu, 316.
Corsica, 295.
Cowes, 276.
Cradle Mount, 75.
Crete, 319.
Crusoe, Robinson, 434.
Cryolite, 101.
Cuba, 187, 190.
Curaçao, 237.
Cyprus, 328.

Delos, 322.
Dingo, 51.
Dominica, 241.
Dori, 371.
Douglas, 277.
Duck Is., 109.
Dyak, 358, 362.

INDEX.

Elba, 297.
Esquimaux, 96, 103, 106, 151.
Etna, Mount, 301.

Falkland Is., 433.
Faroes, 137.
Fiji Is., 392.
Fogo Volcano, 242.
Freemantle, 40.
Friendly Is., 410.
Funchal, 261.

Galapagos Is., 436.
Georgetown, 169.
Geysers, 92, 120.
Gilbert Is., 388.
Glaciers, 102.
Godhaven, 100.
Godthaab, 100.
Gold, 15, 26, 52.
Great Australian Bight, 14, 17.
Great Barrier Coral Reef, 60.
Grecian Archipelago, 321.
Greenland, 95.
Guadeloupe, 240.
Guernsey, 266, 270.

Haiti, 207.
Hamilton, 172; Alexander, 238.
Havana, 193.
Hawaii, 418.
Hebrides, 145.
Hecla, Mount, 115, 118.
Heligoland, 279.
Herm, 270, 273.
Hobart, 77.
Hogolen, 385.
Honolulu, 425.
Hovas, 335.
Hyppolite, 212.

Iceland, 112.
Ida, Mount, 319.
Igloo, 103.
Independence Bay, 96.
Ionian Is., 314.
Isle of Man, 276.

Isle of Wight, 273.
Ivigtut, 101.
Iviza (ē vē'sa), 287.

Jamaica, 213.
Jamestown, 245.
Java, 351, 363.
Jersey, 266, 268.
Jethou, 270.
Jokul, 114; Skapta, 119.
Juan Fernandez, 434.

Kane Basin, 96.
Kangaroo, 50.
Kara Sea, 150.
Kauri Tree (kä'u rē), 90.
Kava (kä'va), 406, 413.
Kingsley, Charles, 230.
Kingston, 215.
Kirkwall, 141.
Knights of St. John, 326.
Kosciusko, Mount, 17.
Kurile Is., 437.

Laccadive Is., 344.
Ladrones, 388.
Lady Eliot I., 60, 66.
Launceston, 76.
Leeward Is., 187.
Lerwick, 143.
Lewis I., 146.
Liliuokalani, Queen, 422.
Lincoln Sea, 96.
Lofoden Is., 156.
Louisburg, 167.
Loyalty Is., 399.
Luzon, 379.

Macassar, 376; Strait, 356
Madagascar, 330.
Madeira, 261.
Maelstrom, 157.
Majorca, 282.
Malay Archipelago, 350.
Maldive Is., 348.
Mali, 349.
Malietoa, 403.

INDEX.

Mallorcan tombs, 284.
Malta, 309.
Manila, 379.
Maoris, 84, 92, 95.
Mari, 309.
Marianne Is., 388.
Marshall Is., 388.
Martinique, 237.
Matanzas, 206.
Mauna Kea, 428.
Mauna Loa, 428.
Mauritius, 336.
Melbourne, 26.
Melville Land, 159.
Messina Strait, 301.
Mestizos, 380.
Mindanao, 379.
Minorca, 287.
Miquelon, 171.
Moluccas, 351, 365, 374.
Monte Pellegrino, 306.
Montserrat, 239.
Moreton Bay, 66.
Morty I., 351.
Mother-of-pearl, 69, 70.
Mount Lofty Range, 42.
Murray R., 14, 18.
Myall tree, 46.

Napoleon, 210, 246, 296, 299.
Nassau, 181.
Nevis, 238.
New Caledonia, 399.
Newfoundland, 160.
New Guinea, 369.
New Hebrides, 397.
Newport, 275.
New Providence, 179, 184.
New Siberia, 151.
New South Wales, 20.
New Zealand, 22, 82.
Nicobar, 351.
Nicosia, 329.
Nova Zembla, 150.

Odin, 132, 133.
Ogygia I., 309.

Orang-outang, 357.
Orkney Is., 141.

Palembang, 361.
Palermo, 306.
Palma, 283.
Papeete, 416.
Papua, 369.
Paria, Gulf of, 227.
Patmos, 323.
Peary, Lieutenant R. E., 96, 98.
Pelée, Mount, 238.
Pelew Is., 383.
Perth, 40.
Peter Botte Mountain, 336.
Petermann's Peak, 96.
Philippine Is., 378.
Pico, Mount, 248.
Poi, 420.
Pointe-à-Pitre, 240.
Ponce, 221.
Ponce de Leon, 224.
Ponta Delgada, 248.
Port Jackson, 31.
Port Louis, 336.
Port Mahon, 287.
Port of Spain, 227.
Porto Ferrajo, 297.
Porto Rico, 220.
Port Philip, 26, 30.
Pribilof Is., 442.
Prince Albert Land, 159.
Prince Edward I., 168.

Queensland, 20, 36, 52, 74.
Quetta, 62.

Reikiavik, 114, 123.
Reunion, 339.
Rhencia, 322.
Rhodes, 323.
Robeson Channel, 96.
Roseau, 241.

St. Denis, 339.
St. George, 442.
St. Helena, 243.

INDEX.

St. Heliers, 269.
St. John, 239, 323, 324.
St. John's, 163.
St. Kilda, 26, 30.
St. Kitts, 238.
St. Michael, 248.
St. Paul, 320; Island, 442.
St. Peter Port, 270.
St. Pierre, I., 171; Town, 237.
St. Vincent, 237; Gulf of, 15.
Samana Bay, 207.
Samoan Is.. 403.
Sandridge, 26.
San Juan, 221.
San Salvador, 177.
Santa Maura, 314.
Santiago de Cuba, 206.
Sarawak, 354.
Sardinia, 288.
Sark, 266, 272.
Scio, 323.
Seals, 108, 442, 444.
Shetland Is., 141.
Sicily, 299.
Singapore, 350, 354.
Skapta Jokul, 119.
Skye, 146.
Snorre Sturleson, 122.
Society Is., 414.
Sokotra, 342.
Solent, 273.
Solomon Is., 389.
South Australia, 20, 40.
Spencer Gulf, 15.
Spice Is., 374.
Spithead, 273.
Spitzbergen, 96, 153.
Sponge fishery, 186.
Staffa, 148.
Stevenson, R. L., 410.
Stewart Is., 82.
Stromness, 143.
Sumatra, 351, 357, 360.
Sunda, Is., 351; Strait, 360.
Swan R., 40.
Sydney, Austr., 31; Cape Breton, 166.

Tahiti, 414, 416.
Tamar R., 75.
Tasmania, 22, 23, 74.
Teneriffe, 255; Peak of, 256, 258.
Tennyson, 276.
Tenos, 322.
Thingvalla, 125, 127.
Thor, 131, 132.
Thorshavn, 137.
Thursday I., 67.
Tierra del Fuego, 431.
Timor Sea, 14; Island, 369.
Tobago, 227.
Tofua, 412.
Torres Strait, 14, 60.
Toussaint L'Ouverture, 210.
Trinidad, 226.

Upernavik, 100.
Upolu, 405.

Valdemosa, 285.
Valetta, 309.
Van Dieman's Land, 74.
Victoria, 20, 26.
Volante, 197.
Volcanoes, 117, 238, 353.

Waikato R., 86.
Wallaby, 50.
Walrus, 106.
Watling I., 179.
Wellington, 84; Mount, 77.
Western Australia, 20, 40.
West Indies, 187.
Windward Is., 187.
Wombat, 80.
Wooloomooloo, 33.

Yahgans, 433.
Yarmouth, 276.
Yarra R., 26.
York, Cape, 15.

Zante, 314.
Zanzibar, 340, 341.

www.ingramcontent.com/pod-product-compliance
Lightning Source LLC
Chambersburg PA
CBHW032005300426
44117CB00008B/904